Narrative Construction of India

Narrative Construction of India

Forster, Nehru and Rushdie

Mukesh Srivastava

RAWAT PUBLICATIONS
Jaipur and New Delhi

ISBN 81-7033-846-8

Published by
Prem Rawat for ***Rawat Publications***
Satyam Apartments, Sector 3, Jawahar Nagar, Jaipur 302 004 (India)
Phone: 0141 265 1748 / 7006 Fax: 0141 265 1748
E-mail: info@rawatbooks.com
Website: www.rawatbooks.com

Delhi Office
4858/24, Ansari Road, Daryaganj, New Delhi 110 002
Phone: 011-23263290

Typeset by Rawat Computers, Jaipur
Printed at Chaman Enterprises, New Delhi

Contents

Preface

This book is about the story of India as narrated by three master storytellers, namely, E.M. Forster, Jawaharlal Nehru and Salman Rushdie. Despite wide differences in historical periods, constituency of readers and styles of narration of these three writers, their works seem to be governed by a common commitment: the will to know India and the desire to represent it particularly to those inhabiting other spaces and times, different from what is here and now, from this country called India. As one works through the intricate mechanisms of narrative production in each case, the underlying structure of relations—historico-political as well as formal or literary—acquires a certain critical visibility.

In each case, I argue, the desire to represent India is stretched to its limits, and then narratively fractured because of the impossibility of such a demand. The specific resolutions worked out by each text are qualitatively different as we move from Forster through Nehru to Rushdie. In spite of such differences, however, one can still locate in each text a subterranean structure of significations characteristic of liberal humanism. Liberal humanism, then, is the key to an understanding of the texts in question, even as it undergoes dramatic transformations in its tortuous route from the colonial period to an incipient 'post-national' one. This can be shown when a text confronts the specific historical task of responding to British imperialism and Indian mysticism, imagining a nation, or even, as in Rushdie, interrogating the received forms of knowledge and behaviour of communities and a whole nation.

The three texts undertaken for analysis here reveal more about themselves in the specific problematic they set up, the set of questions they raise, and the solutions they provide, than the world they seek to illumine. Although they could be read as 'autonomous' texts, each setting up its own narrative scheme and suggesting a range of devices of interpretation, I have found them to be linked by a common epistemology: that of liberal humanism supported in each case by different cultural assumptions which represent a specific stage of the development of capital. Of course, these links are not at all intrinsic to the textual design: they are forged by a critic's understanding of the political thrust which each text potentially carries in its narrative scheme of representation, or actively brings into play as 'events' in a historical or literary account.

This book has four chapters besides 'Introduction' and 'Epilogue'. Chapter 1 is a critical recounting of late Victorian production of the discourse on liberalism in England, and its multiple affiliations and disjunctions with British imperialism in India. It advances the argument that internal contradictions of liberal discourse in England produced a happy blending of the urban middle class and the rural aristocracy, thus providing rich archival material for the rise of E.M. Forster's literary modernism. Chapter 2 is a critical survey of literary criticism available on E.M. Forster's *A Passage to India*. I have deliberately avoided a chronological ordering of this material and tried to present as varied a set of positions on the novellas possible in order to ground my own position on the novel *vis-à-vis* others. The Chapter discusses the novel under three sub-sections, namely, *Mosque, Caves* and *Temple*. My main concern here is to show, through a close reading of the text, that despite its relinquishing of British values and British racism, Forsterian narrative is unable to relinquish the multi-layered discourse on colonialism. It is a narrative, therefore, which makes us realise only too well that there is no place to stand outside the imaginative geography of an India conceived by the West. There are indeed a few places in 'Caves' and 'Temple' where one encounters in the narrative an effort to stretch the limits of its construction and cast an ironic glance at its own epistemological foundations. But every such effort towards self-reflexivity, within the overall design of the novel, ultimately serves to heighten the effect of liberal humanism.

Chapter 3 on *The Discovery of India* by Jawaharlal Nehru is composed somewhat intricately. I have taken certain key concept-metaphors out of this text and tried to discuss them in those discursive and ideological frames which overshoot the internal design of the text. The first section is an analysis of 'the status of the text'. It shows how on close reading *The Discovery of India* reveals extremely complex styles of narration, defying any conventional classification of genres. The text has the merit of often running against the grain of its own logic and manner of storytelling. This particular paradox in the composition of the text becomes decisive, for the text remains neither history, nor fiction, nor autobiography, and finds itself a place among those dubiously privileged artifacts of *pure writing* or *textuality* which seek to undermine the very distinction between history and fiction. Such hybridity of genre, I argue, is a manipulative and dynamic instrument to forge the story of India for a nationalist design.

The second section is an analysis of the relationship between narrative and temporal structure as created by the requirements of the 'coming into being' of a nation, that is, India. *The Discovery of India* can thus be discussed as creating a new sense of national time by producing a double axis in which episodic and configurational dimensions of the narrative establish a link between the reader's and the writer's present, as well as their common national past.

The third section is a critical elaboration of the term 'tradition'. Like the discourse of the nationalism and its several cultural languages, tradition turns out to be a contemporary politico-social and cultural artifact that sutures over gaps and creates a *social imaginary* in the Lacanian sense. In Nehru's handling of tradition, particularly in his commentary on the Hindu epics such as *Ramayana* and *Mahabharata*, we find enacted a series of discourses which might potentially contradict each other. They are, however, held together by the force of the magic idea of synthesis, and by the idea of India's 'tryst with destiny'. On a close analysis these discourses can be shown to be contested, fractured, re-distributed and re-enacted as new resolutions with regard to the politics of tradition are negotiated or effected.

The fourth section is a detailed examination of 'Gandhi and the Phenomenon of Mass Politics' in relation to *The Discovery of India*. Beginning with the early liberal and leftist positions and working through democratic-socialist to existing Marxist positions on Gandhi, I have tried to show how scholarship on Gandhi to this day remains conceptually delimited, and structurally contoured, by the familiar psycho-empirical categories of knowledge that can be found in their germinal forms on Nehru's representation of Gandhi in *The Discovery of India*. Detailed examination of Gandhi is therefore warranted because of the central role assigned by the narrative to Gandhi the man and *not to Gandhian discourse* or *Gandhian political practice* in the grand narrative of Indian national movement. The implications of such a figuration of 'Gandhi' are deep rooted for the story of India and they carry with them a definite political weight in determining the significance of India's bourgeois 'passive revolution'.

The fifth section makes use of contemporary scholarship on political economy to develop the argument that 'democratic secularism' emerged as the only legitimate form of the Indian nation-state because of the deeply ambivalent and contested relations of classes which constituted, and in fact became the very condition of, the *coalitional* form of the Indian state at the time of the departure of the British imperial government. Secularism a la Nehru, which emerged in the gap between traditional loyalties of caste and religion and the requirements of building a modern, democratic nation-state, was constituted out of heteronomous modes of narration, addressing a wide range of people across classes, geographical and social locales, drawing upon a spectrum of cultural and political artifacts for its appeal: the Indian tradition, autobiography, law modernity and scientific spirit, to name a few. In constituting the discourse on the secular, the narrative voice combines the techniques of both individualisation and collectivisation. The technique of individualisation lies in creating a *new form of citizen subject* whose force is derived from self-recognition. This recognition implies a knowledge of the conscience and the ability to direct it. The individualising power of secularism is combined effectively with totalising, or collectivising procedures, as for example, law. Secular law addresses a variety of people as a unit, or homogeneous mass, thereby enabling smooth management of collective life, and the construction of a collective national, particularly Indian identity.

The sixth and final section pulls the entire argument in this chapter together, and shows how each constitutive element of 'the story of India' contributes to its overall design and structure.

Chapter 4 on Salman Rushdie's *Midnight's Children* might be regarded only as a postscript, considering the range of arguments raised in the earlier chapters. However, it remains crucial to my argument in that it tries to show how recourse to an *anti-mimetic* and anti-referential style of narration as against literary realism, or conventional historiography, may turn out to be complicitous when 'new' and 'indigenous' forms of liberalism harnessed to the purpose of international, as against national, cultural production.

There are many strands interlocked in Rushdie's narrative style. At the first sight, it is a parody of the epic, the realist and the autobiographical modes that jostle uneasily and too rapidly in the traditional Indian folktales, and *puranic* modes of story-telling. In this medley of 'surprise' and 'innovation', however, there is definitive sense in which Rushdie carries forward modernist problems of knowledge and representation. The fragmentation of the individual subject within the modernist project of 'alienation' is deftly transformed into a post modernist aesthetic of dispersal of meaning. I have advanced the argument that the problems of meaning, form and representation that best the 'third world' are indeed very different form the slippage of meaning and of the 'real' which currently confront academic discourses on Europe and the United States. This, of course, does not mean that one can find the 'true' meaning of an indigenous variety by applying a purely local, or a more authentic method of inquiry. It is only to emphasise that both meaning and the need for locating meaning are *conjunctural*. Therefore, the so-called epistemological problem of the West is itself a narrowly historical one.

While Rushdie's narration might be, at places, sensitive to some historico-political 'events' which appear to acquire a fantastic, or magical figuration in the text, it often lapses into a solipsistic, anti-representational style, devoid of the crucial multiple conjunctions of a usable past, or indeed of historical agency, both explicit and subterranean. The overall effect of such narratives, seeking to express a transindividual, collective destiny of its 'people' in a parody of both the nationalist-real and the traditional epic seems to be the production of a new artifice: the grafting of a (post) modernist aesthetic on Indian material.

To sum up, 'the story of India' unfolding in the following

pages is simultaneously fascinating and depressing. It is fascinating in its bewildering variety, narrative manoeuvres, craft and ingestive capaciousness as one finds in it a confident theoretical advance from Forster through Nehru to Rushdie. However, it is also depressing because there is nothing, literally nothing—from the brute material production in the factories to the production of culture and literature, of libidinal impulses, and of the unconscious—which may have escaped the jaws of an ever-rising, marauding and dangerously swelling capitalism. Like a true chameleon, capital has changed its colour, form, tone and accent, and has in fact adopted polyphonous voices, created its own controlled oppositions, and erected its humanist, and indeed anti-humanist edifices of narrative to convert every object into a commodity: to split every desire into the desire to either dominate or surrender, tied as it is to an inevitable trajectory of economic, social and symbolic exchange. To read 'the story of India' is also to imply, however faintly, in the following pages, the subtle but sure march of capital in its multiple historical and cultural trajectories from colonialism through nationalism to a period of globalisation in India. One may only hope that, true to the spirit of a sage deeply immersed in an epiphanous meditation, capital will bear the seeds of self-destruction in its own 'mind' one day. The task of a cultural critic is, no doubt, to help speed up this process.

Acknowledgements

This book has been in the works for almost a decade. Substantial portions of the initial chapters were written in Hyderabad at the Central Institute of English & Foreign Languages. Susie Tharu's gracious guidance, encouragement and support for this project would always be a very precious and memorable gift. Probal Dasgupta was very kind in writing long letters from Deccan College as well as from the University of Hyderabad in response to my queries. K.V. Tirumalaesh, Alok Rai, Tejaswini Niranjana, Vivek Dhareshwara, A. Salahuddin, I.S. Dagar, Venkat Reddy, D. Venkat Rao and Pavan Kumar have contributed one way or another to the writing of this book and I must express my sincere thanks to all of them.

At the IIM, Ahmedabad where I spent a couple of years as a visiting professor at the Ravi Matthai Centre for Educational Innovation, Pradip Khandwala, the former director, was most wonderful and willing to share his ideas and arguments till several late nights. Simon Dabhi's friendship has been both enduring and gratifying while Ashok Jambekar's ready help to provide any reference material at the Vikram Sarabhai Library was exemplary. I am also thankful to Harsh Sethi, acquisition editor of Sage Publications for giving me some useful tips on editorial skills. Junaid Quadri at the School of Oriental and African Studies, London University, was immensely kind in his hospitality, as he was equally ruthless and impeccable in his criticism. Donny Alex, Mangala and V.S. Sreedhara, V. Soami Saran have been all along marvellous people with their discussions and friendships. In the University of Chicago, Dipesh Chakravarty, Seely Clinton, Norman Cutler and C.M. Naim offered helpful suggestion on presentations of parts of this book. Dipesh and Clint were particularly most generous in sharing their ideas with me. Mikelle Standbridge at the Chicago Art School was always an exacting critic, as indeed she was charming in her friendship. I take this opportunity to thank them all.

I am most grateful to Jyoti Panjwani for her friendship and for mailing very useful reference material to me from the libraries at the University of Illinois. My elder brother, Madan Mohan Verma, has always been a source of greatest inspiration to me, and my gratitude to him can never be adequately expressed in words. Rajendra Kumar Srivastava, who is always so much more than a friend, has contributed richly in so many ways and I express my heartfelt thanks to him as well.

Moolchand Sharma, Professor of Jurisprudence and Director of National Law University, Bhopal, whose charming, energetic and most delightful presence has completely transformed the atmosphere of my workplace, deserves my warmest thanks. His friendship and support made it possible for me to complete this book in peace. I would far rather remain beholden to him.

Finally, I would like to thank Mr. Pradeep Kumar for his meticulous typing and Rawat Publications for bringing out this publication.

Mukesh Srivastava

A thought comes when 'it' wishes, and not when 'I' wish, so that it is a falsification of the facts of the case to say that the subject 'I' is the condition of the predicate 'think.' It thinks; but that this 'it' is precisely the famous old 'ego'... only a supposition, an assertion, not an immediate certainty. After all, one has even gone too far with this 'it thinks'—even the 'it' contains an *interpretation* of the process, and does not belong to the process itself...

—Friedrich Nietzsche
Beyond Good and Evil

Introduction

Several attempts have been made in the last decade or so to analyse the narrative strategies, which underwrite the politics of cultural representations, particularly within the field of British empire and Indian nation. In fact, the study of British cultural imperialism and the making of the Indian nation together constitute a continuum, with its marked continuities, departures, inversions, silences and gaps as the 'old' ideological and narrative frames are shifted, appropriated, and re-deployed in the form of 'new' commitments of the nation.[1] While one appreciates these labouriously nuanced and critical endeavours to study literary and historical texts of this period as cultural practices which constitute the colonial and national subjects, there seems to be, however, in this critical enterprise, a deliberate omission of the 'political'. In other words, while a great deal of close attention has been paid to unravel the narrative twists, indeterminacies, rhetorical control and other representational strategies, little effort has gone into establishing relationships of these narrative devices with the cataclysmic historico-political transformations taking place in India. And, while there is, no doubt, a keen awareness of history itself being a 'text' in its chosen narrative emphases, and deflections—giving air to the belief that there can be no history, but several histories, often contending with each other—we do not yet find in many of these 'cultural studies' an active and thorough engagement with the historical and political forces in-the-making.

The present study undertakes to broaden the scope of 'cultural studies' without reducing the significance of textual analysis, per se but by integrating it with those forces which have become the very condition of the production of literature, and shaped our literary and cultural responses.

The story of India as analysed in these pages brings together the historico-political as well as discursive operations of the empire and the Indian nation. As is well-known, the naturalness of the historical or cultural is not merely spurious—a matter of false consciousness—but an active and often enabling process of sifting, ordering, and suturing of events from a vast array of traditional source material. Further, in this act of selection and ordering is involved the choices of ideology which are inscribed in the very form of the received historical and/or cultural sources. These issues bring us to the study of narrative forms, which are over-determined by the politics of culture.

Since narratives are always told from someone's point-of view, they create a world in which the 'self' may find a home. Alternatively, however, the home of the self is built by the raw materials supplied by the contours of narratives. Indeed, there is always an active, reciprocal relationship between the demands of the narrative and the formation of the self.[2] Again self may be individual or collective, as for example the self invoked in the 'destiny' of a whole nation, or the 'pulse' of the empire but in either case, the process of its formation is based on a narrative contract between the writer and the implied reader, or between the speaker and the implied listener. The contract lies in the identification of the areas of similarity and difference, unity and departure, and above all in *structuring the field of action* for the self.

The above consideration brings us to a crucial question: how did such a narrative contract become possible? How was it that at a particular historical conjuncture, the traditional Indian 'fuzzy community' gave way to the totalising and hierarchical structure of the empire and subsequently the Indian nation.[3] There is no obvious answer to this question except a conjecture, a possible one, that traditional Indian communities did not reason through those concepts which were employed by the British colonial cultural and administrative machinery. There was no single, united 'India' to be controlled and conquered, since the horizon of belonging and conceivable social action in pre-colonial India was highly elastic and diffuse, allowing a *proliferation of cultural and religious identities without a centralising and homogenising axis of governance.* The internal composition of this community was 'diffused' in the sense that the construction of individual or collective identities was not governed by a hierarchical, fixed socio-political norm, and was subject to vary with changes in the context. Belonging to varying layers of community was not taken as illogical or irrational, and given different contexts the selfhood of a pre-modern person could have been formed around various divisions of caste, community, language, region or religion.

However, the story of the absorption of traditional communities to the logic of colonial modernity and its attendant institutions is a fairly complex one, replete with its own internal contradictions. This can be shown by tracing the genealogy of liberal discourse in England and its transposition, albeit in a distorted form, into Indian political, and socio-cultural formations. In fact, it is quite clear by now from the documented historical 'evidence' of the early colonial period that Britain could not, without infringing the fundamental logic of colonialism, introduce forms of political rule which were current in Europe.[4] What was introduced, on the other hand, was a set of legal identifications which were unprecedented in the Indian context.

In pre-British India, there were innumerable, overlapping local jurisdictions and many groups enjoyed one or another degree of autonomy in administering law to themselves. The existence of *Dharmasastras*, a refined and respected system of written law, did not serve to unify the system in the way the national law did in the West. The relative absence of written records, of professional pleaders and of appeals made even local unification difficult. Further, as Marc Galanter has argued, 'the respective authoritativeness of governmental, *sastric*, and local components was not visualised in a way to provide either the techniques or the ideology for the *ruthless* supersedure of local law'.[5] The system allowed for change, but did not impose it; it allowed the old to remain alongside the new. The relation of the 'highest' and most authoritative parts of the legal system to the 'lower' end of the system was not that of superior to subordinate in a bureaucratic hierarchy.

In contrast to this, the legal measures of the modern colonial system changed the prevailing 'anarchy' in order to impose uniform territorial laws based on universalistic norms, with apportion 'rights' and 'obligations' as incidents of specific transactions. These laws were to be administered by a new hierarchy of courts that were organised bureaucratically, employing new 'rational' procedures, unknown to a large population. Such new legal measures brought about in course of time a new liberal regime, which introduced gradually the *sign system* or *semiotics* of liberal rights (without in any fundamental way altering the prevailing balance of property or economic relations) in the field of socio-cultural reform.

Far from being coercive, or merely inhibiting, the entire gamut of conceptual transformations brought about by the introduction of liberalism formed a structure, or a field of action for the Indian citizen 'subject' as well as his British rulers. The cultural implications of this new regime were particularly far-reaching for the colony, as the internal contradictions of classes, and the political instability within the

English State, threatened a possible disintegration of the empire. This argument has been developed in the first chapter to show how the magic word 'culture'—sometimes endowed with the qualifier, 'national' and at times 'universal'—was inscribed in the grand narrative of liberalism *to bind a tottering empire from within and without.* And precisely here we come up against imperialist designs of liberalism in their most productive sense.

E.M. Forster's *A Passage to India* appears in this particular historical conjuncture where it must negotiate with a new liberal ideal of subjectivity and its attendant fear and anxiety. It was enormously important for liberal discourse in India—to its philosophy as well as its actual practice and therefore to its politics, especially to the politics of subjectivity—to maintain the sense that nothing is, or can be 'closed' or for that matter understood and resolved, except in some extra human, or extra-anthropomorphic realm. More particularly, the universalistic aspect of this extra human dimension is to be noted as an essential strand of late Victorian liberalism, where the universal resides as alien, as outraging taste, as unconcerned with housing humankind, as existing in the silence outside language, and hence as untranslatable into human sounds or human scale. Understood in this light all *syntactic, tonal* and *verbal indeterminacies* of the 'Caves', so delicately and labouriously chiselled by the narrative artistry, can be referred back to the liberal problematic of human consciousness and its 'other'.[6]

Structurally, the spiritual muddledom/mystery is mirrored and augured in the mundane muddle that Hinduism/India is. This is, despite the exalted tone, represented as the opposite of the well-ordered West. In Fielding's retreat to the Mediterranean the strange 'other' is overturned in favour of the 'normal' self:

> The harmony between the works of man and the earth that upholds them, the civilization that has escaped muddle, the spirit

> in a reasonable form... *The Mediterranean is the human norm.* When men leave that exquisite lake, whether through the bosphorous or the pillars of Hercules, *they approach the monstrous and extraordinary*; and the southern exit leads to the strangest experience of all [p.278].
>
> (emphasis added)

Liberalism—both in its philosophical, orientalist mode, or in its overtly political-bourgeois mode—needs such a guarantee of the other to sustain itself. It can not hold together without such a transcendental presence. There is, however, a sort of contradiction in this argument. The problem at one level is that liberalism's dream for the universal (to be realised classically through art, or an ethical guarantee of the conscience through authenticity), a dream which underwrites and empowers its politics, is far too grandiose, majestic and overpowering in its proportions to be held within the confines of its humanist philosophies, or its empiricist dependence upon the knowledge of the senses. Therefore the liberal mind has to acknowledge the presence of 'India' honestly, face up to its challenge, while it has to admit of India's indifference to the founding values of the western liberal world. It must construct other vantage points of knowing the 'truth', if its claim of universality is to be established. In this act of constructing an all-pervasive truth, liberalism sacrifices part of its humanism, as well as its aesthetic, ethical and moral norms and its taste. In other words, Forster's liberalism forces him into a position where he must locate the voice of truth/pure consciousness outside all history and society in an extra linguistic realm where ethical distinctions which are humanist do not hold. Within the narrative scheme of *A Passage to India* it is 'that place where completeness can be found... completeness not reconstruction' (p.282).

As we move from the cultural liberalism of the empire to that of the making of a new nation, the narrative contract initiated by the early liberal discourse of Forster is inflected sufficiently to accommodate the demands of writing a new 'history' of India. *The Discovery of India* by Jawaharlal Nehru is one of the earliest and classic examples of the hegemonic power of liberal discourse, which creates *a new narrative location* for a *willing participation* of the 'people' of India. This performance is effected through a subtle and dexterous mixing of genres. On a close analysis, one discovers in this text an underlying liberal epistemology, at its most productive moment perhaps, an epistemology which reworks its logic to oppose colonial rule, but carries forward the hegemonic function of the new relations of knowledge, power and government brought into play by the requirements of the empire.

All nationalism, or more narrowly, nationalist historiography, is indeed a product of colonialism, but the continuities between them range from the choice of a linguistic mode of expression (modern English and vernaculars), development of a historical consciousness, discovery of tradition or heritage, to the installation of a new state based on the principles of secular democracy and the rule of law. This new regime of administrative, legal and political relations, marked by the arrival of modernity is held together in the text by narrative strategies which foreground culture, or more appropriately, a common cultural identity as the essence of the Indian nation. Also implicit in this characterisation of national culture is a sense of national time. National time can be seen to be the invention of the present moment—a history of the present—which lays out retrospectively each moment of its supposedly collective past in the hope of building a new future. The colligatory principles of narration here invoke once again the familiar concept of culture as a cohesive device to write the story of India.

While it is true that nationalism levels differences of all kinds—cultural, racial, political, geographical and so on—to create a consensus among its citizens who are often addressed, or interpellated, as a homogeneous mass of 'people' in a realm of timelessness, it also generates simultaneously a new order, a new hierarchy of differences. This can be observed by taking a close look at the political function of enumeration. The meticulous task undertaken by the eighteenth century orientalists—codifying, tabulating, comparing, translating and simplifying various classical languages of India in order to 'prove' the authenticity and power of their origin and expression—is well matched by the Nehruvian nationalist project of enumeration of cultures, languages and communities.[7] As with the colonialist construction of 'communalism', nationalist narrative had to rely on the essential, a priori, and fixed characteristics of certain types of races, behaviours, habits, climates and cultures, which could be retrospectively brought into a unison by forging a modern and secular ethos for the new nation. The discourse on 'secularism' is thus predicated on an automatic acceptance of the various types of enumeration set in motion by the colonial machinery of cultural production.

The awareness of different patterns of subjugation and dominance inherent in the narrative structures of nationalist historiography, politics and culture, has triggered a variety of responses in our times.[8] We are in fact now living in a period, which is witnessing resurgence from different versions of Orientalist discourse first set in motion late in eighteenth century Bengal. There is a continuous investment in 'communal' politics, or a politics based on playing upon the 'religious' identity of different communities, and the growth of a socio-cultural climate where a major ideological prop is found in versions of essentialist nativism, in which descriptions of caste, gender, language, tribe and religion et al are offered as eternal truths, even though they may have been, on closer scrutiny, the inventions of yesterday. In addition to this chauvinistic 'revivalism' is an assertive state-sponsored display of Indian tradition especially of the classical, the tribal and the folk representing the truly 'indigenous' art-forms for ready appreciation and consumption in international markets. These efforts at representing Indian literary and art forms some times seem to collaborate with the so-called Gandhian position, in re-establishing the values of a *desi* or *swadeshi* India by using a rhetoric of anti-colonial nativism as against the values of enlightenment, encompassing western reason, science and linear history.

A corollary to the above nativism is the institutionalised production, circulation and criticism of 'third world' literature. This is yet another phase of the 'narrative contract' which has directed its attention to the study of 'colonial subject' through the application of recent developments in literary criticism and critical theory that are ostensibly pitted against bourgeois, patriarchal, colonial and enlightenment value systems. Much of this work—often densely abstruse and heavily dependent on an exclusive access to metropolitan journals, and international library system with interconnected data banks—situates itself within the politics of anti-imperialism and anti-nationalism as well, yet cannot help taking a metropolitan stance which is pathetically distant and indifferent to its 'object of inquiry'.

The above two positions which constitute our critical milieu today have far more complex histories, internal differences and variations than any summary statement here can suggest. But this summary statement is perhaps necessary to understand the situatedness of Salman Rushdie's *Midnight's Children* and, even more importantly, the reception of post-colonial and post-modernist fiction in India.

Rushdie carries forward modernist problems of narrative representations to their limits in his comic treatment of the epic, the realist, and the autobiographical modes that seem to create a simulacrum of traditional folktales, as found in the *puranic* style. Such consummate artistry succeeds in expressing the fragmentation of the individual subject and the impossibility of an objective history. However, as has been argued at length in the Chapter 4 on Rushdie, the problems of form, meaning and representation that beset the 'third world' are indeed very different from the free play of meaning and the slippage of history and the real which confront academic discourses of Europe and North America. Historically, the problem of form in the 'third world' has been to extricate itself from the so-called epistemological crisis of the West, in order to link itself up with interrogative local traditions.[9] We need to make a sharp distinction between the Orientalist and Nationalist museumisation of 'tradition' from those continuously changing, growing and interrogating local practices which do not easily lend themselves to a frozen repertoire of 'heritage' and 'tradition'. They can be seen and understood only as 'lived' reality, at the site of their formation and engagement with a wild variety of indigenous languages and the rich repertoire of ideologically intersecting cultures of India.

Falling far short of these labourious links, Rushdie's narrative—which seeks to express a transindividual, collective identity in parody of both the nationalist-real and the traditional-epic—seems to lapse into the elegance of a new and somewhat sensational style: the grafting of a (post) modernist aesthetic on Indian material. A persistent critique of all forms of essentialism and humanism—which a post-modernist critical practice supposedly entails—cannot extricate itself from the consequences of its own production and circulation. Further, to argue, as anti-humanists of all shades have done, that humanism is shot through with metaphors disguised as concepts, or that it is dependent on a whole battery of rhetorical and figurative devices is very well, but in itself hardly matters much, unless it could be shown that the existing stock of metaphorical devices, and concepts of subjectivity as embedded in humanist practices, have had disabling theoretical and political consequences which could be remedied by the use of a different set of metaphor-concepts. If this is not the point at issue as a variety of 'new' and formal applications of post-modernist critique of conventional historiography and literature seem to suggest, then anti-humanism is likely to do no more than, alas, lock itself into an historical cul-de-sac in which it keeps alive the demand for transcendence simply by never-endingly denying its possibility. Such criticism of essentialism can rapidly become a lament for its loss, a consolation for the limitations of 'the human condition' which is simultaneously a recipe for political quietism.[10]

When we consider the particular case of India, an analytical strategy based entirely upon anti-humanist assumptions of culture (which takes for granted a hegemonic bourgeois social relation as its given condition) is thrown in serious doubt. Liberal notions of equality, law and citizenship, which were introduced by British rule in India, leave us with a peculiar ambivalence in the society where the modes of dominance and subjugation might still be characterised, to some extent, by pre-modern, vastly rural and hierarchical social-political and economic relations. This is of course not to argue that one has to embrace 'modernity' as an answer to the specific ills of Indian society. Far from it. This is rather to suggest that a comprehensive critique of modernity and humanism would underline the need for the specific uses of these categories in places where more severe 'illiberal' forms of oppression are intact. On the other hand it can be equally argued that there is nothing in the logic of the market or profit, that guarantees an automatic transformation of individuals into 'citizens'. Under certain conditions the most feudal system of authority can survive at the heart of the most modern of factories, as Dipesh Chakravarty has persuasively argued:

> Capitalist production—whether resulting in development or underdevelopment—has thrived in a variety of cultures, ranging from the hierarchical to the most democratic one. Perhaps we have long overestimated capitalism's need or capacity to homogenize the cultural conditions necessary for its own reproduction.[11]

This characterisation of the system of social relation and signification poses serious problems of narrative representation and containment of individuals who are radically *different from the citizen-subjects of the 'first world'*. This argument can be developed further to show how power relations in a country like India operate in ways far more different and more complex than through the 'disciplinary' grid of a Foucauldian documentation of the western discourses and institutions such as the mental asylum, prison, and clinic.[12] While the humanist ideal of equality encompasses individual rights and freedom and consequently leads to the formation of a new bourgeois individual 'self' which has very serious and far-reaching limitations, these limitations need to be critically assessed and weighed against the prevalent anti-humanist negative hermeneutics of 'the production of the subject'. It is important to remember that Foucault's work on the production of the modern subject was a direct response to the critical scene in France in the decade 1960-70 which leaned heavily on the existentialist and phenomenological modes of inquiry. His work, in the process of shaping a polemical response to these critical schools, rendered invisible a crucial contradiction in the construction of the modern subject whose full force we can appreciate only if we ask: how does the bourgeois humanist conception of the subject as free, autonomous and self-identical individual function as an appropriate ideology for late capitalist society?. This is hardly considered by 'post-structuralists' who appear to stake all on the assumption that 'unified subject' *is indeed an integral part of contemporary bourgeois ideology, and is thus ripe for immediate deconstructive scrutiny*. One might argue equally that it is indeed in the interest of late capitalism to deconstruct such a 'subject' as meticulously as possible. As I have tried to argue in the fourth chapter on Salman Rushdie the contemporary subject may be less strenuous monadic agent of an earlier phase of capitalist ideology than a dispersed, decentred network of libidinal attachments, emptied of ethical substance, and psychic interiority: the short-lived function of a variety of 'high-tech' acts of consumption such as media images, sexual explosion, advertising, architecture, fashion industry and so on.[13] The unified humanist subject appears in this light to be a straw target, a mechanical repetition of an older liberal epoch of capitalism, before computer technology and electron capitalism scattered our monadic self to the winds into so many splinters, bit and pieces of commodified technique, reified hunger for consumption and automatised operations of desire. The humanist subject, it can still be held, is not simply part of an obsolete history we can choose to leave behind. If it is an increasingly inappropriate object of inquiry at certain levels of post-modern subjecthood, it remains a potently relevant model at others. We have to therefore continue to fight for equality, autonomy, liberty and justice—all constitutive features of liberal humanism—while at the same time being keenly aware of their limitations, and their complicity with the existing system of social relations and significations. The struggle to become a 'citizen' will thus be integrated to the wider struggle to multiply and de-individualise. Renouncing the earlier struggle will mean submission to an authoritarian traditional order that draws upon the cunning of capitalist expansion at those sites of our consciousness, we might not have taken cognizance of.

With these assumptions I have tried to make use of 'theory' in this book. The story of India, as it unfolds from Forster through Nehru to Rushdie displays, like the proverbial assimilative power of 'Hinduism', an uncanny absorptive capacity: ingesting critical concepts and analytical categories one after another within the metaosmotic pores of its huge intestine. However, 'India' of this story gains identity only by negation, displacement and disruption of the narrative authority, which tried to give it its time, habitation and voice. An India of 'our' choice, an India free of narrativistic, ideological and political violence, free of critical miscegenation, and theoretical over-determination as often candidly proposed by the authoritarian love and sympathy shown by its migrant children abroad does not—like the much esotericised entity called 'subaltern'—speak as yet. To do so would be to devise different frames of narrativisation and to invent a new imaginative geography, both of which throw the kind of challenges that can be met only with the writing of a new book.

Notes

1. See for instance Partha Chatterjee, *The Nation and Its Fragments* (Colonial and Post-colonial Histories) (New Jersey: Princeton University Press, 1993) and Dipesh Chakrabarty, *Provincializing Europe* (Post-colonial Thought and Historical Difference) (New Delhi: Oxford University Press, 2001).
2. Hayden White, *The Content of the Form* (Baltimore: Johns Hopkins University Press, 1987). Also see Michel Foucault's later work, especially the *History of Sexuality* (vol.I) as example of the formation of 'self' by the demands of narrative, and in turn, by discursive regimes.
3. The phrase is from Sudipta Kaviraj. See Kaviraj, 'On State, Society and Discourse in India' in James Manor O (ed.), *Rethinking Third World Politics* (London and New York: Longman, 1991), pp.72-99.
4. This has been argued in many social and economic histories critical of the early colonial period. One such authoritative history would be Ranajit Guha, *A Rule of Property for Bengal: An Essay on the Idea of Permanent Settlement* (Delhi: Orient Longman, 1982; 1st ed. 1963).
5. Marc Galanter, *Law and Society in Modern India* (Delhi: Oxford University Press, 1977), p.16.
6. Several variations of this are to be found in existentialist, and some versions of 'post-modernist' voices confronting the

ontological 'presence' of India. See Martin Heidegger, *Being and Time*, translated by J. Macquare and Edward Robinson (Oxford: Basil Blackwell, 1985) as the most provocative statement of this genre.

7. The Orientalist project via William Jones et al is too well-known to need special mention here. For one authoritative account see David Kopf, *Orientalism and Bengal Renaissance* (Berkeley: University of California Press, 1976). Nehru shows, however, much greater ingenuity in the style and rhetorical devices used for enumeration. The narrative style of *The Discovery of India* 'prefigures' the contemporary disjointing of language and time, or language and linearity, in order to produce the India of 'future' that would answer the call of its liberal citizen-subject.

8. The school of the 'subaltern' historiography led by Ranajit Guha is well known. But the reaction to this by 'new' traditionalists, as well as secular modernists, presents a wide spectrum of positions. Of special mention would be Ashis Nandy 'History's Forgotten Doubles' *History and Theory* 34 (May 1995), and Aijaz Ahmad, *The Lineage of the Present* (Delhi: Tulika, 1996).

9. This is an extremely interesting if rare and 'new' area for research that goes a long way ahead of traditional 'folklore' and 'popular culture' studies, beyond a mere critique of 'Orientalist discourses'. Mahasweta Devi's fictional work is of course well-known. G.N. Devy's work on Indian mythology would be considered a step in that direction. Also see the currently ongoing work on the Kabir tradition in Amarkantak in Madhya Pradesh, India.

10. An excellent review of such criticism of anti-humanist essentialism appears in Tony Bannet, 'Texts in History: the determinations of readings and their contexts' in D. Attridge, G. Bennington and R. Young (ed.) *Post-Structuralism and the Question of History* (London: CUP, 1987) pp.63-82.

11. Dipesh Chakravarty, *Rethinking Working Class History* (Delhi: Oxford University Press, 1989), pp.xi-xiii.

12. For many hazards of 'quick' and (mis)applications of Michel Foucault (despite Edward Said's *Orientalism*, a classic of the genre, that was extremely interesting and provocative) see James

Miller, *The Passion of Michel Foucault* (New York: Simon & Schuster), esp. pp.286-319.

13. Baudrillard, whose critical stance sometimes appears to be a symptom of what it seeks to analyse and critique, has recorded such 'acts' of consumption prevalent in high-tech, late capitalist societies, under the mysterious designation of the 'hyperreal'. See Jean Baudrillard, *America* (London: Verso, 1989); and *Cool Memories* (London: Verso, 1990).

1

Many Voices of English Liberalism and the Question of India

In his essay, 'The Challenge of Our Time', Forster describes himself as belonging to 'the fag end of Victorian liberalism'.[1] This statement, important though it is for an understanding of *A Passage to India*, is undercut by the interplay of several other currents of thought from within and outside liberalism. As Lionel Trilling puts it, 'for all his long commitment to the doctrines of liberalism, Forster was at war with the liberal imagination.[2] Trilling's critical comment on Forster shares many assumptions with other contemporary critical voices.[3] Taken together, these voices enable us to pose three major questions: first, what does it mean to be a Victorian liberal, secondly, what was the nature of the liberal imagination? and lastly, what would it mean to be a liberal and yet be at war with it? With specific reference to *A Passage to India* it is important to raise such questions, since (as I shall argue in the next chapter) it is precisely the dilemma of liberal humanism, or the internal contradictions of the liberal tradition, which can be shown to be at cross purposes in the novel. Put differently, *A Passage to India* can be discussed as a stage in which several contradictory currents of liberal thought in England came into collision, pushing liberalism to its limits.

Having said that, it can be further shown how such tensions within liberal discourse engaged with, and in part are enabled by the larger and often hidden commitments of the narratives of Imperialism. It is true that Imperialism was not a monolithic, inhibitory and definitive phenomenon to which all problems arising within English liberal discourse can be simply referred; it is, on the contrary, the complexity of Imperialist narratives and their ability to fashion new tools, concepts, images and vocabularies for dealing with native cultures which must be considered carefully, if we are to account for the multi-dimensional and enabling conjuncture of the tensions with liberalism at home and its shaping influence and requirements in the colonies.

Writing in 1959, Eric Stokes, an English historian, acknowledges the crucial, interactive and reciprocal nexus of the urgencies of Imperialism in British India with the nature of liberalism in England. The shaping of an 'English' character, the rise of the 'gentleman' and the hammering out of the protestant ethic into a new wave of individualism, all draw on colonial investments in economic, cultural, political and aesthetic spheres. The scope of Stokes' analysis is limited to an official, somewhat magisterial, recounting of historical events and their affiliation with political institutions. Despite that, it is a useful pointer towards what we might study as a subterranean regime of discourses, institutions and relations of power. According to Stokes:

> It has been my conviction that British rule in India was not a disconnected and meaningless fragment of English history, but that even from the most insular standpoint it holds a mirror unto nature, reflecting in *English character and mind a way that often escapes the Englishman confined within his domestic setting...* I would like to think it [Utilitarian movement] counters the

> prevalent tendency to be interested in the Utilitarian solely as abstract, novel, and political theories, to the neglect of their practical aims and influence... the nature of these practical aims was deduced logically from their abstract theory, and that both fall into a system *whose completeness is more obvious in Indian than in English history*.[4]
>
> (emphasis added)

India certainly played a significant part in fashioning English civilisation—its unequivocal emphasis on order, sense of moral duty, firmness, manliness and sexuality—even as India was believed to act as a disturbing force, 'a magnetic power placed at the periphery tending to distort the natural development of Britain's character as a great commercial power.'[5] In addition, the question of empire often produced an authoritarian counter-current into the mainstream of liberal opinion. As a result, several liberal thinkers were either led into maintaining double standards with regard to freedom—one for the colonies and the other for home. John Stuart Mill is a glaring example. Others such as Chatman wondered whether 'the possession of a despotically-rule empire might not prove fatal to the cause of liberty in England.'[6] Indeed considering the indifference and hostility which greeted the demands made on behalf of the colonies, it is remarkable how many of the movements of the English life and English ideas tested their strength and fought their early battles upon the ground provided by the Indian question. For Adam Smith, the much-despised 'mercantile system' had its origins in the East India Company, which he denounced as barbarous. The cause of Free Trade was hotly debated in the struggle for the abolition of the company's commercial functions. Other contemporary English movements of ideas such as Evangelism, which laid the foundations of character for the typical nineteenth century Victorian Englishman, owed a similar debt to the Indian question. The militant Christianity of Clapham which had taken up the cause of Indian missions was a tremendous force in public life. A number of Christian missionary groups that arose in the wake of Clapham—the Grands, the Stephens, the Thorntons, and others—were to send forth generations of Indian civil servants stamped with the Evangelical assurance and earnestness of purpose, if not always the old religious conviction. Critical accounts document the mode in which *Indian experience hardened certain traits in the English character.*[7] The fierce, downright exterior, the instinct for his own caste and race, a consciousness of religion, the sense of moral code and a constant dwelling under an unwritten law of duty—all the images of English character that the imagination summons the picture from the Victorian age in England as much as from Forster's novel—are all traits and qualities which were historically hammered and chiseled out of an active engagement with the Indian question. It is this particular liberal current of English thought which shaped its own destiny out of a multilevel contact with India—even as it was to shape the course of action in India for generations to come—that needs a critical attention from us.

The word 'liberal', or the phrase 'liberal humanism', has been turned into a blanket sign often carrying widely different and contradictory associations. For our purposes, considering the particular tradition which Forster is drawing upon, it is desirable to carefully chart its trajectory and then go on to show how *A Passage to India* draws upon this tradition, inflecting it further to generate a peculiar combination of discourses which were relatively unknown until the 1920s.

In a fundamental sense the word 'liberal' is derived from the French Revolution with its uncompromising slogan 'Liberty', 'Equality', 'Brotherhood', or 'Death'. In the early nineteenth century when the word made its first appearance in the context of English thought, a liberal was identified as a revolutionary thinker, more usually known as 'radical' because he or she attacked social institutions at their roots, with the aim of either reforming them altogether or abolishing them and establishing new ones. It was from about 1813 that the cause of freedom and reform gathered momentum. In the parliamentary battle of 1813 the free-traders had stripped the company of its commercial monopoly over India, and separately, Wilberforce and Charles Grant had gained freedom for Indian missions. By 1818, liberalism as a force was emerging in England. The romantic poets had set about the task which Shelley described in his preface to *Prometheus Unbound*: 'the cloud of mind was discharging its collected lightning, and the equilibrium between institutions and opinions was about to be restored.'[8] It was in 1818 that Macaulay revolted against his father's Torysim and declared himself a radical liberal. Also, in the same year, James Mill published his *History of British India* and became a candidate for high office in the Company's Home Government. The radical movement was especially inspired by the ideas of the lawyer Jeremy Bentham, and from him the most energetic part of it was labelled 'Utilitarian', because as his disciple John Stuart Mill put it, he asked about any institution or idea the practical question, 'What is the use of it?' and decided the correctness of policy in accordance with the answer.

However, to understand the specific articulation of liberalism with the so-called 'external factor', or more precisely, imperialism, it is necessary to ask: what is capital as a whole in the specific circumstances of British social development? It is certainly not an undifferentiated and abstract category. It is rather an imperialist formation with an accompanying and sustaining relationship to the civil society, with its moral, social, and cultural preferences, values, and tastes. Further, the late nineteenth century liberal thinker was not isolated professionally. The professional life of a colonial administrator, writer, or economist was not cut up into specialised compartments as it is today. The result was an active, reciprocal reinforcement of one area of activity by the requirements of another. Herbert Sussman has observed of Victorian literature that it represented the 'end of hope in the blessings of the machine'.[9] This shift, marked by the new upper-middle class generation coming of age, and shaped by the 'gentle manly' ideal was, more relaxed, more cultivated, and more detached from economic struggle than its predecessors. Fathers who had spent their lives reading the Bible and making money with equally dedicated intensity very probably had agnostic children who were suspicious of the effects of money accumulated from the vast land holdings, or from the trade venture in the overseas.

A sharp reaction to this 'commercial society' produced another realm—that of *aesthetics* and of a universal humanism as the *answer to the ills of a beleaguered humanity*. For their social and cultural values, and criticism, members of the generation turned to men like Matthew Arnold—men of letters who were both new style professional men and social thinkers. Their criticism of mid-Victorian England, as Wiener has argued, 'was more widely influential than similar criticisms on the continent or in America, contributed in a major way, to the containment of industrial values and the shaping of a new cultural tradition for twentieth-century Britain'.[10]

Symptomatic of this 'social criticism', was the work of Anthony Trollope, whose strategy was to appeal directly to universal values of humanity, which transcended mere politics. This is best expressed in his novel *Doctor Thorne*:

> England is not yet a commercial country in the sense in which that epithet is used for her; and let us still hope that she will not soon become so.... England a commercial country! Yes, as Venice was. She may excel other nations in commerce, but yet it is not that in which she most provides herself, in which she most excels. Merchants as such are not the first men among us; though it perhaps be barely open, to a merchant, to become one of them. Buying and selling is good and necessary; it is very necessary; and may, possibly, be very good; but it cannot be the noblest work of

man; and let us hope that it may not in our time be esteemed the noblest work of an English.[11]

This represents *the capture of liberalism by imperialist design par excellence.*[12] The Imperialist venture in the colonies required commerce, economic expansion, free trade, and along with it a breakdown of the pre-existing socio-cultural inertia which seemed to obstruct such a venture. Hence, the telling emphasis on individual enterprise, freedom, democracy and equality—all those liberal values which served to consolidate the expanding military, naval and economic regime. By the same token, however, it was equally significant to preserve the 'cultural' superiority of the 'Englishness' which was shaped and firmly established by more than a generation of thinkers. The mystique of 'Englishness', 'English culture', 'the English nation', was not merely a desperate attempt to save a dilapidated edifice from going to pieces; neither was it of a decorative, functional value. Rather, the 'English' emerged as a plane of cultural and social investment for several advancing interest groups as the rising imperialist bourgeoisie strove to maintain stability, order, and harmony, both against the working classes at home, and against the far spreading radical-liberal tide in the colonies. The ethos of *the public school* as well as its self consciously 'rural' surrounding, imparted the much needed cultural preservations, which was, like a double-edged weapon, to achieve a double function: first, to check the tide of liberal wave from becoming too unwieldy, too rebellious against the gentry-bourgeois coalition at home; and secondly, to consolidate the British empire by churning out a *'British national culture' as the universal norm, as the torch-bearer for the rest of the humanity.* Although less than one in twenty Englishmen ever passed through the public school, they became an archetypal national institution. 'When we are criticising its products, 'noted a defender in 1929, 'whether by way of praise or blame, it is really to a great extent, *the English character* that we are criticising.[13] After examining in detail the faults of the public school, the Clarendon Commission turned to their greater merit:

> These schools have been the chief nurseries of our statesmen; in them, and in schools modeled after them, men of all various classes that make up the English society destined for every profession and career, have been brought up on a footing of social equality, and have contracted the most enduring friendships, and some of the ruling habits of their lives; and they have had perhaps the largest share in moulding the character of an English gentleman.[14]

This process of shaping English gentleman who was to advance the cultural tradition of England, along with its commercial enterprise abroad, had been firmly established by the turn of the century, and was carried forward in the twentieth century, even as the 'cultural' side of this programme had to stretch and reshape itself in its multiple encounters with the East. The cultural custodians of late Victorian England—Mill, Arnold, Ruskin and Carlyle—though each different from the others in his own way, contributed to the nationalization and the preservation of the English cultural tradition. As a result, we see that the contradiction within the liberal tradition, or the differences in their individual positions were absorbed by the over arching concern *for the moral quality of a truly English life*. This was a phenomenon of extraordinary significance in the sense that despite different articulation of culture and society in England, and even apparently contradictory solutions to the specific problems suggested by these liberal thinkers, all *of them contributed in one way or another to what I like to term the 'imperialist design of liberalism'*. This I would like to considered at some length in the following pages.

John Stuart Mill, whose concern for individual liberty over the social order impressed Forster's own writing a great deal, chose to react against the current of 'practical reason' and 'industry' as automatic vehicles of 'human goodness'. In his famous essay on Bentham he wrote:

> All he [Bentham] can do is but to indicate means by which, in any given state of the national mind, the material interests of society can be protected; saving the question of which others must judge, whether the one of those means would have, on the national characters, any injurious influences...[15]

> The question had to be saved for others because as Mill argued 'practical reason' was inadequate to understand what would be harmful for the national mind and the national character. Bentham was ignorant of, or chose to ignore:

> The sense of honor, and personal dignity—that feeling of personal exaltation and degradation which acts independently of other people's opinion or even in defiance of it; the love of beauty, the passion of the artist, the love of order, of congruity, of consistency in all things.[16]

The love of art, order, beauty, and personal exaltation—virtues which were coterminous with the 'national mind' and the 'national character—could never be assessed by a mechanical application of mere 'practical reason'. The 'personal' was in a deep sense always above the political, hence the parameters of judgment drawn from the public life and public rationality would be inadequate to judge the particular quality of an individual. However, to recognise the reality of the 'culture of the human spirit' is one thing; to learn how to nourish that culture without the demands of practical qualities may be altogether a different matter. Indeed, in the ultimate analysis it may turn out that the so-called demands of practical politics may shape and determine the very existence of the culture of the human spirit. Hence, the emphasis on an 'educated', 'mentally superior' minority representation in *Mill's scheme of universal suffrage* which—and this was exceptional in his time—included female suffrage. This system of minority representation turns to be a way of reorganising franchise to compensate for its extension. Mill, of course, regarded, universal suffrage to be inevitable as well as desirable, but when in 1858 it was suspected that working-class majorities would be neither deferential nor altruistic, he also feared the extension of franchise and doubted the democratic assumption underlying it, the assumption that the most valuable representation is the most accurate reflection of social facts, so he writes:

> The natural tendency of representing a government, as of modern civilization, is towards collective mediocrity: and this tendency is increased by all reductions (of the property qualification) and extensions of the franchise, their effect being to place the principal power in the hands of classes more and more below the highest level of instruction in the community.[17]

Here, the accumulation of numbers leads to a devaluation of the idea of representation and of political practice. Therefore, his reposed parliament based on the concept of 'minority representation', *would not correspond to any empirical social reality* but would, rather, directly *represent value to the population.* The state, in his scheme, represents value; first, by constructing its institutions in such a way that *they teach the population what it should want* instead of *passively mirroring what it does want*. The state does stand for a normative value to be realised by the whole nation as he makes clear in 'the minority of instructed minds scattered through the local constituencies, would unite to return a number, proportional to their own numbers, of 'the very ablest men the country contains' ['On Representative Government', p.260].

> The national institutions should place all things that they are concerned with, before the mind of the citizen in the light in which it is good that he should regard them: and as it is for his good that he should think that every one is entitled to some influence, but the better and wiser to more than others, it is

> important that this conviction should be professed by the state, and embodied in the national institutions [p.283].

The state and its accompanying *national institution* will become *the shaping agencies of value and will determine what is inherently good for every citizen*. It was this representation of value to a mere social fact or political participation, which led Mill to argue against their demand of self-government in the British colonies. It cannot be overemphasised that for all of Mill's 'revolutionary ideas', he never, thought Indians capable of ruling themselves. The 'culture of the human spirit', the 'national mind' and the British 'national character' had always to evade the question of Indian freedom. So, he wrote in 'On Representative Government':

> If the smaller nationality, supposed to be the more advanced in improvement, is able to overcome the greater, as the Macedonians, reinforced by the Greeks, did Asia, and the English India, there is often a gain to civilization; but the conquerors and the conquered can not in this case live together *under the same free institutions*. The absorption of the conquerors in the less advanced people would be an evil; these must be governed as subjects, and the state of things is either a benefit or a misfortune, according as the subjugated people *have or have not reached the state in which it is an injury not to be under a free government*, and according as the conquerors do or do not use their superiority in a manner calculated to fit the conquered for a higher stage of important... [p.364].
>
> (emphasis added)

This is typical of the schizophrenic practice, especially after the 1880s, when for a variety of reasons imperial rule occupied the English imagination with much greater intensity, and united late 19th century liberal intellectuals in Britain. Personal exaltation, free institutions, beauty and art, were the issues related to a particular stage of development, or a higher stage of improvement which, they argued, fell out side the scope of the 'subjugated race'. Hence, liberal though he was, John Stuart Mill—as a particularly telling case in point—could still say that 'the sacred duties which civilized nations owe to the independence and nationality of each other, are not binding towards those to whom nationality and independence are certain evil, or best a questionable good'.[18]

This is indeed a *classic instance of the Imperial* design of liberalism.

Another great Victorian liberal, sixteen years younger than Mill, believed that politics and culture ought to be so divided that if either must take precedence in that age then it should be the latter. Also, unlike Mill, who though of individual liberty and freedom as the greatest virtue, he laid stress on the state which ought to be 'the union of our best selves' in order to promote and establish a culture, which represents 'the best that is known and thought in the world.' This was Matthew Arnold, who described himself as 'a liberal of the future'. In his classic, *Culture and Anarchy*, which constitutes his definition of culture, Arnold described *a truly 'national' culture as one, which 'seeks to do away with classes altogether*'. However, his social criticism was predominantly aimed at the middle classes—his 'barbarians' and 'populace' receive but a glance in comparison with the steely gaze directed at his 'philistines.' The 'master thought' of his writings, he confessed, was the 'bad civilization of the English middle class. With the ever growing importance of this class, its bad civilization—narrow and materialistic—would poison national life: 'England has no national purposes or ideals, other than the instrumental ones such as freedom and work':

> Freedom, like Industry, is a very good horse to ride;—but to ride somewhere. You seem to think that you have only got to get on the back of your horse Freedom, or your horse Industry, and to ride away as hard as you can, to be sure of coming to the right destination..[20]

By the time (1870) *Culture and Anarchy* gets written Arnold's cultural project is crystallised in the form of a state, which would transcend all classes. No accumulation, or combination of mere social facts, argued Arnold, will add up to either culture or values. Like Mill, he added, if England is to be saved from anarchy, if it is to deal for instance with working-class demands for the franchise without disintegrating through intensified class conflict, *the state must become the representative of some thing other than social facts.*

'That something' is, in Arnold's phrase, the 'best self', by which 'we are united, impersonal, at harmony' [p.95]. Certain individuals, Arnold assured us, have already managed to rise above their social and personal selves:

> Therefore, when we speak of ourselves as divided into barbarians (aristocrat), philistines (middle-class) and populace (working-class), we must be understood always to imply that within each of these classes there are certain number of aliens, if we may so call them,—persons who are mainly led, not by their class-spirit but by a general humane spirit, by the love of human perfection.[21]

The 'aliens', as the epithet indicates, are even more thoroughly defined by their asocial characteristics than John Mill's intellectual elites who had 'mental superiority' by virtue of which they could be given plurality of votes in the system of universal suffrage.[22] These 'aliens' serve the same function as Mill's intellectual elites in that they embody the things to which politics should be devoted but which are necessarily excluded from politics under descriptive systems of representation. This could be substantiated by showing how one whole chapter of *Culture and Anarchy*, 'Doing as one likes,' is devoted to refuting the Utilitarian reliance on individual liberty as the producer of value and to showing how ubiquitous Utilitarian assumptions are in English political thought. Thus, the Hyde Park rioter in his demand for franchise is merely extending the logic of his betters, not introducing a new principle of representation:

> *He has no visionary schemes of revolution and transformation*, though of course he would like his class to rule, as the aristocratic class like their class to rule and the middle class theirs... The rough has not yet quite found his groove and settled down to his word, and so he is just asserting his personal liberty a little, going where he likes, assembling where he likes, bawling as he likes, hustling as he likes, just as the rest of us,—as the county squires in the aristocratic class, as the political dissenters in the middle class—*he has no idea of a state*.[23]

The answer to the ills of a nation, a nation beleaguered with anarchy, lay in the empowering of the state: an organ which, for Arnold, represents our 'best self', by which 'we are united, impersonal, at harmony' [p.95]. Arnold's way of pitting the best self against the ordinary self, then, and associating the former with the state is very close to Mill's method of counterpoising 'the instructed mind' and 'disinterested action' with personal and class-bound action. Arnold draws on Mill's ideas, then widespread in liberal, intellectual circles, and builds on that a new argument about the content of political representation. *While Mill uses education in general to describe the process by which one rises above his persona, class-bound self, the magic word 'culture' will do the job for Arnold.* 'Culture', for Arnold, is the keyword—a word that gives a wholly different emphasis to his project of national, and thereby imperial regeneration.

Through this line of enquiry, as we have seen, culture, especially English culture, a realm of values, becomes opposed to society, a realm of facts, as it also links directly by the same logic, literature and the state. However, and this is significant, unlike those of the English Romantics and other liberal lines of inquiry preceding Arnold, this culture is *secular* and not *religious*. Consequently, culture and state become all the more interdependent:

> We want an authority, and we find nothing but jealous classes, checks and a deadlock; culture suggests the idea of state. We find no basis for a firm state power in our ordinary-selves; culture suggests one to us in our best self [p.96].

To read this resounding conclusion of Arnold in our own times, no matter how much we strive to read it against the grain and however accurately and richly we account for its historical roots, is to undertake a prodigious task. For the task involves the burden of unloading a colossal imaginative power at work for more than a century, which *divided the realm of value from that of bare social existence,* naturalizing the superiority of the former over the latter. Indeed, it enabled generation of thinkers, artists, poets, statesmen, and politicians to shape their worlds around the *mystique of culture* as a panacea for all human problems. This unique discourse on culture, coming as it did at a very crucial juncture of English history, (just around the time when there was vociferous demand for social and political equality and universal suffrage) took the wind out of the sails of socio-political struggles, as it apparently represented universal interest as against mere sectional or regional one. Also, by the same token, culture, or more precisely, English *national* culture, achieved a disinterested, normative value against which all-struggling societies, including the colonized ones such as Indian, Arab or African, had to measure themselves. In other words, by equating culture with state power and representing such a move as apolitical, even humane, Arnoldian discourse subordinated in a single stroke all those social and cultural systems which *did not lay claim to universal knowledge* as essentially inferior, and therefore as unfit to represent the common interest.

The significant point of Arnoldian discourse is that it demonstrated clearly how European liberal culture often, if not always, *characterized itself in such a way as simultaneously to validate its own preference while also advocating those preferences in conjunction with distant imperial rule.* Imperialist culture should not be seen, therefore, either as an effect of English liberalism, or as being coterminous with late Victorian emphasis on the cultural as against the political; but rather as a *plurality of responses to the definitions of culture* and society that were principally arrived at the late Victorian period.

Frederic Jameson while writing about 'production of the subject' in the formation of new academic disciplines, has arrived at this formulation in a totally different context:

> Culture itself as a system, but also the individual texts and works of arts and literature that are 'included' in it, are both best grasped as responses to situations, as solutions to contradictions, as answers to questions. This conception of the structure of culture—but also of the individual cultural or literary text—is reinforced by a number of important contemporary philosophical currents.. It usefully neutralizes two traditional but equally problematical conceptions of art: on the one hand, art can no longer be seen as autonomous... If it is in one way or another a reaction to a situation we must necessarily reconstruct that situation in order to grasp it fully. On the other hand, however, the work of art can on this view no longer be seen as a mere document about a context or a situation either, as some mere 'reflection' of a real social state of things, from which we can at best obtain information. For if the work is an answer, a solution, a reaction, *it is a form of praxis; it can no longer be grasped passively; it must be seen as an active intervention in a concrete social situation and grasped as a problem or dilemma.*[24]
>
> (emphasis added)

In other words, if we want to grasp the power of Arnoldian discourse, or more generally, the liberal discourse on culture of his time we have to read it as an active process of reconstruction of the entire cultural field; a reconstruction in which there has been a continuing investment. It is in this sense that we can associate the contradictions within liberalism and the continuing imperialist cultural practice. However, as we shift attention from Arnoldian conception of 'culture' to E.M. Forster's meticulous inflection of this Victorian term, the site of the formation of culture, art and order has changed, but not the fundamental premise of the argument. As Forster has it:

> I have no mystic faith in the people [Mill's, or Arnold's nation-state]. I have in the individual. He seems to me a divine achievement and I mistrust any view that belittles him. If anyone calls you a wretched little individual—and I have been called that—don't you take it lying down? You are important because everyone else is an individual too—including the person who criticizes you. In asserting your personality you are playing for your side...[25]

Thus, the individual is perfectly right to repel any 'maiden aunt' who tries to unburden on him the load of culture. This however doesn't mean that 'nothing is happening...' it means only that if the individual can not use culture to create the inner order of his own mind, then it is better for him to reject it. However, what constitutes this 'inner order' and the 'individual'—his tastes, social and political positions, alliances and interests—is not even taken cognizance of, let alone analysed. Hence, the continuation of Arnoldian liberal emphasis on the transcendent, universal status of art, despite an apparent contradiction:

> Art is valuable not because it is educational (though it may be), not because it is recreative (though it may be), not because everybody enjoys it (for everybody does not), not even because it has to do with beauty. It is valuable because it has to do with order, and creates little world of its own, possessing internal harmony, in the bosom of this disordered planet.[26]

Two things come to a sharp focus here. One, Forster would have us treat art as 'autonomous,' creating 'little worlds of their own'; two, he would like the reader to 'hear' the personal voice of the author; to hear him 'talk' through his book.[27] With issues such as these we come to the mode of liberal thinking which is elegantly assimilated to *literary modernism*. Literary modernism finds its fullest articulation in the *concept of voice* as the locus of unique, personal identity, and in particular, the projection of the artist's voice as a personal, private style, as unmistakable as your fingerprint, as incomparable as your own body.[28] Style, as voice, proclaims its allegiance to the individualized body and individualistic personality, so that the modernist aesthetic becomes organically linked to the conception of a unique self and private identity.[29]

For a critique of these issues, particularly as they interweave with the liberal tradition as much as they are inflected by the colonialist narratology generating a new aesthetics in its own right, we shall turn to the next chapter where we undertake a detailed discussion of E.M. Forster's novel *A Passage to India*.

Notes

1. E.M. Forster, *Two Cheers for Democracy* (1951), Abinger edition., ed. O.Stallybrass (London: Edward Arnold, 1972), p.151.
2. Lionel Trilling, *The Liberal Imagination: Essays on Literature and Society* (1948;rpt. London: Secker & Warburg, 1951), p.34.
3. Apart from Trilling, Several criticism have found Forster to be at war with the liberal tradition, while inhabiting it at the same time. Foremost among them are H.A. Smith, 'Forster's Humanism and the Nineteenth Century' in *E.M. Forster: A Collection of Critical Essays*, ed. M. Bradbury, pp.106-16; Brijraj Singh, *The Development of a Critical Tradition: From Pater to Yeats*. (Delhi: Macmillan, 1978). For a very comprehensive

examination of this question, see Michael Bentley, *The Liberal Mind, 1914-29* (Cambridge: CUP, 1977), p. 28-67: also see his essay 'The Liberal Response to Socialism, 1918-29', in *Essays in Anti-Labour History: Responses to the Rise of Labour in Britain*, ed. Kenneth D. Brown (London: Macmillan, 1974), pp.42-73.

4. Stokes' book provides very useful source-material to demonstrate the shaping influence of Indian question on the 19th century English economic, social and moral values, see Eric Stokes, *The English Utilitarians and India* (London: OUP 1959), p.vi.
5. Ibid, p.x.
6. Ibid.
7. Among several studies along this line such as Allen Greenberger, *The British Image of India* (London: OUP, 1969), Dennis Kincaid, *British Social Life in India*, 1608-1937 (London: Macmillan, 1939), L.H. Mayers, *An End of the Hours* (London: OUP, 1938) and George Orwell, *Burmese Days* (London: John Chapman, 1935), to name only a few, Ashis Nandy's seems to be a highly stimulating and critical account. Nandy's argument is that the aggressive rulers are themselves caught in the 'image' they are required to live by in order to rule over their subjects. Also, in his analysis of the psychology of colonialism, Nandy discusses the production of 'models' of 'official' dissent—models that might apply to Fielding's situation in Passage: 'It is possible today to be anti-colonial in a way which is specified and promoted by the modern world-view as 'proper', 'sane' and 'rational'. Hence, colonialism creates a culture in which the ruled is constantly tempted to fight its ruler within the psychological and ideological limits set by the latter.' See Ashis Nandy, *The Intimate Enemy: Loss and Recovery of Self Under Colonialism* (Delhi: OUP, 1983), p.xii.
8. P.B. Shelley, 'Preface' to *Prometheus Unbound*, reprinted (London: Longman, 1978).
9. Herbert Sussman *Victorian and the Machine* (Cambridge: CUP, 1968), p.91.
10. Martin Wiener, *English Culture and the Decline of the Industrial Spirit* 1850-1980 (Cambridge: CUP, 1981, pp.30-31.

11. Anthony Trollope, *Doctor Thorne* (1858) (London, 1934), pp.11-12, quoted by Wiener, p.31.
12. The 'Capture of Liberalism by Imperialism' nullified the former's radical aspect, and gave the working-class the task of 'recovering and accentuating that radicalism as a necessary part of its own political advance'. This 'second bourgeois revolution' remains in that limited sense on the historical agenda, but 'it is surely not the case that recognizing this entails a general ideological retreat to old-fashioned radicalism:. Tom Nairn, *The Break-up of Britain.* (London: Verso, 1981).
13. Bernard Darwin, *The English Public School* (London: Macmillan 1928). For further elaboration on how 'English' character as embodied in English moral and ethical values was constructed by the crucial nexus between the British Parliament, the British Education System, and the Christian missionaries in the 19th century, and how its specific articulation through the diffusion of English literature in India became the universal norm of behaviour, see Gauri Viswanathan, 'The Beginnings of English Literary Study in British India: *Oxford Literary Review*. Vol.IX no.2 (1987).
14. Quoted in T.W. Branford, *The Rise of the Public Schools* (London: Everyman, 1967), p.15.
15. See John Stuart Mill, 'Remarks on Bentham's Philosophy' G.L. Williams (ed.), *John Stuart Mill on Politics and Society* (London: Fontana Press, 1976). pp.99.
16. Ibid p.112.
17. John Stuart Mill, 'On Representative Government', *Utilitarianism, Liberty, Representative Government*, 3rd edn. (London: Everyman, 1910) p.259.
18. John Stuart Mill, *Disquisitions and Discussions*, Vol.III (London: Longman Green, Reader & Dyer, 1875), pp.167-8.
19. Matthew Arnold, 'My Countrymen' (1866), quoted in Martin Wiener, (op.cit.), p.36.
20. Ibid.
21. Matthew Arnold, *Culture and Anarchy*, ed. D. Wilson (London: Routledge and Kegan Paul, 1960), p.109.

22. In 'On Representative Government', although Mill writes of 'instructed minds' receiving representation 'proportional to their own number', he quickly revises himself with a plan to have votes 'weighed as well as counted.' This 'plurality scheme' as he calls it, is designed to combat the 'twin evils' of universal suffrage, 'that of too low a standard of political intelligence, and that of class-legislation, 'by giving plural votes to people with 'mental superiority.' Mental superiority, claimed Mill, 'could be ascertained by a number of signs: occupation, education, and voluntary examination, at which any person whatever... might prove that the came up to the standard of knowledge and ability laid down as sufficient, and be admitted, in consequence to the plurality of votes' (p.286): Thus by the introduction of this measure, although the representatives of the 'instructed' would not obtain a clear majority, they would have sufficient numbers to prevent the 'class legislation' of the representatives of the 'uninstructed'.
23. *Culture and Anarchy*, ed. D. Wilson (London: Routledge and Kegan Paul, 1960), pp.80-81.
24. Fredric Jameson, 'The State of the Subject III', *Critical Quarterly* Vol.29, No.4 (Winter 1987), pp.16-25.
25. E.M. Forster, 'Does Culture Matter?' in *Two Cheers for Democracy*, (op.cit), p.21.
26. E.M. Forster, 'The Challenger of Our Time' in *Two Cheers for Democracy*, pp.148-69.
27. Ibid, pp.90-111.
28. Forster's conversation with Indian students, Quoted by John Colmer in his book, *E.M. Forster: The Personal Voice* (London: Routledge & Kegan Paul, 1975), p.193.
29. Fredric Jameson, 'Post-modernism and Consumer Society' *The Anti-Aesthetic: Essays On Postmodern Culture*, e.d. Hal Foster (Port Townsend, Wash: Bay Press, 1983), p.114.

2

A Passage to India: The Critical Reception

I

Critical scholarship on *A Passage to India*, despite being rich, diverse, and even mutually antagonistic, is unanimous on one point: the all-inclusiveness of this work. The novel is shown to possess an absolutely inexhaustible potential for interpretation given its highly complex symbolic pattern.

W.H. Mason's account, for instance, echoes several other critical voices, in its search for an unfathomable and impenetrable core of meaning which frustrates reason, form, and any straight forward critical approach. He writes:

> The more we respond to *A Passage to India* the more we see it as a novel of successive planes of interest. As with the receding arches in the Indian sky, so with the perspective of meaning in the book.[1]

Yet the differences of opinion and 'successive planes of interest' seem to be finally merged, or so it is suggested, when one 'learns' to appreciate them as necessary parts of the overall design of the novel, or as integral parts of its artistic wholeness.[2]

In the extensive studies of Forster's aesthetic achievement—characters, plot, imagery, metaphysics, language, even mysticism—the underlying assumption seems to be that politics is something that great literature transcends.[3] Thus, in a foreword to G.K. Das' study of Forster's Indian sources, John Beer concludes: '... his long account of the matter recalls us to the fact that Forster's basic preoccupations always extended far beyond politics.[4] And for John Colmer, writing a centenary essay on Forster in 1979, politics has at best a dubious place; it belongs, and then only questionably, to those most oppressed by the political situations the novel represents: 'It is perhaps natural for Indian writers to be especially critical of Forster's alleged political deficiencies but in general political statements do not belong to the novelistic realm.'[5] So, the hallmark of great art, it is argued, has its intrinsic ability to resist any single or decisive interpretation. While changing methods of 'textual analysis' and the ongoing march of 'historical context' will definitely expand the scope of critical insight, a great work of literature such as *A Passage to India* would remain irreducible to any 'cult' interpretations, be it psychological, aesthetic, historic or sharply political. For, it is in the very fabric of 'art' to subsume and cancel these conflicting positions simultaneously.

Forster's own account of the novel, for what it is worth, bears testimony to this position. He disparaged the possibility of any single approach, however meticulously researched, and cast a quasi-mystic, contemplative and amorphous halo around his book. Though he acknowledges the significance of the local and historical elements in the novel, he sees so in a manner which reduces them to influence in a background or a setting:

> The book is not really about politics, though it is the political aspect of it that caught the general public and made it sell. It's about something wider than politics, about the search of the human race for a more lasting home, about the universe, as embodied in the Indian earth and the Indian sky, about the

horror lurking in the Marabar Caves and the release symbolized by the birth of Krishna. It is—or rather desires to be—philosophic and poetic.[6]

The 'search for the human race for a more lasting home' in the symbolic description of 'the Indian sky' and 'the Indian earth' is itself deeply political. Its narrative energy, as I am going to argue later, was drawn out of an 'imaginative geography' of India and its authority established by an already existing inventory of self-referential and self congratulatory historical as well as literary accounts of Europe on India. It was this particular 'discovery' of India, where the grossly materialistic, mechanised, industrial civilization of Europe, it was said, could regain its lost spirituality and thus revitalise itself.[7]

The order of art, it is further assumed by the critical scholarship in the Forsterian vein, will ultimately escape the dusty roads of mere 'interpretation', even though this 'order' may be elusive, merely 'glimpsed' and never seized for sure.[8]

Much of this speculation has obviously ill considered the deeper and far-reaching implications of the politics of literary production. Neither has it shown an awareness of a number of questions bearing upon the status of the writer or speaker, the position of reader, the diffusion of cultural norm, literary and artistic value containing historical contexts as discursive construction, and the choice of 'aesthetic' or 'literary' form itself being shaped by such contingencies. On the other hand, a great deal of critical energy is spent, in addition to establishing the purely aesthetic concerns, on trying to locate the 'truth' of the authorial voice, whether what Forster wrote was right or wrong, whether sexual assault on Adela really happened.[9] Whether the Marabar Caves, for instance, are truly impressive and mysterious as Forster described them, and whether Anglo-Indian behaviour was exaggerated by him. When *A Passage to India* was first published, civil servants bound for

India, seeing themselves being caricatured there, threw their copies overboard, declaring that 'Anglo-Indian society was no longer 'like that'.[10] 'This dramatizes fully the conditions the novel reflects, where the audience is inevitably a part of the play. Also from the very beginning, national allegiances and political ties resulted in conflicting responses to questions of representational authenticity. So Nihal Singh wrote at the time of its publication: 'The author's pictures are faithful and vivid. That is particularly the case in regard to the Anglo-Indian characters he has created.'[11] The contrary Anglo-Indian view was expressed by E.A. Horne simultaneously: 'They are not even good caricatures.. most of what he [Forster] knows about [Anglo-Indians] their ways and their catchwords, and has put into his book, he has picked up from the stale gossip of Indians.'[12]

The rhetoric that informs these oppositional *judgements* reveals the assumption they share: that the novel can be judged by the accuracy of its ethnography. The comments rehearse a debate familiar to cultural anthropology—the value of representation based on experience versus those derived from other texts. On the other hand, to reverse the verisimilitude of the authorial representation, it is assumed by another brand of critics that, to free the novel from historical and textual lineage is to remove it from the literary arena and grant it 'scientific objectivity'—a mark of high achievement indeed. Sylvia Land, an English critic, writes: 'The Indians in this book are not, as in all other Anglo-Indian novels, deplorable but unavoidable pieces of the scenery. They are not cast for the roles of simple villains and clowns. They are men with different conventions from Englishmen—how different has never been revealed before.'[13] Similarly, a more overtly political position, but based upon the same standards of authenticity, was argued by Nirad Chaudhuri:

> Aziz would not have been allowed to cross my threshold, not to speak of being taken as an equal; Godbole is not an exponent of Hinduism, he is a clown.[14]

What these judgments have in common is a belief in the absolute distinction between literature and culture, text and experience, aesthetic fiction and political truth. However, what should be clear from the foregoing sampling of responses is that the contours of the novel are moulded by the critical preconceptions its readers bring to the text, and the particular 'language' they speak. In the glaring instance of this phenomenon, one reviewer, who found the racial politics of the text unbelievably unreal, tried to rewrite the plot of the novel. Unable to understand how a white woman should have 'sexual fantasies' about an Indian, he remarked: 'My private theory is as follows: The hallucination was not Adela's but Aziz's'[15] This radical rewriting of the text ironically confirms the politics of all reading. Yet critical scholarship on this text continues to adhere to the norms of objectivity and fair play, sympathy and cultural understanding. Yet another critic, testifying to this could affirm, 'I have never seen so accurate, so penetrating, and so sympathetic an account of the divergent characters and lives as this. It is sympathetic with both sides.'[16]

Thus, we find how significant it has been to assess the novel—political as it is acknowledged to be—by the yardsticks of justice and fairness. V.A. Shahane went on to edit a volume of essays to present 'the Indian' side in order to redress the balance against the Anglo-Indian view that had been dominant earlier. In the introduction to his volume, Shahane wrote:

> One of the basic reasons for this volume is the need to project the Indian image. It is my belief that the essays by the Indian writers presented here bear the indelible stamp of 'Indianness' which may seem refreshing in the context to Forster's great masterpiece.[17]

For these commentators, the novel was indeed a recognised political event, but its politics according to them lay in the representation of the truth of Imperialism. The criteria for judgment were invariably based upon finding a correspondence between the authorial presentation and/or British Imperialism on the one side, and Indian reality on the other. Indeed as a text book for the Indian Civil Service, the novel became a filter through which the Imperial regime was viewed. Nirad Chudhuri claimed that *A Passage to India* had 'possibly been an even greater influence in British Imperial politics than in English Literature'. For him, the politics of the novel were determined by the ways it could be put to use: 'Mr. Forster's novel became a powerful weapon in the hands of the anti-imperialists, and was made to contribute its share to the disappearance of British rule in India.'[18] A compendium of objectivity, accuracy, and sympathy, this special kind of fairness, forecloses other interpretive possibilities, and makes possible the type of literary praise we now read with cultural embarrassment as in Rose Macaulay's paean to the novel's truthfulness: 'He can make even these brown men live.'[19]

Based on the above survey of criticism it would be of course right to say that a great deal of criticism on the novel available today has ignored debates around the complex web of relations between Imperialism and production of knowledge which led to the crucial changes in the form of narrative and modes of address. It has also ignored the concurrence of the rise and consolidation of modernist aesthetics with the development of colonialism and nationalism in Europe. Further metropolitan control of saturating hegemonic systems like 'culture' or the representation of 'other cultures' in works of art and literature are ill considered by such criticism. It remains largely unaware of the complex and heterogeneous terrain of Indian material which is either simply elided or narrativised by the text in a particular style. Consequently, such critical writing cannot but remain content to point out the general and hegemonic outlines of the text as more complex, even fractured, and repeat the theme of 'appropriation of other cultures' as an inescapable phenomenon of the narrative of imperialism.

This phenomenon is demonstrably visible in the rapid advance in colonial discourse theory which has analysed variously—from psychoanalytic, post-structuralist, neo-Marxist and deconstructive positions—the production of a native consciousness, or the construction of 'the other' in the colonies. It has also argued that 'the other' was an inevitable construct designed to produce, shape and consolidate the consciousness of 'the self' itself. Further, born in a colonialist epistemology and tied together in a reciprocal relationship the demands of the 'self' and 'the other' reinforce each other. Hence, they cannot be simply relocated or traced back to a source: they are dispersed over the text's surface, often in mutually contradictory, multiple and ambivalent ways.

Such advance in critical theory that seeks to establish alternative protocols in disciplinary studies and posits nothing less than new objects of knowledge and new theoretical models that upset or radically alter the prevailing paradigmatic norms, poses a serious problem, however, when applied to the specific texts. Take, for instance, Homi Bhabha's 're-reading' of *A Passage to India* as follows:

> What emerges from the dispersal of work is the language of a colonial nonsense that displaces those dualities in which the colonial space is traditionally divided: nature/culture chaos/civility Ouboum or the owl's death call.. These are the inscriptions of an uncertain colonial silence... It is from such an uncertain invitation to interpret, from such a question of desire, that the echo of another significant question can be dimly heard. Lacan's question of the alienation of the subject in the other: 'He is saying this to me, but what does he want?'[20]

What emerges from such critical writing ultimately is a sense of the language of 'colonial nonsense' being 'uncertain' and hence to be best understood as a 'question of desire.' Nowhere does a reader, however, get an inkling how such re-readings help articulate or demystify the cultural politics of imperialism, except by a microscopic analysis of the question of presence and splitting it into a contradictory 'difference'. So Bhabha goes on:

> The articulation of nonsense is the recognition of an anxious place between the human and the non-human, between the sense and non-sense, which no dialectic can deliver in that sense, these 'senseless' signifiers pose the question of cultural choice in terms similar to the Lacanian 'vel', between being and meaning, between the subject and the other, 'neither the one nor the other'. Neither, in our terms, 'work' nor 'word' but precisely the work of the colonial word..[21]

Such dazzling operations on the colonial presence could outmatch the mystic echo emanating out of the Marabar Caves as the staging of the colonial signifier in the narrative uncertainty of culture's in-between: between sign and signifier, neither one nor the other, neither sexuality nor nationality, neither memory nor desire is to be seen as the writing of cultural difference:

> In the context of the strange play of cultural memory and colonial desire in the Marabar Caves, Derrida's words are uncannily resonant. 'It is neither desire nor pleasure but between the two. Neither future nor present but between the two. It is the hymen that desire dreams of piercing, of bursting in an act of violence that is (at the same time or somewhere between) love and murder.' It is an undecidability that arises form a certain culturalist substitution that Derrida describes as anti-ethnocentrism thinking itself as ethnocentrism.. For neither can the epistemological object of cultural identity nor the dialectical, structuralist sign of arbitrary difference contain the effect of such colonial nonsense.[22]

What reigns supreme in these passages is the metaphysics of undecidability, a persistent 'desire' to be playful and make a fetish of all 'essentialism'. Such criticism, if anything, *is both culturally and politically irresponsible* as it refuses to grapple with the voice of the 'otherness' in the novel in all its complex opacity. However, it must be added that as a result of a decade of colonial discourse studies percolating into disciplinary pedagogy and its powerful adjuncts, and as a result of the imbrications of techniques of knowledge with power, no self-conscious critique would claim to represent per se the voice of the unmediated 'other' or 'marginality' in the larger post-colonial field; neither can one make a similar unproblematic claim for a monolithic, ponderous presence of the colonizer. But does such a realisation, of necessity, prevent us from the re-formation of, un-originary but politically self-conscious, boundaries of 'the other', hybrid and contestatory as they always are, in favour of paralytic, self-absorbing parodies of a deconstructive practice as above?

So would it seem from another recent theory-conscious study of the novel, which discusses *A Passage to India* mainly as 'a crisis of voice'. Betti London, in her exhaustive study of the novel, writes:

> What I want to argue in this study, however, is that modernism's ruling constructs must themselves be read problematically, and that they are problematised within modernism—within the modernism we are empowered to perceive. *I chose voice for my locus because of its peculiar centrality to modernism's textual productions and literary history and to the more recent theoretical challenges to modernism's canonical authority.* In this larger context voice itself is in question—the subject of contested meaning: organic center of the text, agent of aesthetic unity, site of a personal presence, instrument of ideology, effect of mechanical reproduction. My title *The Appropriated Voice*, marks

> the convergence, or collision, of these competing understandings.[23]
>
> (emphasis added)

The orthodoxy of literary modernism which autonomises art is unwittingly replaced by yet another orthodoxy with qualification—namely *the centrality of voice as problem.* What has remained untouched in the exercise is the materiality of such proliferation of voices, as well as their sources. Moreover, we see again the dazzling operation of splitting of the signifier at work here:

> Yet for me what remains most troubling about Forster's novel—and what constitutes its greatest interest—is its resistance to being placed. The contradictory currents it articulates on both the political and aesthetic fronts make it difficult to determine whether the critics' cherished decorum—the mark of artistic autonomy—is something the novel embraces or violates. For the novel's voices prove neither unitary nor stable, existing in a continual state of struggle and realignment.[24]

In its refusal to be 'placed', one might as well argue, the text regains its lost colonial authority, as a testament of spiritual silence. Whose interest does it serve to conclude that 'the novel's voices prove neither unitary nor stable..?'

This reminds us of Robert Scholes' chiding against narrative indeterminacy—Scholes having apparently become something of a revisionist in matters narratological—'narrative is not just a sequencing, or the illusion of sequence.. narrative is a sequence of something for somebody.'[25] To this one might add and by somebody, and within the world, within history, whatever be the discursive discontinuities of such a history.

Yet another cultural critic, sensitive to developments in colonial discourse theory, has surprisingly taken a U-turn, and mildly lauded the achievements of the novel. Abdul R. Jan Mohamed argues that colonialist writings is divisible into two broad categories; the 'imaginary' and the 'symbolic'[26]. An 'imaginary text is one which refuses to admit the possibility of cultural 'syncretism', of a rapprochement between the self and the other, whereas the 'symbolic' text's openness towards the other is based on 'a greater awareness of potential identity and a heightened sense of the concrete socio-political-cultural differences between the self and the other.[27] The 'symbolic' writer's understanding of the other proceeds through self-understanding, he is freer from the codes and motifs of the deeper, collective classification system of his culture. Yet, in the final analysis, his success in comprehending or appreciating alterity will depend upon his ability to bracket the values and bases of his culture.' He may do so very consciously and deliberately, as Forster does in *A Passage to India*, or he may allow the emotions and values instilled in him during his social formation in an alien culture to inform his appraisals of the other, as Kipling does in Kim. These two novels offer the most interesting attempts to overcome the barriers of racial difference.'[28]

Judged by the criterion adopted by Jan Mohamed, *A Passage to India* is a 'symbolic' text as Forster is able to bracket the values and bases of his own culture. Forster mercilessly satirises the cruder imaginary forms of colonialist racism and does not present us with stereotypes. The retreat of Anglo-Indians into the 'simple Manichean emotion of the 'imaginary', their negation of free intellectual inquiry and accommodating civilized personal relations is also castigated by Forster: '[Fielding] was still after facts, though the herd had decided on emotion. Nothing enrages Anglo-India more than the lantern of reason if it is exhibited for one moment after its extinction is decreed'. Also, Forster's representation of the Indians' 'cruder attempts' to overcome the effects of racial designation—for example, the servility of the colonized, the easily wounded pride and vanity of Aziz, the historic outbursts of Mahmoud Ali in court, and other such manifestations of self pity—are equally acerbic and penetrating. The result is thus, according to Mohamed, a genuinely self critical and powerful portrayal of India:

> ..the ambiguity of the caves—the absolute 'nothing' which infers in them and the experience of which is the goal of Jain religion-comes to *represent the essence of Indian metaphysics.. The caves represent the fundamental, unconscious identity from which all natural and social differences emanate and to which they all return* when they can escape their phenomenal manifestations. Mrs. Moore and Professor Godbole experience this kind of unity...
>
> *A Passage to India* also abounds in conscious rejection of the chaos that, from Forster's viewpoint, attains the discovery of transcendent identity. The echo returns to tell Mrs. Moor that 'everything exists, nothing has value', and she is gradually terrified by the realization that everything—the concepts of eternity and infinity, the wisdom of 'talkative Christianity', and even her affection for her children and Aziz—is 'boum'... The 'India' that had said 'come', that is the embodiment of an unpalatable metaphysical calculus of identity and difference, *now says 'no' to the possibility of overcoming racial alterity..* The metaphysical preoccupation of A Passage to India is 'a culmination of problems that Forster had been examining throughout his work, and his decision to cast his concerns in terms of Indian philosophy is innocent and logical'.[29]
>
> (emphasis added)

This interpretation of the novel clearly privileges two vantage points of entry into the novel and naturalises them. They are: the objective, rational and self-critical voice of Fielding as the norm of judgment (he was still after the facts, even as the lantern of reason had been putout by the Anglo-Indian community in the face of danger against their race) and second, the mystique of the caves as representing our collective 'unconscious' which levels off the play of all social and cultural differences. 'Nothingness' in this reading of the novels is taken as a real possibility, if not a solution to overcome the barrier of racial difference.

On a closer reading, however, it can be shown how both the entry points are internal, constitutive parts of the discourse of colonialism. Inheriting the tradition of a liberal humanist Enlightenment, the normative voice of 'free intellectual inquiry and civilized personal relations' can hear only what is 'fair' and 'rational' according to its own historically constructed narratives of taste, value and judgement. Similarly the 'nothingness' of the Marabar Caves, and its attendant ever-haunting echo which ruptures the boundaries of self and the other, and disrupts a carefully guarded rational consciousness, may turn out to simply be a neatly-crafted aesthetic device—a literary technique which, instead of being innocent and logical, underwrites the western metaphysical desire to regain the totality of its lost self. Even in as devious and divergent a form, as 'nothingness', which is conflated with the goal of mystic Jain philosophy of India, *the burden of the quest itself represents narratively the colonialist desire to 'resolve' the internal contradictions of liberal rationalist humanism by projecting them on its 'other' as a unitary whole.* Written into this 'rebellion' of the mystic other, therefore, can be seen the narcissistic operations of the colonialist 'self' which blunts the resisting edges of 'the other' in the very process of naming it as its alterity, as 'nothingness.'

It is desirable at this place, prior to making yet another 'interpretation' of the novel, to say what the novel is about, or alternatively, what the novel is said to have 'achieved'. This achievement of the novel, once represented, can be further allowed to contend with all those things which the narrative is either constrained to elide, or represent with a very particular focus, and in a certain style that, was coterminous with the consciousness created by colonialist epistemology.

Considering the 'achievements' first of all, it can be said that the novel does attempt a critique of British colonialism in India. The Anglo-Indian community is satirised for its racial chauvinism as much as for its own hollowness, its empty imperialist sloganeering and its 'fear psychosis' leading the British to rally around 'race' and 'nation' under stressful conditions. Forster was well aware that due to the severe economic crisis in Britain during the industrial expansion, the lower and lower-middle classes in England were badly affected, but it was mostly these classes which chose to migrate to the colonies. This migration brought them an opportunity to move up in the social scale and inherit the social mores and values of English upper-middle class. The pucca-sahib code was then firmly established to confirm their class position. Bureaucrats such as the Burtons and Turtons, Heaslop, Major Calendar, and McBride who wielded enormous repressive political power over the local populace are shown as quasi-comical characters, suffering from a psychological anguish deep within themselves. Unable to adjust themselves in the profoundly different socio-cultural 'reality' of India, they are devoid of poise, discrimination, intelligence and good will, which in Forsterian vocabulary can be gained only by a 'developed heart'. Seen in this light, what the British empire lacked completely was kindness, humanity, understanding and a desire to communicate (virtues embodied in Fielding) which would have made all the difference. As Mrs. Moor puts it in the novel: 'One touch of regret from the heart would have made him (Ronny) a different man, and the British empire a different institution' [p. 70].

At another level, however, a solution based on the golden heart, and human virtues issuing out of the creed of liberal humanism is put into question and even suspended. The narrative organization, curiously, at once inherits and interrogates liberal humanism. Mrs. Moore's experience in the Marabar Cave from which she can never recover fully, is a powerful ironic inversion of all those formal and thematic devices which try to pull the disparate, contradictory elements of novel together into a unified whole. The smooth, shapely arches that were symbolic of friendship, and the spirit of personal allegiance to God in the Mosque are to be shattered by an ever-haunting echo emanating from the caves. The Temple is a progression from the vision of 'nothingness' of the caves, from terror, to peace. It relocates the boundaries of the lost self even as the boundaries of 'self' and 'world' are pretty much blurred here. Though the birth of Krishna in the Temple might provide a means to alleviate the horrendous effect of the echo, the formal harmonies of the mosque and its arches can never be restored. Thus we discover that a profound desire which underwrites the narrative, the desire to create symmetrical design and integrative symbolism to make a coherent statement about India, to envelope the whole of India within its scheme, as it were, is thrown into contradictions by that very narrative, as the novel can be shown to hold open-ended, paradoxical and multivalent meanings, discharging ideas and images, which cannot be contained within the confines of the formal pattern, and a world-view fashioned by optimistic liberal humanism.

The contradictions of liberal humanism, often expressed in a deeply ironic, comic and meditative tone, seem to create the impact of an apparent 'objectivity', a certain distancing of the reader from the 'events' of the narrative. Confronted by the breakdown in the established values as a result of the circumstances obtaining after the First World War—the ravages of European mercantile competition, intensified class conflict within British society, and the consequent social disintegration—the reader is able to look outside England, in the East no doubt, for peace, harmony and over-arching metaphysical order in the true Judeo-Christian tradition. However, the reader (and reader here is an European one, quite unmistakably) gets frustrated in this effort, as the fundamental value system of India—its sexuality, morality, ethics, culture, education, definition of selfhood—is shown to be essentially 'different' from that of the West. Hence, the search for harmonies is futile unless one learns to master the baffling mystery of India which alone can nullify the disturbing effects of the echo and render intelligible the chaotic unfolding of the birth of Krishna. 'The God who was, will be, is not, is.'

The narrative voice oscillates thus between the mystery of India and the limitations of a liberal-democratic humanist world order which leads to it. As Benita Parry puts it:

> The text reveals the crisis of liberal humanist ideology; its importance as a code in an embattled social situation where moderation and compromise are not possible, its inadequacy as an explanation of a universe more extensive than the environment made by human intervention, and the insufficiency of its insights into the potentialities of its mind whose experiential range exceeds ratiocination and sensory cognition.[30]

This puts the 'achievements' of the novel squarely. A foray into new and astonishing perceptions (though often mediated by the known sterilities of liberal humanism) enabled by a contact with India becomes the 'central' motif of the novel. Thus if immersion in pure mysticism wastes 'secular' proficiency, adherence to 'rationalism' atrophies other possible facets of human personality; and if empiricism can provide a rigorous arrangement of appearances, it misses essences, and if, to quote Parry again, 'exclusion and definition led to functional and aesthetic excellence, only the suspension of discrimination and the abolition of barriers will facilitate the making of a total explanatory system.[31]

Thus considered, we find that the 'achievement' of the novel would seem to lie in locating a paradox at the heart of the 'human condition', a lived contradiction between the known, definitive categories of western rationalism, and the baffling, non-definitive, non-evolutive, and non-empiricist 'reality' of life as revealed by an encounter with India.

This thesis finds ample support from the dominant resolution of the novel itself. Fielding and Aziz have to part company at the end of the novel as friendship between them, symbolically a friendship between England and India, turns out to be an impossibility:

> 'Why can't we be friends now?' Said the other [Fielding] holding him affectionately. 'It's what I want. It's what you want'.
>
> But the horses didn't want—they swerved apart; the earth didn't want, sending up rocks through which riders must pass single file; the temples, the tank, the jail, the place, the birds, the carrion, the guest-house, that came into view as they issued from the gap and saw Mau beneath: they didn't want it, they said in their hundred voices, 'No, yet, 'and the sky said, 'No, not yet there' [p.336]

This is symbolism par excellence. This demonstrates the principle of autonomy of art. Note the delicacy of ironic vision, a calm, resolute distance from action, and the priority of accent and tone over sense. All these aesthetic virtues help convey no doubt an ontological void, a crisis of faith, meaning and action which must be faced in the domain of spiritual loneliness. One might say that ultimately a discourse of poetic order alone, the rhythmic pattern 'No, not yet... No, not there' creating internal distance within space as well as time, can envision the novel with its much-needed epiphany, as neither Aziz nor Fielding opens up a perspective on decolonization. Indeed it is as if this perspective, a willingness to come together, was denied by the very earth and sky, which they inhabited.

Reading against the grain of the 'achievements' enumerated above, three points can be briefly listed here which I will elaborate in the later sections. First, the supposedly 'central' paradox in the novel, often expressed in the metaphor of a 'mystery-muddle' opposition, or opposition between skeptical-mysticism versus humanist liberal-rationalism, is a relatively minor, insignificant phenomenon within the overall rich and complex fabric of the novel. Suffice it to say here that this *debate which was internal to late 19th century England—the debate concerning a rationalist truth versus a poetic truth or 'truth' of mood; scientific rationality versus mysticism and free will versus determinism*—has been projected onto the Indian scene.[32] Such thematic representation of the 'paradox' is itself a product of the colonial-liberal imagination which is historically produced and socially circulated as knowledge gained out of a direct, unmediated 'experience' of the non-western world. Critical scholarship elides significant issues that constitute the fabric of the novel; for example, the question of caste within the Hindu society as represented in the iconic figure of the punkhawala, and the Brahmin, Godbole; communal strife between Hindus and Muslims mediated by the British bureaucratic machinery; the crucial nexus between princely India and Imperialism; the newly emerging nationalist intelligentsia and its conflictual relationship with both imperialism and the vested interests of a 'feudal' or 'princely' India; the development of an Indian past, or better, the reconstruction of Indian history and its spontaneous seepage into the novel; and above all, the representation of *bhakti* in the novel as an idiom of spiritual realization, or conversely, as a strategy of socio-political containment as against the variously deployed and historically changing, even subversive, roles of *bhakti* in Indian history. Each of these issues which shape the narrative configuration at crucial junctures in the novel have remained, by and large, invisible to literary critics and need to be attended to.

Secondly, the much celebrated ironic distancing of Forster's narrative and a highly sophisticated use of language—now comic and playful, now somber and meditative, creating odd turns and inversions in the plot, enabled by a subtle modulation of tone, syntactic variation and multiplicity of voices, can be analysed for its effects on different reader-positions.[33] This particular 'aesthetic' achievement of the novel, seen as skilful and sensitive handling of a complex subject-matter, and arising out of Forster's engagement with literary modernism, and symbolism of the Bloomsbury group, strikes a contradictory note.[34] Such techniques draw careful attention, on the one hand, to the text's surface, to its exteriority. This brings into sharp focus the linguistic mechanisms, literary devices, rhetorical strategies, and tropes which produce the effect of coherence in the novel, or disrupt its coherence willfully. The added significance of such aesthetic craftsmanship lies in its manoeuverability and its ability to suggest that 'meaning' or 'reality-effect' in a novel is internal to its narrative structure. Therefore, the values we choose to read into the novel themselves very according to how the verbal arrangement of the text is achieved. This insight, when applied to the text in question, serves as a pointer towards the significant realisation that the 'India' of this novel's imagination—academic, political, or both—is born out of the specific British anxieties to represent it in a certain manner. However, on the other hand, these very 'techniques'—and here lies the contradiction—also serve to reinforce and consolidate the dominating historico-cultural frameworks within which the novel is produced. This claim can be substantiated by showing how, in the novel, indeterminacies or facile pluralities are manufactured by the narrative as if they were built into the very conditions of human existence, and exceeded far beyond the pale of ordinary human grasp. Seen in this light, the switches and turns of the narrative do not seem to work to wrest the novel away from the plane of an autonomous other-worldliness of art. Indeed they betray the politics of the novel instead.

Thirdly, a few pages have been written about the so-called historical background of the novel, to suggest that it subsumes and shows a keen awareness of Indian history.[35] Such a claim has confused history with a mere backdrop, or an inert, often decorative, setting. For, in no way does it take cognizance of those multiple enabling and inhibiting forces of unequal cultural, economic, and political exchange which shaped the contemporary experience in its narratives, plots, values and goals. Far from being a merely casual, or unilaterally determining 'ground', history has entered the portals of the novel in multiple ways, often in ways which have had nothing to do with its author, with some 'real' events at the time of its writing, or before. These ways, *are the traces of history, which will*, for their illumination, *require the making of continuous inter-textual connections, reinterpretation and re-formation of the text's surface.* To do history in this sense would be different from saying that all academic, cultural and political discourse on India, which *A Passage to India* represents overtly or inheres covertly, is trainted with or violated by the gross political fact of British imperialism. The association of imperialism and culture, and the ensuing politics which bears upon the production of literature and history, often creates internal constraints within a field of scholarship which might prove to be highly 'productive' not 'unilaterally inhibiting'.[36] To show this productivity at work, one has to turn one's attention not to a mindless chronology of authors, books, gazettes, and records as *historical facts*, but to multiple distribution of awareness into various fields of knowledge which delimit the horizon of thinking and action within a particular historical conjuncture. It is to map this particular terrain of awareness, and to demonstrate the deposition of traces of such willed history, even in its internal contradictions, ambivalences and discontinuities, that we proceed to an analysis of *A Passage to India* in the next sections.

II
Mosque

The opening of the novel is a grand performance in irony. By its carefully judged allusions to cave and sky, it would seem to propose the cosmic at the expense of the mundane, the positive at the expense of the negative and the numinous in the garb of raw materiality:

> Except for the Marabar Caves—and they are twenty miles off—the city of Chandrapore presents nothing extraordinary. Edged rather than washed by the river Ganges, it trails for a couple of miles along the bank, scarcely distinguishable from the rubbish it deposits so freely [p.9].

So run the first two sentences: flat, casual, the tone pitched so low as though deliberately to deny the reader any expectation. And yet, paradoxically, the style achieves the opposite of what it pretends. The first sentence mentions, as though casually, the Marabar Caves, which apparently are extraordinary. It is true that they are waved away from our attention at this moment, but a reader is likely to remember a name attached to the word 'extraordinary' in the very first sentence. And then the second sentence conveys movement, however sluggish, graphically by the precision of its verbs: 'edged rather than washed' and 'deposits so freely'. We discern animatedly in the rubbish, the place may be squalid but it lives. As the narrative advances, we are led to yet another instance of irony; the description appears this time to be the apotheosis of squalour and abasement, as though we are being made to feel that the very triviality and meanness of the city of Chandrapore endows it with an essential import:

> So abased, so monotonous is everything that meets the eye, that when the Ganges comes down it might be expected to wash the excrescence back into the soil. Houses do fall, people are drowned and left rotting, but the general outlines of the town persist, swelling here, shrinking there, like some low but indestructible form of life [p.9].

This is another instance of a Forster disclaimer that covertly asserts as much as it openly repudiates, and is as much honorific as pejorative—'the double turn' in Trilling's phraseology. The importance seems to issue from the suggestion that there is no frontier between human life and that of lower form. And when the catalogue of Chandrapore's mediocrity and featurelessness comes to a climax in 'the very world seems to be made of mud, the inhabitants of mud moving', the subdued extravagance of the conceit evokes a vitality that the actual itemizing or the catalogue would seek to deny. The reader is thus supposedly being led to a position in the very opening chapter of the novel from where a direct, uncontradictory and total comprehension of India is denied. Instead the textural markers draw up a scenario of a mysterious, if somewhat quizzical, world to the western eye.[37]

The second paragraph opens: 'Inland, the prospect alters'. And indeed it does. We are on the heights, looking down on the native city, enjoying the privileged view of it from the British quarters. What we now see is not much of the human dwellings, but, instead, a forest of trees. Verbs and participles express energy and exultation:

> They rise from the gardens where ancient tanks nourish them, they burst out of stifling purliens and unconsidered temples. Seeking light and air, and endowed with more strength than man or his works, they soar above the lower deposit to great one another with branches and beckoning leaves, and to build a city for the birds [pp.9-10].

As against the shapelessness of the 'real' India of the bazaar and inhabitants of mud, moving about confusedly in the excrescence which can not be washed off by even the river Ganges, since the 'Ganges happens not to be holy here', we are shown the stony imperiousness of the civil station. The arrangement of the English habitation is shot through with the soulless symmetry of the bungalows and the right angles of the Raj. So we pass from the river to the city, from the city to its vegetation, from the vegetation to the sky, which unites all and is yet remote with its own existence. The next paragraph emphasizes its separateness, its variety of colour and depth of mystery. The sky is not merely a home as it is in Europe:

> There stars hang like lamps from the immense vault. The distance between the vault and them is as nothing to the distance behind them, and that farther distance, though beyond colour, last freed itself from blue [pp. 10-11].

The mystical description of the sky contributes to a panoramic vision which appears to imply a dimension beyond the physically human; and this vision is contrasted with a description of the earth which despite its vastness, does not share the secret of the overarching sky, that 'settles' all human conflicts. In the last paragraph, we return to the earth, with the insistence that despite its remoteness the sky is the supreme power of India. The earth by herself can do little—only 'feeble outbursts of flowers':

> But when the sky chooses, the glory can rain into the Chandrapore bazaars or a benediction pass from horizon to horizon. The sky can do this because it is so strong and so enormous. No mountains infringe on the curve. League after league the earth lies flat, heaves a little, is flat again. Only in the south, where a group of fists and fingers are thrust up through the soil, is the endless expanse interrupted. *These fists and fingers are the Marabar hills containing the extraordinary caves* [p.11].

The style of narration here might as well be coterminus with the chanting of the Vedic hymns, or with a solemn description of the creation of the universe. Sky is transfigured into a principle of numinosity, a vehicle of spiritual thought. People, so far, have been insignificant, indeed absent, from this majestic unfoldment of the grand passage to India: ironic, yet meditative.

However, if this were taken as final 'meaning' of the opening chapter announcing its programme of a *spiritual revelation through art*, the novel would certainly not have attracted a prolonged critical attention.[38] And here, the Forsterian 'double turn', a balancing mechanism, a subtly delicate exercise in self irony strikes once again. We discover on closer examination that the sky cannot after all remain uncontaminated for too long, and it must have its centrality challenged in two ways: first, by the attempt to go beyond—to push the prose into conveying an unconveyable, illimitable distance beyond colour itself. Secondly, it is challenged by returning to the earth, to the mud of the Chandrapore bazaar that was itself, earlier on, an indestructible form of life. The sky draws its size from the prostrate earth and its impression of infinite space is in fact created for the eye and the mind by the line of the earth's horizon.

Inscribed in Forster's pictures of a repulsive landscape, confusing bazaar, 'ethereality' of the civil station, and overarching sky that settles everything, is an economy of representation which all but ignores the ordinariness, the unheroic, routine, yet pulsating rhythms of every day life.

The *ideological function* of this mechanism, that is, *of representation of space*, has been to present it as a metaphysical 'fact of life' before which those who have fashioned the colonial world are themselves, as the narrative representation of the civil lines shows, only passive spectators in a mystery not of their own making.[39]

Thus considered, the very architecture of the mosque holds out the promise of a 'secret understanding of the heart', unfolding vistas of immortality in spiritual unison of two souls for whom only 'instinctive wisdom', not 'ratiocination', or 'logical thinking' can be the attribute of divinity. It is a very personal, intense feeling achieved not from the Koran, nor from the notion of a powerful God emphasised by Islam, but mainly from evocations of a spiritual mood by mosque architecture; its profound simplicity, grandeur and the sublime sense of peace it conveys. Like temple architecture which suggests something very specific about the nature of the Hindu religious outlook, Forster's intimations of the spirit of Islam derives in part from the 'structural features' of the mosque. He writes that whereas a cathedral seeks to locate God within its interior, a mosque is more truly exalted because its uncomplicated structure suggests the omniscience of God:

> A mosque embodies no crisis, leads up through no gradation of church and choir, and employs no hierarchy of priests. Equality before God, so doubtfully proclaimed by Christianity—lies at the very root of Islam...
>
> The Christian has a vague idea that God is inside the church, presumably near the east end. The Moslem, when his faith is pure, cherishes no such illusion, and attaches no sanctity of it beyond what it is conferred by the presence of the devout.[40]

Islam means peace: 'whatever the creed may have done, the name means peace, and its buildings can give a sense of arrival which is unattainable in any Christian church.'[41]. It is this particular association with the mosque, and in the exaltation of the personal emotions laid bare in the presence of God, which unites Aziz and Mrs. Moore, in spite of the cultural and political polarities of their respective positions within a colonial setting. The culture of the heart enshrined in the mosque becomes a metaphor for the 'subversion' of racial authority, and thus the space within the enclaves of a mosque acquires specific meanings in the narrative design. In this scheme of things, Aziz can learn to recognise himself—his identity, emotion, religion, pathos—as a reflection of the mosque masquerading as Islam. Consider the following lines which introduce a reader to the mosque, and Aziz's relationship with it:

> He was an athletic little man, daintily put together, but really very strong. Nevertheless walking fatigued him.. At the edge of the civil station he turned into a mosque to rest.. He had always liked this mosque. It was gracious and the arrangements pleased him.. The covered part of the mosque was deeper than is usual; its effect was that of an English parish church whose side had

been taken out. Where he sat, he looked into three arcades whose darkness was illuminated by a small hanging lamp and by the moon... Elsewhere some Hindus were drumming—he knew they were Hindus, because the rhythm was uncongenial to him.. But the mosque—that alone signified, and he returned to it from the complex appeal of the night, and decked it with meanings the builder had never intended. Some day he too would build a mosque, smaller than this but in perfect taste, and near it, under a low dome, should be his tomb, with a Persian inscription:

Alas, without me for thousands of years, the rose will blossom and the spring will bloom. But those who have secretly understood my heart—they will approach and visit the grave where I lie [pp.87-88].

The narrative representation of mosque *as a place for rest effects a curious gerrymandering*, and not merely *a gross Orientalist misunderstanding*, of the variously deployed traditional functions of the mosque. In its anxiety to weave a symbolic pattern around the mosque, and forge a theme of aesthetic unity that transcends racial and cultural difference, *the narrative cuts the mosque loose from its traditional social space, and relocates it within a personal, one might even add, English personal domain.* For elaboration of this claim we should consider briefly how the mosque has been described, and said to have discharged its functions traditionally.[42]

Throughout the history of Islam the basic features of the mosque have been repeatedly reinterpreted and adapted to a wide range of geographical, cultural and historical contexts. Egyptian mosques for instance, with richly decorated street facades took on strong public presence beginning already in the Fatimid era (969-1171), and in the Indo-Islamic style of the Mughal period (1526-1858). The Hindu influence emerged in a courtyard that was frequently the primary spatial element and a sanctuary reduced to an elaborated pavilion or arcade wall. The giant iwan of the sanctuary, the portals, and the arcades were articulated with ogee arches, onion domes, and polychromed masonry bearing the ornamental lineage of both traditions.[43]

Thus, in its long history, the mosque has been subject to a series of contingencies: Like Islam itself, the vitality of the mosque tradition must be seen or tied to its syncretic potential. While its 'contemplative and liturgical functions have barely altered through time, its specific political and social roles have varied widely according to the historical and cultural contexts.'[44] So too, have climatic and technical exigencies continually reshaped and delimited its exterior form. The aesthetic component, coordinating and unifying these diverse elements, has given expression to the particular significance of the mosque in space and time. Today, 'the evolution of the mosque continues as the technique of the modern technology and contemporary society interact with several ongoing traditions of Islam'.[45]

As in the grand opening of the chapter, in Forster's description of the mosque, the societal and collective principles are transformed into aesthetic and personal ones; the covered part of the mosque was 'deeper than is usual: its effect 'was that of an English parish church'.. he looked into three arcades 'whose darkness was illuminated by a small hanging lamp and by the moon'.. and he tried to 'symbolise the whole into some truth of religion or love'.

'Hindus dislike the arch of European and Muslim architecture, 'we are told by Forster's friend J.R. Ackerley, because 'the arch never sleeps'[46] but the tension in the arch gives the image its appeal for Forster, since it suggests a deliberate selection or naming of the friend [who never comes but is not entirely disposed] and the response of the other to this initiative. Mrs. Moore and Aziz make such a selection of one another in the shadow of the mosque. Fielding and Aziz begin to 'build' their relationships beneath the Mughal arches of

Fielding's garden house. In each case we have a sense of stressful form that modernist aesthetics would expect us to regard as triumphing over the human inertia of non-relationships. Hence, sharply definitive, black upon white, the ninety-nine attributes of God stand out upon the mosque's arcade. These numinous moments of an 'Islamic Vision' can be seen as detached from life, from cause and effect, from the social performance of language, in the delicately chiseled incantatory phrases—'never stopping to analyse', from the 'divine lips of beauty' and 'the nightingale' as if they had defied the rules of temporal narration and taken a life of their own: 'his heart began to glow secretly. Presently it burst into speech—you understand me, you know what I feel' [p.45].

This numinous moment, which at once offers a 'passage' through the thickets of human dishonesty, enables Mrs. Moore to see the mosque in a new, redemptive light. While referring to the mosque within her own mind she puts her son's humanity to the test. But in the second such moment the moonlight is itself transformed. As a reflected radiance on the Ganges, the moon belongs 'neither to water, nor moonlight', but stood like a luminous sheaf upon the fields of darkness' [pp.52-53].

The last part of Aziz's fantasy, 'Some day he too would build a mosque' which is followed by the Persian verse that is to be inscribed on his tomb, suggests an instance of double irony. It lies in a carefully controlled satire implicit in Aziz's fantasy, with its marked exaggerations, pathos, self-pity and disproportionate emotions, which turns against itself, and in the process reveals more about the authority of its own representation. The effect is indeed of vicariously produced humour, but produced at whose expense, we need to ask ? The effect of Aziz's fantasy is consistent with pity and pathos; it is of a piece with Ghalib, his bulbul, and the narcissistic masochism characteristic of the theme of 'Mughal decadene' in India within the grand narrative of imperialism.[47]

In this fictional account, the 'humorous' indulgence of the narrator masks the cruder racial theme. Aziz's discourse becomes frantic as he senses his loss of social ground; he attempts to dominate all the conversational slots. When, for example, he soars off on a treacherous flight of fantasy, imagining himself a benevolent ruler dispersing justice from the halls of Fielding's house, the narrative deflates Aziz in a condescending way: 'His face very tender—the tenderness of one incapable of administration, and unable to grasp that if the poor criminal is let off he will again rob the poor widow' [p.71]. the voice could be that of any British official speaking of the Indian as of a child, and carefully spelling out its every word. Similarly, in an effort to pose his Mughal imperial connection, when Aziz begins to improvise in a reckless way, inventing a legend about emperors who so loved water that they made it run uphill, the narrator seems compelled to offer a petty connection: 'He was wrong about the water, which no emperor, however skillful, can cause to gravitate uphill; a depression of some depth together with the whole of Chandrapore lay between the mosque and Fielding's house' [pp.71-72].

If the narrative, then, authorises itself at the expense of Aziz, it does so in part by mimicking the frantic logic of Aziz's improvisations. *But does this voice represent an act of narrative patronage, or is it merely calculated mimicry and irony*? No doubt, the ideal reader implied by the narrative is positioned to take this instance as one of humorous irony. For in the very next sentence, the narrative displaces its 'British' voice by representing, in the form of others, the modulations of its tones: 'Ronny would have pulled him up, Turton would have wanted to pull him up, but restrained himself. Fielding did not even want to pull him up; he dulled his craving for verbal truth and cared chiefly for truth of mood...' [p.72].

This brings us back to the issue of narrative representation as an all powerful cultural force which is inscribed in the forms and tones of the discourse inherited by Forster. By choosing to focus on Islam as embodied in Aziz, and further *showing this as antagonistic to Hinduism* ('the temple of another creed would have bored him. He knew they were Hindus, because the rhythm was uncongenial to him'). Forsterian liberalism becomes coeval with the British colonialist machinery in India which created ethnic and religious types, and essentialised them.[48] In this divisive scheme of things *Islam served to designate a pathological condition.* It captured for the colonialists what they had conceptualised as a basic feature of Muslim society: its religious bigotry, and its fundamentally irrational character, somewhat like tribalism and factionalism. Islam in the colonialist perception was given, endemic, inborn. It is the legacy of such knowledge which is seen to operate even in the best of the liberal minds, which is why Forster could write with impunity:

> All illness proceeds from Hindus, Mr. Haq said. He spoke with disgust of the hot sun, the cow dung and marigold flowers, and the encampment of sadhus, some of whom strode stark naked through the streets:
>
> Aziz liked to hear his religion praised. It soothed the surface of his mind, and allowed beautiful images to form beneath...... He recited a poem by Ghalib. It had no connection with anything that had gone before, but it came from his heart and spoke to theirs. They [Aziz's Muslim friends] were overwhelmed by its pathos; pathos they agreed, is the highest quality in art; a poem should touch the hearer with a sense of his own weakness, and should institute some comparison between mankind and flowers... Whatever Ghalib had felt, he had anyhow lived in India, and this consolidated it for them: he had gone with his own tulips and roses, but tulips and roses do not go. And the sister Kingdoms of the North—Arabia, Persia, Ferghana, Turkestan—stretched out their hands as he sang, sadly, because all beauty is sad, and greeted Chandrapore where every street and

> house was divided against itself, and told her that she was a continent and unity... [pp.109-110].
>
> (emphasis added)

Writing in 1959, Forster outlined the circumstances that led to his first Indian visit:

> My connection with India is peculiar and personal. It started because I made friends with an Indian, and but for him I might never have gone to that country or written about it. His name was Masood, he was a Moslem, who had come over to go to Oxford. We saw a great deal of each other and travelled in Italy and France and when he returned to India it was agreed that I should go to stay with him. That I did in 1912, and twelve years later when *A Passage to India* came out I dedicated it to him.[49]

Before meeting Masood, Forster had virtually no contact with India, let alone Indian religions or history, but soon after his meeting with Masood he immersed himself in reading about India to prepare for the upcoming journey. Curiously, it was this particular section of the Muslim Society (as represented by Masood, the Grandson of Sir Syed Ahmed) and its genealogy that shaped Forster's Narrative on Islam in India.

This marks a return to 'production of narrative' from genealogical sources which may include a variety of genres—histories, biographies, letters, memoirs and diaries—to appreciate how the Forster-Masood entente becomes *a paradigmatic case for the study of the formation of a monolithic Islamic community in India* as bequeathed by the English liberal imagination. Islam in India—inclusive of its architecture, social mores, cultural ethos, traditional customs and politics—is narratively conflated with the ideology of a microscopic aristocratic minority of Muslims in India. Tuned to British cultural, educational and political requirements, this minority identified its own interests with those of their rulers, *setting aside the vast heterogeneous Muslims as irrational, barbarous, bigoted and reactionary.*

The response of the lower classes of the Muslim community to colonialism was, however, vastly different, as was indeed their perception of Islamic culture and its sociopolitical goals. The Wahabi and the Faraizi movements, for instance, which Forster does not mention anywhere in his writing, constituted the core of lower-class Muslim response to colonial invasion. Described variously as 'communists' and 'red-republicans', these movements concentrated their attack on the vested interest within the Muslim community. In addition to being a 'persistently belligerent class' and 'a source of permanent danger to the Empire' the Wahabi government, under Bakht Khan, had abolished duty on such articles of common consumption as salt and sugar; it penalised hoarding and offered *bighas* of rent-free land to the families of those soldiers who happened to die in the fight against the British.[50] The Wahabis had also set up compact organisations in rural Bengal and Uttar Pradesh consisting of both Hindus and Muslims. The purpose of this organization was to forge a close link between the rural districts of Bengal and the jihad camps in the Frontiers in order to drive away the alien rulers.[51] People marched regularly from Bengal to the frontier and actively participated in the 'holy war' against the British. Those who could not join the jihad were urged to 'resist passively and refrain from all intercourse with the *kafir* rulers'[52].

As their number swelled, and the sons of tailors, butchers, hide-merchants, petty traders, weavers, artisans, milkmen, shopkeepers joined them in large numbers, they began to pose a serious threat to Muslim aristocracy and the British administrative machinery. In a sense, the *Fairazi* movement was more directly concerned with the aspirations of the poor and the oppressed. Although some of its members were engaged in small business dealing in rice, jute, hides and tobacco, almost all the rest came from the lowest strata of the society, e.g. *Jolahas*, *Kulus* and the like. This was precisely the reason why the founder of the movement, Hazi Shariatullah, came to be derided by its opponents as the pir [Sage] of the Jolahas. The *Faraizi* principle of equality induced many from the lower occupation groups to discard their 'caste' affiliations and join the movement.[53]

Significantly, the *Ulemas* did not equate nation with religion, and in fact, some of them, after the Russian revolution of 1917, believed that 'there was *no difference between Islam and Communism*, as both of these emphasised society based on equality and justice'[54]. The followers of the Deoband School, mostly among the rural poor, did not evince a sharply polarised Muslim consciousness. Also, their social customs, belief patterns and politico-economic interests were common with the Hindu lower-classes. The Muslims belonging to the aristocracy, on the other hand, complained about their rural brethren that:

> Nearly all of them have Hindu names; their manner and customs are those of the Hindus; they celebrate the *Pujas*.[55]

It is noteworthy that the homogenization of Islam in India which effaced various regional, linguistic, economic, cultural and political differences under a single religious ideology, often masquerading as communal consciousness or Muslim culture, was *an interested class-position of the Muslim aristocracy*. In Forster's narrative, however, it was this particular position which becomes decisive as the sources of his information about Indian Muslims were confined to the aristocracy of Delhi, Lucknow and Aligarh[56]. In this scheme of the 'history' of Islamic rule in India, which coincided with the British colonial machinery, Babur and Akbar would indeed be assigned the highest place as the true custodians of 'universal humanism', so urgently needed for the British liberals themselves. To illustrate, the following dialogue between Aziz and Adela is in order:

'..One of the dreams of my life is accomplished in having you both here as my guests. You cannot imagine how you have honoured me. I feel like the Emperor Babur.'

'Why like him?' she enquired rising. 'Because my ancestors came down with him from Afghanistan. They joined him at the heart. He also had often no more elephants than one, more sometimes, but he never ceased showing hospitality...'

'I thought another Emperor is your favourite—I forget the name—you mentioned him at Mr. Fielding's: what my book calls Aurangzeb.'

'Alamgir? oh yes, he was of course the more pious. But Babur—never in his whole life did he betray a friend, so I can only think of him this morning.'

At this juncture the narrator's intervention puts the conversation immediately 'in perspective'. The signals are marked for the reader, before this exchange becomes too unwieldy, hence the following interdiction:

...At last he [Aziz] was talking about what he knew and felt; he was again the Oriental Guide whom they appreciated.

Much as Forster's narrative is known for irony, its 'double turn' and switches, the 'oriental' reader here finds it rather dim-witted, flat; and the effort to put the conversation in perspective itself ['At last he was talking about what he knew and felt'] becomes ironical, revealing in the process the insurmountable difficulties of trying to help on, to 'guide' the narrative, as it were. But it must run on for a little while more:

'I always enjoy conversing about the Moghul. It is the chief pleasure I know. You see, those first six emperors were all most wonderful men, and as soon as one of them is mentioned, no matter which, I forget everything else in the world except the other five. You could not find six such kings in all the countries of the earth, not, I mean, coming one after the other—Father, son.'

'Tell us something about Akbar.' 'Ah, you have heard the name of Akbar. Good. Hamidullah—whom you shall meet—will tell you that Akbar is the greatest of all. I say, 'Yes, Akbar is very wonderful, but half a Hindu; he was not a true Moslem, which makes Hamidullah cry, 'No more was Babur, he drank wine.' But Babur always repented afterwards, which makes the entire difference, and Akbar never repented of the new religion he invented instead of the Holy Koran.'

'But wasn't Akbar's new religion very fine ? It was to embrace the whole of India'. 'Miss Quested, fine but foolish. You keep your religion, I mine. That is the best..' 'Oh, do you feel that, Dr. Aziz? 'She said thoughtfully. 'I hope you are not right. *There will have to be something universal in this country—I don't say religion, for I'm not religious, but something, or how else are barriers to be broken down*? [pp.142-3].

(emphasis added)

Three fundamental issues pertaining to the construction of grand narrative of Islam in India are thrown up by the above dialogue. One, the issue of being a 'true Muslim', or the purity of the Islamic practice which was often extrapolated to the Afghan, Persian or Turk genealogy, Indian Muslims being only a derivative 'residue' of original, virgin moment. Two, the tracing of the Mughal ancestry to a chronological dynasty of rulers from Babur to Aurangzeb who represented the ethos, splendour and legitimacy of the Muslim Community. Three, Adela's proposition that the religion of 'universal humanism' as said to have been practiced by Akbar 'embraced the whole of India' or alternatively, that its 'secular' import lay in the practice of unity among differences which the narrative juxtaposes with the contemporary moment of political crisis in India.

Each of these issues deserves to be treated separately to show how the construction of the discourse on Islam was/is made possible by the complicity of the Muslim aristocracy with a liberal-colonialist epistemology. We also need to demonstrate, how in a dialogic situation the narrator's ostensible 'distance' from his characters serves only to reinforce the narrative authority.

First, we are told that Aziz was like 'the Oriental guide' who was, 'talking about what he knew and felt.' It was an authentic version of the 'little man daintily put together' which his sympathetic interlocutors 'appreciated'. As with the true 'oriental' who always 'overrated hospitability', Aziz's subject-position is already assigned to him. The reader knows the passionate, oriental guide before the narrative sets up a dialogic situation to confirm the expectancies already created about him: Like the victim of a pathological condition evoking sympathy, Aziz always transgressed his emotional scale as he begins:

'One of the dreams of my life is accomplished.. you cannot imagine how you have honoured me. I feel like the emperor Babur' [p.141]. We need to ask exactly whose desire it was to seek purity of Islamic origin and of its contemporary ritual practice [Babur drank wine, we are told, and even Akbar was only half a Muslim]. To locate the 'origin' of Islam in India in the 10th Century Mughal Dynasty headed by Babur coming from Afghanistan is yet another instance of tampering with historical boundaries. The content of such history may be the object of ridicule and comic satire, as we see in the positioning of Aziz by the narrative, but the forms of such historiography, its periodisation, and its logic are upheld as given. Ishtiaq Ahmed's 'alternative' version of Indian Muslim community might serve here as a useful point of departure. He writes:

In reality the Muslim community in its fourteen centuries of history has been influenced by diverse outlooks and traditions besides the Islamic. That such were to happen is not surprising considering the fact that Islam spread to various parts of Asia and Africa, and in the process *local traditions and culture lent their own imprint to the Islamic identity* which evolved in the process. Furthermore, from the very outset *Muslims were not a cohesive society* but comprised several sects and sub sects and ethnic and linguistic variations. South Asian Muslim identity presents a good example of multi-dimensionality, cultural diversity and ethno linguistic and sectarian heterogeneity. *The result is plurality and ambiguity rather than consistency and conformity* to which Muslim theorists assumed in their (ideal) vision of the Islamic community.[57]

(emphasis added)

Some basis for accommodating 'deviations', 'inconsistencies' and 'ambiguity' in Islam, however, has exited within the logic of the grand narrative of colonialism itself. The standard view in which the colonialists as much as the Muslim aristocracy, middle class intellectuals, and later the nationalist invested their faith, was that the perfect period in Islamic history [The Golden Age of Islam] ended with the demise of the prophet (632 AD) and the end of the pious caliphate. The implication of such a view was that subsequent Islamic society was a divergence from the ideal model, and an effort to conform as much as possible to the ideal society was considered the bounden duty of all good Muslims. Also, within the logic of this argument the 'duty' of the Islamic State and 'Muslim tradition' were inseparable, each endorsing the other, resulting in a natural and spontaneous political system in which the state was the preserver and guarantor, not only of Islamic tradition, culture and history, but also of Muslim identity. By the end of the nineteenth century colonialist historiography cast the somewhat diffuse and decentralized Islamic regimes of south Asia, into the dominant behaviour pattern of Islam. Indeed this pattern was qualified by a manufactured religious bigotry, as the conflict between different religious groups were extrapolated as the distinctive feature of the Indian Mughal past.

Secondly, it is somewhat surprising that despite Forster's stay in India and his acquaintance with, if not sound reading of, Indian myths, philosophies, religious and musical traditions, he seems unaware of Sufi ways of life. For Sufi practices undercut in many ways the dominant textual authority of Islam and interrogate the representation of the imperial Islamic genealogy that had subordinated the diversity of Islamic histories, customs, and cultural and social practice to a single, centralised Mughal state power. *A Passage to India*, we can thus infer, is complicitous with a particular 'reading' of the middle period of Indian history which was distinguished not only by its periodisation in terms of European experience (ancient, medieval, modern), but also in its 'discovery' of certain fixed traits, or features, corresponding with each period. As Gyanendra Pandey has argued, such historical (re)construction, was

> Characterised by an emptying out of all history—in terms of the specific variations of time, place, class—from the political experience of the people, and the identification of religion, or the religious community—as the moving force of all Indian politics. The communal riot narrative(s) serve to substantiate this reading of history.[58]

Finally, how was Akbar's new religion, in Adela words, 'to embrace the whole of India'? This theme of 'unity in diversity' has a certain ring of contemporaneity in the Indian nationalist emphasis of '*secularism*'—a creed whereby the state will guarantee the freedom of all religions within the realm of the private experience of its citizens. Adela's fear—which is conflated with that of the implied reader's within the narrative setting, that India will fall apart without the inevitable victory of such a 'secular' creed [There will have to be something universal in this country—I don't say religion... but something, or how else are barriers to be broken down?]—is a preemption of the present day nationalist fear of 'fissiparous regional and communal tendencies'. 'The emphasis upon universal, or secular for that matter, is an ideological effect—the displacement of the particular and specific to the positional authority of the universal.[59] As the ethical universalism uncannily prevails over the multiplicity of the local, the sign of identity and reality found in the work of Empire is slowly done. Eric Stokes describes the mission of work—that medium of recognition for the colonial subject—as a distinctive feature of the imperialist 'mind' which, from the early nineteenth century, effected 'the transference of religious emotion to secular purposes.[60] But this transference of 'affect and object is never achieved without a disturbance, a displacement in the representation of Empire's work itself'.[61]

For a consideration of the above 'displacement' in the work of Empire, accompanied by a simultaneous mechanism of 'othering'—as it obtains in the high moment of symbolism, the opacity of the caves, and the magical effects of the echo—we proceed to the next section of the novel, that is, the Caves.

III
Caves

Robbe Grillet's comments on solitude strike a curious parallel to narrativisation in the 'Caves' section of *A Passage to India*. In Grillet's description of a characteristic New French Novel, solitude becomes the metaphor for the ultimate incommunicability of all human action. As he puts it:

> Let us, as an example, recapitulate the functioning of 'solitude'. I call. No one answers me. Instead of concluding that there is no one there—which could be an observation, pure and simple, dated and placed, in space and time—I decide to act as if, for one reason or another, he was refusing to answer. From then on the silence that follows my appeal is no longer a real silence, it has become pregnant with content, with depth, with a soul—which immediately plunges me back into my own soul. The distance between my cry, as I hear it, and the mute (perhaps deaf) interlocutor to whom it is addressed, becomes a sort of anguish, my

> hope and my despair, a sense to my life. Henceforth nothing will count for me save this false vacuum and the problem it causes me. Should I go on calling? Should I call more loudly? Should I use other words? I try again... I very soon realize that no one is going to answer, but the invisible presence that I continue to create by my cry forces me to go on, for all eternity, sending out my unhappy cry, into the silence. Its echo soon starts to deafen me.[62]
>
> (emphasis added)

Negative sentence structures abound in the 'Caves' and the use of such forms seems to open towards 'indeterminacy'. For example, the first extended discussion of the Marabar caves, even before they are brought to the reader's vision:

> 'Are they large caves?' she asked.
> 'No, not large.'
> 'Do describe them, Professor Godbole.'
> 'It will be a great honour' ... After an impressive pause he said: 'There is an entrance in the rock which you enter, and through the entrance is the cave.'
> 'Something like the caves at Elephanta?'
> 'Oh no, not at all; at Elephanta there are sculptures of Siva and Parvati. There are no sculptures at Marabar.'
> 'They are immensely holy, no doubt,' said Aziz to help on the narrative.
> 'Oh no, oh no.'
> 'Still they are ornamented in some way.'
> 'Oh no'.
> 'Well, why are they so famous? We all talk of the famous Marabar Caves. Perhaps that is our empty brag.'
> 'No, I should not quite say that.'
> 'Describe them to this lady, then.'
> 'It will be a great pleasure.'
> He forewent the pleasure, and Aziz realized that he was keeping back something about the caves... [pp.91-92]

This escape from question and identification is repeated in the 'lies' of the Indian characters, which open ways towards what might be, what may be wished, what might have been all routes out of the determined. Gillian Beer's discussion of such escape deserves to be mentioned here. She considers 'nothing' as a word of power in this text. As the narrator persists with this theme; 'But nothing in India is identifiable, the mere asking of a question causes it to disappear or to merge in something else' [p.101] the word 'nothing' acquires two natures. 'Set above, it expresses stasis, vacancy: nothing.' But as soon as 'it' becomes part of a sentence, it makes the whole organisation of that sentence restless and unstable, expressive of contrary impulse.'[63]

On first reading the significance of this sentence might be construed as 'It is not possible to identify anything in India'. But there is another organisation linking as a shadow form in that sentence, the possibility that Only in India is Nothing Identifiable.[64] This seems to echo Aziz's statement, mentioned earlier, pertaining to Akbar's religion, which sought to marry Hinduism and Islam: 'Nothing embraces the whole of India, nothing, nothing....' This diagram of meaning is 'unstable', like an 'optical illusion'.[65] It alternates between 'There is nothing that embraces the whole of India' and—particularly with the force of the reiterated nothing—'nothingness embraces the whole of India'.

The effect is reinforced when the caves are described prior to any action. The reader is told:

> Having seen one such cave, having seen two, having seen three, four, fourteen, twenty-four, the visitor returns to Chandrapore uncertain whether he has had an interesting experience or a dull one or any experience at all. Nothing, nothing attaches to them, and their reputation—for they have one—does not depend upon human speech [p.138].

In these two examples, language may fail but its practitioners (readers) try to make it serve the 'truth' as they have come to understand it. In this instance, 'Nothingness' begins to predominate in the sense over 'There is nothing' that attaches to them': 'Nothing is inside them, they were sealed up before the creation of pestilence or treasure; if mankind grew curious and excavated, nothing, nothing would be added to the sum of good or evil' [p.138].

The narrative alternates: it retreats from us and also wants to confront. In the process it disrupts the normal chain of signifiers and subverts fixed orders, as it produces echoes and disturbance of received meaning and refuses to answer questions that are framed by it, or might be implicitly derived by the reader.

In the face of this highly aestheticised drama of the human predicament where solitude is charged with ambivalent metaphysical dimensions of both presence and absence, the disruption of all human consciousness, and all ethical and religious order, seems to be the only possible 'resolution' in the narrative. This effect is kept throughout at a high key, from the early hints about the caves, through the traumatic experience of Mrs. Moore, to Fielding's wonderment at their intransigent, and ineluctable presence. As Mrs. Moore enters the caves she finds that:

> The crush and the smells she could forget, but the echo began in some indescribable way to undermine her hold on life. Coming at a moment when she chanced to be fatigued, it had managed to murmur: 'Pathos, piety, courage—they exist, but are identical, and so is filth.'... 'Everything exists, nothing has value': If one had spoken vileness in that place or quoted lofty poetry, the comment would have been the same—'ou—boum'... [pp.160-61]

This calls forth attention to the dimensions of 'experience' which can be authenticated by their psychological truthfulness alone—expressing a hunger for perfection, a discontent with the limitations of the present and an aspiration to possess the future inspite of the 'void' that seems to envelop them. The 'awakenings' of Mrs. Moore and Adela dislocated by an Indian that confounds their expectation thus take on cataclysmic form and results in derangement and delusion, the one (Mrs. Moore) mimicking in her feelings and behaviour the ascetic stance of isolation from the world, but 'misunderstanding' its meaning and meaninglessness, the other (Adela) assailed by the sudden knowledge of her sexuality and 'interpreting' it as sexual assault. However, the narrative's 'disbelief' in the purely mystical must represent this moment as touching upon the fringes of humanity, as *interrogating the limits of liberal humanism without quite being able to find its other.* And so we have an interesting play of the 'numinous' and 'mundane', an exalted narrative tone that suddenly rings hollow against the flat voices of Aziz and Adela, 'dwarfs shaking hands.' So 'non-mystical' does the register of narration become that when Godbole makes one of his brief and not-quite-congruous appearances, asking an incredulous Fielding about the success of the Marabar expedition and about a name for his new school at Mau his arcane words concerning good and evil have quite the opposite effect to that of his 'funny little song' to Krishna at Fielding's ill-starred tap-party. There, his voice was succeeded by the 'silences'; a moment of unparaphrasable and otherworldly meaning, cherished and endorsed by the narration. But here, within a more prosaic rhythm of narrative events and voice, Godbole's gnomic words strike us, and the exasperated fielding, as lapidary and unhelpful:

> Good and evil are different, as their names imply. But, in my own humble opinion, they are, both of them, aspects of my lord. He is present in the one, absent in the other, and the difference between presence and absence is great, as great as my feeble mind can grasp. Yet absence implies presence, absence is not non-existence, and we are therefore entitled to repeat, 'Come, come, come, come'! And in the same breath, as if to cancel any

beauty his words might have contained, he added, 'But did you have time to visit any of the interesting Marabar antiquities? [p.186]

This cutting-out of the transcendental seems very conscious, even to the point of parody. Godbole is absurd here, and his argument, in its compression and apparent irrelevance, sounds partly like an empty jingle.[66]

Fielding, after seeing the hills, experienced nothing himself, and plunges instead into moral self-scrutiny and his characteristically prosaic mode of discontent, doubt, and frustration. Of course the Marabar echo remains, and its lesson of a dimensionlessness beyond the ethical. For a while, until the sound of her own pragmatic voice gives her a self-restoring purchase on truth and factuality, Adela is haunted by it: 'The sound had shouted after her when she escaped, and was going on still like a river that gradually floods the plaint.. Evil was loose' [p.200]. And, for Mrs. Moore, the Marabar struck a gong to mark her final alienation from the world of relationships, judgments, and words like 'duty', 'good', and 'love'. But what is brought out now is not so much the annihilating power of the despairing vision as its strange pettiness—as though to match the narrative's later focus on legal process, political dispute and social and personal fumblings. This is seen as '*the twilight of the double vision*', the doubleness being the simultaneous perception of the horror of the universe and its refusal to be grand—grandeur being a quality by which even an infinite horror can make at least some appeal to the 'human' imagination.

This brings us back to the central thematic of liberalism, raised earlier, to ask: how important is it to liberalism—to its philosophy as well as its actual practice and therefore to its politics, especially to the politics of subjectivity—to maintain the sense that nothing is or can be closed, or for that matter understood and resolved, except in some extra human, or extra-anthropomorphic realm. More particularly, the universalistic aspect of this extra human dimension is to be noted as an essential strand of late Victorian liberalism, where the universal resides as alien, as outraging taste, as unconcerned with housing humankind, as existing in the silence outside language, and hence as untranslatable into human sounds or human scale. Understood in this light, much of syntactic, tonal and verbal indeterminacies, of 'The Caves', so delicately and labouriously cherished by the narrative artistry, can be referred back to the liberal problematic of human consciousness and its other.[67]

Structurally, the spiritual muddledom/mystery is mirrored in the earth that upholds them, the civilization that has escaped muddle, the spirit in a reasonable form...

> The Mediterranean is the human norm. When men leave that exquisite lake, whether through the mosphorous or the Pillars of Hercules, they approach the monstrous and extraordinary; and the southern exit leads to the strangest experience of all [p.278].

Both the spiritual and human muddle ('They did not do one thing which the non-Hindu would feel dramatically correct; this approaching triumph of India was a muddle, a frustration of reason and form', p.280) lie at a certain critical distance from 'the civilization that has escaped muddle.. in spirit in a reasonable form, with flesh and blood subsisting' [p.275]. Both are therefore also inextricably connected to 'the spirit in reasonable form', are indeed part of its structure.

Liberalism in its Orientalist mode, or its overtly political bourgeois mode—needs such a guarantee of 'the other' to sustain itself.[68] It cannot hold together without such a transcendental presence. There is, however, a sort of contradiction in this argument. The problem at one level is that liberalism's dream for the universal (to be realized classically through art, or an ethical guarantee of the conscience through authenticity) a dream which underwrites and empowers its politics is far too grandiose, majestic and overpowering in its proportions to be held within the confines of its humanist philosophies, or its empiricist dependence upon the knowledge of the senses. *Therefore, if the liberal mind has to acknowledge the presence of India honestly, face upto its challenge, it also must admit of India's indifference to the founding values of the Western liberal world.* It has to construct other vantage points of knowing the 'truth', if its claim of universality is to be established. In this act of constructing an all-pervasive truth, liberalism must sacrifice part of its humanism, as well as aesthetic, ethical and moral norms, and its taste.

In other words, Forster's liberalism forces him into a position where he must locate the voice of truth/pure consciousness outside all history and society in an extra linguistic realm where ethical distinctions, which are, after all, humanist do not hold. This could also be interpreted, as an act of challenging the authority of all significations, where the artifice of signification as well as culture inscribed in its imperiled[69]. But within the narrative scheme it is 'that place where completeness can be found.. *completeness not reconstruction*' [p.282].

The philosophical basis of such an anthropomorphic vision, its linguistic and cultural assumptions and its cohesive strategies are analysed in detail by Derrida in his critique of Rousseau and Levi-Strauss.[70] The restoration of 'Ancient Night' *of pure experience, or the total emptiness of 'subject' in its Jain and Buddhist variation as the 'other' side of the nostalgia for the lost unity*, can be shown to be discursively constructed, and historically circulated. For Derrida, 'the other of the signified is never contemporary, is at best a subtly discrepant inverse or parallel—discrepant by the time of a breath—of the order of the signifier'.[71] He puts this 'experience' under erasure:

> As for the concept of experience, it is most unwieldy here. Like all the notions I am using, it belongs to the history of metaphysics and we can only use it under erasure. 'Experience' has always designated the relationship with a presence, whether that relationship had the form of consciousness or not. Yet we must, by means of the sort of contortion and contention that discourse is obliged to undergo, exhaust the resources of the concept of experience before attaining and in order to attain, by deconstruction, its ultimate foundation. It is the only way to escape 'empiricism' and 'naïve' critiques of experience at the same time.[72]

For Derrida the concept of 'experience' is a theological idea, an idea that we need to fulfill our desire for plenitude and authority. He remarks that Levi Strauss, like Heidegger, is afflicted with this nostalgia:

> One perceives in his work a sort of ethic of presence, an ethic of nostalgia for origins, an ethic of archaic and natural innocence, of a purity of presence and self-presence in speech—an ethic, nostalgia, and even remorse which he often presents as the motivation of the ethnological project when he moves towards archaic societies—in his eyes...[73]
>
> (emphasis added)

The 'ethnological project' of Forster's text, when inflected by its peculiar turns of indeterminacy, gains further strength as it conceals the overt politics of Imperialism. Within the ambitious scheme of posing a challenge to its own liberal humanist legacy—an act which ironically consolidates the mission of discovering 'the other' in its ineluctable skepticism or the moment of surrender—the 'surrender' Forster acknowledges to the infectious spirit of India—is seen at its dramatic moment in the representation of the trial scene. The trial scene is the staging of a series of events where the politics of such 'surrender' can be laid bare.

The trial scene had political overtones of contemporary events taking place in India, particularly the *Jallianwallah*

Massacre in Amritsar in 1919. The introduction to the Penguin edition of *A Passage to India* directly refers to this incident which came in the wake of Indian nationalist resistance to a series of acts, called the *Rowlatt Act*, which gave the Imperial police stringent powers of arrest and search. Apart from overtly political import of this scene as it appears in the novel, which has been given detailed critical attention by various writers, some critics have singled out the re-appearance of Mrs. Moore in spirit as the Hindu Goddess 'Esmiss Esmoor', and the 'iconic', if invisible, figure of the Punkhawalla as the key moments of the trial scene.

Setting the metaphysical aside, we need to focus attention on how discursive constructs of race and gender are interwoven in the way Forster stages the 'rape' and the eventual trial of Aziz in the court. Further, we need to investigate how the figure of the *Punkhawalla* emerges from this setting as an object of an anthropological gaze relegating the burning caste question in India to the realm of a comical romance.

The charge of sexual assault on Adela, like the event itself, is interestingly never mentioned directly; it is either elided or referred to by the English as an 'insult', a clearly motivated circumlocution. Later in a moment of vision, during the trial, Adela returns to the caves and retracts her accusation of Aziz, but the reader never learns what if anything actually happened there. *Where we would have the naming of a crime and its perpetrator, exists only a gap.* That Forster deliberately created this gap is clear from the original version of the scene, where an assault definitely occurs; the reader is in the cave with Adela and feels the hands that push her against the wall and grab her breasts; she smashes the assailant with the field glasses before running out of the cave and down the hill.[74] In the published version, not just the violent physical attack but the entire scene inside the cave is omitted. Many critics choosing to interpret this gap as an 'illusion' read Adela's experience in psychological terms, basing their reading on Fielding's description of Adela as a prig, and on her realizations just before entering the cave that she has no love or sexual passion for Ronny, the man she is engaged to marry, and that Aziz is 'a handsome little Oriental' [p.152]. At one point after the retraction, she responds to Fielding's hallucination theory by comparing her experience to 'the sort of thing... that makes some women think they've had an offer of marriage when none was made' [p.240]. *Thus, it is that sexuality and repression enter the gap at the 'center' of the novel.* Adela in this version becomes a hysterical, repressed, overly-intellectual new woman who fantasises and is haunted by sex ghosts. In this reading we might as well say, she thinks she has been assaulted because she wants to be raped.[75]

The narrativisation of this event presents a curious ambivalence as to the sexual norms of bourgeois society. On the one level, it recognises the way in which society, in Michel Foucault's terms, had appropriated bodies and pleasures and deployed a sexuality that served to control individuals. *The event is thus inscribed in the modern society's construction of sexuality, and its attendant strategies*: a 'hysterization of women's bodies' and a 'psychiatrization of perverse pleasure'.[76] At another level, however, the narrative's resistance to the modern system of sexuality is shaped by the sexual discourse of the period, including the concept of repression. As Patricia Joplin has argued, rape in this novel becomes an act of violence, a transgression of boundaries, that 'enact the rivalries at work within the culture and the novel upon the body of a woman who is herself potentially silenced, elided'.[77] With this in mind we can return to Adela's 'unspeakable' experience in the cave—the experience that she speaks as violation or rape, and read it not in terms of sexual desire or repression, but in terms of a deployment of sexuality within a discourse of power which intersects race and gender. Within this discourse, what is at stake is both gender difference and racial difference in a multiplicity of force relations criss-crossing the social and textual field. To read the event in the cave from this perspective *is to pay close attention to what it means to be rapable, a social position that cuts across biological and racial lines to underwrite culturally constructed definitions of sexuality in a colonial setting.*

Recently feminist theorists have argued that any discussion of rape must recognise its integral relationship to the social construction of gender and the social division of power, both of which are grounded in sexuality. Developing Foucault's perception of sexuality as a form of power over the body, they define it more specifically as 'social sexing': 'that social process which creates, organises, expresses, and directs desire, creating the social beings we know as women and men, as their relations create society'.[78] Emphasised in these analyses is Foucault's failure to recognise the different sexual experiences of men and women in our society: to recognise that, 'the system of power... has the bodies of women as its object of privileged appropriation, a sexual differentiation that affects every aspect of their being'.[79] 'Representation of the world', notes Catharine Mackinnon, 'like the world itself, is the work of men; they describe it from their own point of view, which they confuse with the absolute truth... Power to create the world from one's point of view is power in its male form'..[80]

Within this epistemology, power includes the power to name the other as object and objectification makes sexuality a material reality of women's lives, not just a psychological, attitudinal, or ideological one. At issue is both the construction of the female subject and the effect of this construction on women's experience of their own being: *the ways in which women internalise a male image of their sexuality as their identity as women, making epistemology and ontology one.* The process of being reduced to an object, constantly aware of being looked at, acted upon causes women to split themselves in two, to watch themselves as women from the male perspective, affecting both their realisation and their presentation of self[81]. Women then, materially as well as psychologically, are both object and separated from themselves as object, a thing and nothing.

In this formulation of gender, rape plays a significant role, as it is the social perception, which underlies rape. Rape is sexual essentially because it rests on the very social difference between the sexes. Men rape women in so far as they belong to the class of men, which has appropriated the bodies of women. In Mackninon's words, 'To be rapable, a position which is social, not biological, defines what a woman is'.[82]

When we turn to '*The Caves*' in order to understand the deployment of sexuality, it criss-crosses racial lines. For the first part of the novel English and Indian are locked into a discourse of race in which each objectifies the other, although in any direct confrontation the English maintain the position of acting subject. At the same time, however, English and Indian men share a discourse of sexuality that inscribes their subjectivity by objectifying and silencing women. After the 'insult', relations shift to place the Indians explicitly in the category of woman, where their bodies and subjectivity are appropriated for social ends. During the farcical trial scene—all but hides Aziz's point of view—Mr. Mc Bryde, the English lawyer remarked:

> That the darker races are physically attracted by the fairer, but not vice versa—not a matter for bitterness, not a matter for abuse, but just a fact which any scientific observer will confirm...(p.21)

What McBride likes to call 'just a fact' was closer to the expression of a great fear, which swept under the English carpet the embarrassing 'fact' about the Eurasians who were very, very seldom the children of white mothers. Similarly when Fielding produces a 'bad effect' at the English club by asking about Miss Quested's health, his transgression consists of pronouncing her name; for since the 'insult' she, like Aziz, was always referred to indirectly, by elision. By reversing the figure, we can perceive the act of elision as embedded in the cause rather than the effect of the rape. Elision or negation of the individual human being functions as a part of a rhetoric of difference that objectifies the racial as well as sexual other, and creates the space for rape to occur. Rape law, for example with its assumption of a single, 'objective' fact of the matter, determinable by 'evidence', rather than a 'split or gendered perspective that reflects the gendered nature of the exchange, has worked 'to discredit the woman's perception of the encounter's meaning.[83] Whose subjectivity becomes the objectivity of 'what happened' is a matter of social meaning, that is, it has been a matter of sexual politics.'[84]

Thus, when Adela 'improvises' an explanation for her experience in the caves, she does not recognise the act as such; *she is given a text* ('assault by an Indian'), the oldest story around, to which she makes her experience conform. *But in the logic of empire, the superimposed effect* (the story Adela tells) *assumes the privilege of cause.* For Adela to recognise the conditions of improvisation—to acknowledge her own story as improvised as she seems to do at the trial—is to subvert the political machine. Among the Anglo-Indians it is to make herself unheard: 'I didn't catch that answer' [p.229], the superintendent declares when Adela departs from her carefully rehearsed testimony. In what appears to the British as inexplicable improvisation, Adela explodes 'the flimsy framework of the court' [p.231]. But even this explosion is contained within the staged ceremonies of recuperated British ideals.

Adela's 'experience' in the caves brings to surface the theatricality that governs colonial discourse and that supports its sexual politics not only in her own melodramatic rendering of it but in Anglo-India's 'personal' and political response. The 'exalted emotion' she generates, reads like a catalogue of literary cliches: the unselfish devotion ('what can we do for our sister? [pp.179-801]), the ennobling sorrow ('she is my own darling girl' [p.180]), the regrets ('why don't one think more of other people ?' [p.180], the self-accusation ('to refuse, and then give in under pressure, that is what I did, my sons, that is what I did' [p.185]). The discrete actions speak here in a single voice, and when political considerations supplant Adela's private tragedy, the stage language remains the same: 'They had started speaking of 'women and children' that phrase that exempts the male from sanity when it has been repeated a few times' [p.183]. In their eyes, the chilly and half-known features of Miss Quested vanished, to be replaced by all that is sweetest and warmest in the private life [p.183].

The Anglo-Indians exercise power by a form of narrative control. With the script already written, they need only cast the characters and rehearse their lives. Predictably, they need only cast themselves in all the desirable roles: hero, victim, martyr, loyal friend. 'Miss Quested was only a victim, but young Heaslop was a martyr; he was the recipient of all the evil intended against them by the country they had tried to serve; he was '*bearing the Sahib's cross*' [p.185]. Similarly, Aziz cast as villain, plays the part 'acting the criminal' as soon as he is apprised of the plot: he 'lies' about evidence, tries to turn away, sobs and breaks down at his arrest. And similarly again, given a choice between the only available roles, 'to avenge the girl' or 'save the man' [p.165], Fielding accepts the apostate's part; there being little option indeed to join a different play. Such rhetorical procedures control unauthorized readings, and even create the desired text. When Fielding questions Turton about the source of the charges Against Aziz, the collector will not speak Adela's name 'Miss Derek and—the victim herself', [p.163].

Ironically, then, *it is Adela's charge against Aziz rather than her 'experience' in the caves that subjects her to a 'rape'*. For the charge puts her in Anglo-Indian hands where she is 'examined', or perhaps more accurately, a 'proper' voice is extracted from her. The episode then marks a progressive silencing of Adela because her 'illness' with its hysterical symptom, fixes her gender position and restricts her vocal independence. In fact, in Anglo-Indian eyes, Adela never really has a voice at all, for they can not recognise a voice governed by competing narrative demands. As woman, Adela remains 'another bad case', an actor who panics under pressure and forgets her lines. Years after the event, they continue to proclaim, 'that Marabar case which broke down because the poor girl couldn't face giving her evidence—that was another bad case' [p.261].

Aziz too is a highly sexed character and his sexuality like Adela's, is mediated by the othering of the Oriental as well. Once accused of rape, he disappears as speaking subject, appearing only as the object of Anglo-Indian gaze. Both his body and his possessions, including his letters, are appropriated by the police and used against him. He is reduced to his skin colour, his body, by implication his sexuality. In discussing Aziz with Fielding, McBride asserts that while the schoolmaster sees the Indians at their best, when they are boys, he, the policeman, 'knows them as they really are after they have developed into men' [p.169]. From this perspective of a 'scientific observation' Aziz loses his status as man and with it the power to protect women, even his dead wife. When McBride appropriates the photograph along with his other possessions, it ceases to signify Aziz's ability to exchange women in a ritual of male bonding; instead it indicates his reduction to sexual object. In response to Fielding's identification of the photograph, McBryde 'gave a faint, incredulous smile, and started rummaging in the drawer. His face became inquisitive and slightly bestial. 'Wife indeed, I know these wives !' he was thinking' [p.172].

When Aziz regains his freedom, he reclaims his violated wife and with her his manhood, setting the stage for the separation that ensues between Fielding and him, a separation precipitated first by Fielding's friendship with Adela after the trail and later by his marriage not to Adela—which is what

Aziz mistakenly believes—but to Stella, Ronny's sister. Once the misunderstanding is cleared, Fielding tries to recapture their previous closeness by '[Forcing] himself to speak intimately about his wife'—by evoking, that is, the sexual discourse that had united them before. By now, however, Aziz no longer wishes intimacy with any English person and Fielding has 'thrown in his lot with Anglo-India by marrying a country woman' [p.319]. However great Fielding's initial disregard of the rich racial discourse, he perceives his marriage as committing him to the system that defines him as English and male, and he accepts its limitations. He can no longer, in his words, 'travel as lightly' [p.317] nor can he risk flirting with the other. Aziz is reduced to a 'memento, a trophy' [p.319]. Just as Fielding's defiance after Aziz's arrest was contained by the relations of power that made Ronny and Him antagonists who spoke the same language, the form of his resistance corroborates rather than undermines the system. It illustrates Foucault's idea that resistance is never in a position of exteriority in relation to power; it exits within the power/knowledge apparatus that 'depends' upon it and is subject to its discourses.[85] In his defence of Aziz, Fielding relies on the power of evidence and knowledge, which he believes will triumph, unable to recognise, as Hamidullah does from the position of the feminised and colonised object, that evidence and knowledge would not work to free them ('If God himself descended... into their club and said you [Aziz] were innocent, they would disbelieve him' [p.73] Unable to cross the boundaries that separate subject and object, to enter fully into the category woman, Fielding, for all his good intentions and his exposure of the system, thus enacts the story of the failure to understand and align himself with the mode of resistance of 'the other'. To understand this we should examine Fielding's attempt to 'reform' Aziz's sexuality. The fielding seal of containment is brought down on another aspect of Aziz's sexuality: his coarse but surely understandable attitude to

Adela after the trial. In the dialogue between them Aziz tells Fielding that he would forgive her if she wrote to him:

> 'Dear Dr. Aziz, I wish you had come into the cave;
> I am an awful old hag, and it is my last chance...' [p.245]

Fielding shuts him up: 'Oh, I wish you wouldn't make that kind of remark... It is one thing in you I can't put up with.' Does Fielding object simply because the remark is so ungentlemanly? (Earlier he had 'found a touch of bad taste in Aziz's reference to a lady's breasts'—p.117). Or because he cannot allow a white woman to be insulated by a native? Either way, Aziz is put in the wrong, and the source and standard of right behaviour is the white man's. He might see eye to eye with Aziz on this point, but for a lofty, ascetic standard that smacks of another form of the snobbery that Fielding finds so reprehensible in Aziz:

> ...Sexually, [Aziz] was a snob. This had puzzled and worried Fielding. Sensuality, as long as it is straightforward, did not repeal him, but this derived sensuality—the sort that classes a mistress among motor-cars if she is beautiful, is among eye-flies if she isn't—was alien to his own emotions [p.235].

These details are aspects of a larger issue, for they occur during the time when Fielding puts pressure on Aziz not to sue Adela for damages. Surely a desire for compensation, even for retribution, would have been understandable, even justifiable, but the narrative placement of Fielding makes it appear as though he had every right to reform the crude thinking of Aziz on this matter. Fielding may be at odds with all the club but in this instance he out-Englishes the lot of them: 'The insensitiveness about Adela displeased him. It would from every point of view, be right to treat her generously' [p.254].

Every point of view? And surely Fielding's moral high ground is unpleasantly compromised by the methods he uses to get his own way:

> Fielding was not ashamed to practice a little necromancy. Whenever the question of compensation came up, he introduced the dead woman's name. Just as other propagandists invented her tomb, so did he raise a questionable image of her in the heart of Aziz, saying nothing that he believed to be untrue, but producing something that was probably far from the truth [p.254].

Together these details suggest not only that 'the Oriental' lacks moral refinement, but that he cannot be trusted to reach a right decision without an Englishman's guidance. The narrative distribution of roles, however skilfully accomplished, then reinforces the liberal commitment to justice: one must ridicule one set of colonial administrators, but at the same time make sure that a more subtle breed of advisors, such as Fielding, is still necessary for the moral refinement of the Oriental. In doing this the narrative enactment of the trial scene and its aftermath has shifted but simultaneously internalised the requirements of the liberal colonial project. Adela's sudden release from aphasia releases Aziz to the more insidious tyranny of an unwritten law. '*You always get the scale wrong, my dear Fellow*', says Fielding to Aziz with unbearable condescension. And Aziz always will, because this law is a tribal secret; he incurs his so-called friend's displeasure. The reader, it is assumed by the narrative, is also privy to the secret.

The *Punkhawalla* who provides the scene of fantasy in the drama of the court-room, is a figure of truth to the precise degree that he is the object of a colonialist anthropological gaze. Strangely, however, the narrative function of this lowly untouchable is crucial to the outcome of the trial scene. Although described as having 'no bearing officially upon the trial' [p.217] he is strategically positioned on a raised platform across from the assistant magistrate, who is also seated on a platform as a sign of colonial authority. The assistant magistrate is everything the untouchable is not; he is a western educated native. The untouchable was produced not through his contact with western knowledge but with the filth and garbage of the city. Whereas the 'little assistant magistrate' is a 'cultivated, self-conscious, and conscientious' Indian civil servant [p.217], the *Punkhawalla* does not participate in the trial but is there merely to operate the hand-pulled fan.

Yet in the narrative representation of the events leading upto the climax of Adela's discovery, it is he, the untouchable, who is empowered to elicit the truth about the 'innocent' Aziz. Adela sees him when she first enters the courtroom, and it is his highly imposing 'natural' and 'dignified' presence that opens up Adela's mind which had been sealed by the delimiting Englishness of her own race. In the narrative description, this lowly untouchable emerges as a redemptive figure, arising from the underworld, who is counterposed to our temporal world of 'evil':

> Almost naked, and splendidly formed, he sat on a raised platform near the back, in the middle of the central gangway, and he caught her attention, as she came in and he seemed to control the proceedings. He had the strength and beauty that sometimes come to flower in Indians of low birth. When that strange race nears the dust and is condemned as untouchable, then nature remembers the physical perfection that she accomplished elsewhere, and throws out a god... Something in his aloofness impressed the girl from middle class England, and rebuked the narrowness of her sufferings. In virtue of what had she collected this roomful of people together? Her particular brand of opinions, and the suburban Jehovah who sanctified them—by what right did they claim so much importance in the world, and assume the title of civilization? [pp.217-218]

This is then made out to be a case of classic opposition between nature and culture, and the romantic triumph of the former over the latter. In the narrative Adela's response to the cross-examinations is shown to be interlocked with this realization, and the resolution is cast in quasi-mystical, high aesthetic terms: 'then nature remembers the physical perfection that she accomplished elsewhere, and throws out a god'. The moment of unexpected response of Adela caused by this visionary intervention of the *Punkhawalla* disrupts the legal discourse and acts as a narrative turning point for Aziz's transformation from a 'good' colonial subject into an anti-British nationalist. 'I am an Indian at last'.

The *Pankhawalla*, on the other hand, cannot but remain silent, unaware of his own activity of fanning. He scarcely 'knew that he existed and did not understand why the court was fuller than usual, indeed he did not know that it was fuller than usual, didn't even know he worked a fan, though he thought he pulled a rope' [pp.217-18]. This rhythmic action of pulling the fan corresponds to the cyclic notion of time; the repetitiveness of labour in the face of ineluctable, intransigent laws of production; he exists in a mythological world which escapes historical time:

> Then life returned to its complexities, person after person struggled out of the room to their various purposes, and before long no one remained on the scene of the fantasy but the beautiful naked god. Unaware that anything unusual had occurred, he continued to pull the chord of his punkah (sic), to gaze at the empty dias and overturned special chairs, and rhythmically to agitate the clouds of descending dust [p.231].

This dramatises the high point of debate in colonial discourse theory around the figure of the subaltern—the impossibility of his/her own speech in the face of the discursive onslaught of the coloniser and his native counterpart.[86] Yet in appropriating the *Punkhawalla* for its own purposes, the narrative represents clearly a time which negates the historico-cultural specificity of his presence. *He is absorbed into a frozen scale of timelessness that reinforces, in its moment of high aesthetics, the Orientalist displacement of other cultures into the realm of myth.* As such, even as he is represented as a condition of transformation of Aziz's personality, a laudable achievement indeed within the scope of narrative, the *Punkhawalla* remains a figure of 'truth' only to the extent the narrator's founding epistemology can permit. When the *Punkhawalla* does return the colonizing gaze, it is to no effect; the room is empty and the chairs, overturned. The crucial point in the trial scene is that the scene does not offer us a mere reversal of colonising operations but rather a fractured one, in that it represents also a time when educated 'natives' such as Amrit Rao and the transfigured nationalist Aziz were emerging as historical actors although the 'subaltern' was described in the mythology of the lowly God, or what Gandhi was to later describe as '*harijan*', when constituting the Indian nationalist discourse on the untouchable.[87] The ill-treatment given to the emerging contemporary nationalist intelligentsia shows yet another instance of narrative control, where the permission to narrate is inscribed in the founding values and system of knowledge of British Empire.

IV
Temple

In the last two sections we saw how appropriating all the voices in the novel, colonial discourse performs ultimately to a hall of mirrors. The novel's most devastating critique of Imperialism from the variously positioned liberal endeavours of 'goodwill plus culture and intelligence', and from an all-encompassing figuration of the mystic other, may only work to strengthen the tentacular hold of the founding values of the Empire. The final section of the novel demonstrates yet another twist of the narrative in its fashioning of the apparatus of complex symbolism, to present a voice so absolutely 'other' that it defies an attempt to be absorbed.

The 'Temple' section of the novel begins with a kind of programme note to orient the reader to the curtain's rising on a radically changed setting and scene: 'Some hundreds of miles westward of the Marabar Hills, and two years later in time, Professor Narayan Godbole stands in the presence of God' [p.283]. This marks the narrative effort to explore yet another 'passage', away from the unfathomable horrors of the caves, through a solecism, if possible. The walls of the palace at Mau where Professor Godbole dances before God, testify to error and inadvertency:

> The inscriptions which the poets of the state had composed were hung where they could not be read or had twitched their drawing pins out of the stucco, and one of them.. consisted, by an unfortunate slip of the draughtsman, of the words, 'God si love'. God si love. Is it the final message of India? [pp.282-3]

Verbs and prepositions, messages, connectives of any kind are sought to be made 'unstable' here. Syntax is a requisite, but is breakable. In the scene at the beginning of the 'Temple' section of the novel where Godbole confronts the misspelling hung comically on the palace wall, *language has been jostled from the outset*; God is not born yet—that will occur at midnight—but he has also been born centuries ago, nor can He ever be born.. *He is, was not, is not, was*. And what the singers are chanting, in a numbing litany, seems as much the willed negation of meaning and sense as the celebration of a divinity:

> Tukaram, Tukaram,
> Thou art my father and mother and everybody.
> Tukaram, Tukaram,
> Thou art my father and mother and everybody.
> Tukaram, Tukaram,
> Thou art my father and mother and everybody.
> Tukaram, Tukaram,
> Thou art my father and mother and everybody.
> Tukaram...

And yet syntax and the equivalent of syntax remain: the corridors at Mau are not confused, they open into a formal courtyard, there are hard, white pillars, vaulting, detailed chandeliers of pink glass, a pale blue turban on Godbole's head, a gold pince-nez at a slight angle to—not the universe—but his nose. We are made to know where we are; and though the simple opening sentence ends in the phrase 'Godbole stands in the presence of God', thus casually encapsulating the eternal, it began on a quite different perspective, 'Some hundreds of miles westward of the Marabar Hill, and two years later in time... '—that firmly lays down the lineaments of material space and time.'

The misdirected chaos of the ceremony provides the event with its radiance, its escape from syntax:

> They sang not even to the God who confronted them, but to a saint; they did not do one thing which the non-Hindu would feel dramatically correct; this approaching triumph of India was a *muddle* as we call it, a *frustration of reason and form* [p.282].

But the 'triumph' of such disorder is not in itself an untrampled revelation of the real. On the other hand, as we saw in the earlier section, it is inscribed in the founding values of the Empire as much as in its epistemological requirements of building 'passages' to the other, non-western worlds. If 'is' has to be broken for radiance to come, 'si' correspondingly tends to collapse back into the all-too-mundane mode of 'is'. Following the irregularity of 'chance', either by a trick of memory or a telepathic appeal—it does not matter which—Godbole's mind comes into possession of two random images, of Mrs. Moore and a wasp:

> He impelled her by his spiritual force to that place where *completeness can be found. Completeness, not reconstruction.* His senses grew thinner, he remembered a wasp seen he forgot where, perhaps on a stone. He loved the wasp equally, he was imitating God. And the stone where the wasp hung—could he... no, he had been wrong to attempt the stone, logic and conscious effort had

seduced, he came back to the strip of red carpet and discovered that he was dancing upon it [pp.283-84].

The event is staged as a breezy movement: a quick passage from the random image, 'a tiny splinter' towards 'completeness' and then the sudden discovery that effort is inimical to 'completeness', that 'reconstruction' is the normal human mode—like the normal mode of narration itself, which falls within the bounds of space and time. The picture of Godbole trying consciously to adopt the position of God as he invokes Mrs. Moore to express the real in a moment of numinosity, develops *the romantic idea of the artist in the direction of the iconic, but the narrative must ultimately thwart this effort.*[88] So, even Godbole fails: and this narration is not his, nor is it in itself iconic. Like Godbole, narrative must submit to 'the rules of time.' While expressing in all its indirections and ingenuities, its discontent with those rules: 'it does not seem much, still, it is more than I am myself', reflects the Brahman Godbole at the end of the ceremony [p.288] suggesting to the reader that *all narrative, while conditioned by time and syntax remains true to its energies 'by always seeking to test its limits; by making each 'is' dance to the cymbals and become a little more than itself.* And as if God does not show up, which is always already known within the limits of the narrative scheme, literature, like all thought, must return to the conditions of history: 'it is only a game with words, really, a religious pun, not a religious truth' [p.269]. (emphasis added)

The 'consequence' of this is that the narrative succeeds in domesticating the 'uncanniness' of India (India's challenge to liberalism) as it translates both in its mundane (social) and exalted (spiritual) versions into the spiritual complement, threat to humanism, than other. In the process the narrative also naturalises the empire, not necessarily in the narrow, 'political' sense of the British Government in India, but in the broader, infinitely more enduring sense of the Empire of Enlightenment. Colonial rule, within the rules of this logic, is only a symptom of the human condition itself. The 'contradictions' and the 'irrationalities' that arise from empire, and from the divisions between Orient and Occident are represented as merely specific scenes in the majestic play of truth, of the mystery of the universe itself. The temple, the wasp, Godbole, and Mrs. Moore appear in this theatre as the predictable uncanny complement to Fielding and his creed of rational humanism. One can be a Fielding and reverentially acknowledge the power of a Godbole: 'There is something in religion that may not be true, but has not yet been sung... something that the Hindus have perhaps found' [p.274]. One may similarly start one's journey from realism, and march forward to the labyrinthine rhythms of symbolism; but one must not—the novel prohibits it—treat this transition as a requirement of the narrative of Orientalism, or worse, as an epistemological effect!

After considering this attention should be drawn to those 'switches' and 'turns' of narrative which seem to problematise a simple pattern of Orientalist 'otherness'. In spite of Forster's avowed allegiance to Brahmanic Hinduism, and its fundamental principles of 'unity in diversity', *the text succeeds in opening up a new dimension of religiosity which undercuts the assumption of the grand narrative of Hinduism as invented in the late 18th century by the Orientalists, and which obviously served as Forster's archival material.* The discourse of bhakti, for instance, as it is enacted by the text, is situated in ambivalence. While, on the one hand, it seems to feed into the Enlightenment's anxiety of discovering 'the other' of reason which could not be encompassed by its merely ethical and human concerns, *it also interrogates the boundaries of the 'self' and the 'world' fashioned by liberal epistemology* to celebrate non-Christian, non-Brahmanic modes of worship. First of all, it strikes one as immensely curious that in the *Gokul Ashtami* festival which is celebrated to mark the birth of Krishna, devotees are singing in chorus a popular hymn in praise of Tukaram (1608-78), an untouchable poet-saint of Maharashtra. This displacement/ re-figuration of god is in keeping with the deeply entrenched traditional and popular forms of *bhakti* in India, where the sprawling, often mutually contradictory styles of worship *defy the standard, iconic presence of a single God*. The narrative confusion of Krishna with Tukaram interrogates not only the grandiose Hindu tradition of worship, it also, more interestingly, undercuts the assumptions about the purity of caste in such a performance. In this 'carnivalesque' inversion of the pure form of *bhakti*, one finds a significant shift from the solemn seriousness of Christianity to an uncouth merriment which included filth. When the villagers of Mau glimpse the silver image of the infant Krishna, 'a most beautiful and radiant expression came into their faces, a beauty in which there was nothing personal, for it caused them all to resemble one another during the moment of its indwelling, and only when it was withdrawn did they revert to individual clods' [p.289]. *In this style where performance takes over the thematic of worship, the boundaries of subjectivity dissolve*; God is drawn into the collective swirling waves of ecstasy as a diffuse, all-pervasive phenomenon, not a transcendent, formidable figure. It incorporates jollity as well as joy: by sacrificing good taste, this worship achieved what Christianity has shirked: the inclusion of merriment. All spirit as well as matter must participate in salvation, and 'if practical jokes are banned, the circle is incomplete' [p.291]. The ceremonies include roles for all social ranks, from the rajah to the untouchables, who provide the 'spot of filth without which the spirit cannot cohere' [p.289]. Even the flies—a low but indestructible form of life that so annoyed Aziz in Chandrapore—here enjoy divine hospitality, freely claiming 'their share of God's bounty'. At the end of the celebration of Krishna's birth we are told:

At the birth it was questionable whether a silver doll or a mud village, or a silk napkin, or an intangible spirit, or a pious resolution had been born. Perhaps all these things! *Perhaps all birth is an allegory*! [p.291]

In this dramatization of the event, the boundaries of the self, as well as of the world circumscribed by tradition, custom and law are stretched, inverted and interrogated without re-affirming 'the other' of the Occidental religious 'self'. Further, it marks a *shift in the gendering of God* when the *bhaktas* repeat these lines endlessly:

Tukaram. Tukaram.

Thou art my father and mother and everybody...

The significant inflection of gender, of imparting an androgynous nature to god, draws upon the interaction of bhakti and Sufism in North India. Taking their cue from the idiom of mysticism in various Hindu and Islamic traditions, the *bhaktas* and the *Sufis*, shared many philosophical conceptions. These shared conceptions can be read as *counter-systems*, opposed to classical and orthodox system in their views about caste, gender, or the idea of God. For instance, the Vedic or Brahmanic gods were not localised, but in *bhakti*, they are worshipped in local forms and the Gods are given families, complexions, individual temperament. They are thus as human as they are divine.

Also, the moment God begins to be addressed in the mother-tongue (as happens at the ceremony in the temple) the language of children and the family, all sorts of human emotional experiences become relevant to religion, and all the family relationships become part of the *bhakti* repertoire. Thus God becomes a mother, a father, a child, a lover, all rolled into one at the same time. *Bhaktas* in this transformative performance are called upon to shed their defence, *and one of the last things they overcome in these shared, syncretist traditions, is maleness itself. The male saints wish to become women and a powerful symbology of femaleness is produced* which connects it not to the rejuvenation and recovery of all the 'true', ancient or 'original' sources of knowledge, and to salvation, but to a 'commonly and easily internalisable mode of devotion'[89]. It is not the 'temple' (despite the rituals) which *Bhakti* finally inhabits but the devotee's 'heart'.

The Temple shows a more skilful use of Forster's narrative—it is designed as a process of 'maturation' for the reader. It grows progressively more subtle, restful, tolerant and multiple in its tone and accent. Yet precisely, by this mechanism, by being capable of taking in more, *and ironically glancing sideways at its own construction, Forster's liberalism gains authority and validity.* Moreover, the growth and maturation of the reader involves his/her working through the multiple levels at which the problems of East and West, culture and difference and language and signification are articulated. The narrative resolution is achieved by a powerful, almost reverential tone, in which some of the major characters strive to grasp the nature of mystic reality, and are shown to be at the end of their spiritual tether. Yet each one of such effort dramatically represents what India itself has become in the European liberal problematic. As Talal Asad has shown in another context, in competition between 'unequal languages' the weaker is almost always forcibly transformed, for translation generally operates in one direction alone[90]. In the terms the novel articulates, this means not only the suppression of native languages, but within the English speaking community, the absorption or appropriation of heretical modes of discourse. The novel's display of heterogeneous utterances, and ironic distancing, augured all along in a triad structure of Mosque, Caves, Temple sequence, thus merely *conceals the monolithic edifice* of the Empire of Colonialism. The novel demonstrates that the intended 'dialogue' between cultures must remain an unrealizable goal. Even the artist's 'dialogic imagination' must adjust itself to the monological imperative of colonialism, indeed be shaped by the enunciative strength of its discourse. In the politics of the text, the individual voice thus becomes the contested zone.

Seen in this light, the story of *A Passage to India* performs an allegory of rhetorical consolidation and retrenchment. It dramatises and enacts the curtailment of narrative possibilities demanded by a colonial regime. Hence, the similarity of its plots and theatricality of its means. Those characters committed to the possibility of cultural interchange, as disclosed in the opening chapters' carefully staged vignettes, follow their own circuitous paths to a common disillusionment. Those who attempt to speak 'in a different voice' (Fielding, Mrs. Moore, Godbole) to remain Observer-participants outside the political domain, betray the impossibility of maintaining 'ethnographic disinterestedness'. For the novel's dramatic structure works to disclose the intransigence of culturally bound discourse—discourse that marks the interests served by such a neutral stance. And the novel's final 'act' reveals what its fictions of 'autonomy' conceal: in the colonial theatre, exchanges between noncombatants are always marked politically. Making voice the site of such markings, the novel replays its melodramatic possibilities in a different register.

Notes

1. W.H. Mason, *A Passage to India: A Reassesment* (London: Macmillan, 1969), p.9.
2. Several critics have suggested this. See especially Wildfred Stone, *The Cave and the Mountain: A Study of E.M. Forster* (Stanford and London: Stanford Univ. Press, 1966) Malcolm Bradbury writes in his Introduction:

The novel produces the sense that art, faced by social confusion, can produce coherence chiefly through the *exploration of its own symbolic ordering powers...*

3. E.K. Brown writes: The main effect in *A Passage to India* is, I believe, of order in the universe, but order that can be merely glimpsed, never seized for sure (op.cit), p.113
4. G.K. Das, *E.M. Forster's India* (London: Macmillan, 1977) p.15.
5. John Colmer, 'Promise and Withdrawal in *A Passage to India*, in Das and Beer ed. *Forster: A Human Exploration*, (London: CUP, 1979) p.118.
6. See E.M. Forster, *The Hill of Devi and Other Indian Writings*, Abinger Edition 14 (London: Edward Arnold, 1983), p.289.
7. For a powerful and illustrative advancement of this argument, see Edward W. Said, *Orientalism* (New York: Pantheon, 1978). Ch.2
8. F.R. Leavis's concluding remarks about the impact of the novel may be of special interest: '... In its touch upon racial and cultural problems, its treatment of personal relations, and in prevailing ethos the book is an expression, undeniably, of the liberal tradition; it has as such its finesse, its strength, and its impressiveness; and it makes the achievement, the humane, decent and rational—the civilized—habit, of that tradition appear the valuable thing it is. See Leavis in Bradbury (ed.), p.729.
9. For a detailed exploration of such ventures to determine the 'truth' of sexual assault on Adela in caves, see J.A.H. Moran, 'E.M. Forster's A Passage to India: What Really Happened in the Caves' *Modern Fiction Studies* Vol.34, No.4 (Winter 1988)
10. Paul Scott, 'How Well Have They Worn', *Times* (London), 6 January 1966, p.15.
11. Nihal Singh, 'Indians and Anglo Indians: As Portrayed to Britons,' *Modern Review*, September 1924.
12. E.A. Horne, 'An Anglo-Indian View, '*New Statesman* 16 August 1924. Horne's objections reverse a standard English response, as the continuation of his critique confirms:—'just as the average Englishman who goes out to India picks up most of what he knows about Indians from other Englishmen'.

13. Sylvia Land, 'A Great Novel at Last'. *Time and Tide*, 20 June 1924. Quoted in Gardner, pp.224-5.
14. Nirad Chaudhuri, 'Passage to and from India' 1924 reprinted in *Perspectives on E.M. Forster's A Passage to India*, ed. V.A. Shahane (N.Y: Barnes and Noble, 1968).
15. E.A. Horne, (Op.cit), p.248.
16. Henry Levinson, 'India's Moral Stand', *Saturday Review of Literature*, 16 August 1924, Quoted in Gardner, p.258.
17. V.A. Sahane, Focus, p.13, quoted in Bette London, *The Appropriated Voice: Narrative Authority in Conrad, Forster, and Wolff*. (Ann Arbor: The University of Michigan Press, 1990) p.176.
18. Chaudhuri, 'Passage To and From India', p.115.
19. Rose Macaulay, 'Women in the East' *Daily News*, 4 June 1924.
20. Homi Bhabha, 'Articulating the Archaic: Notes on Colonial Nonsense' in *Literary Theory Today* (ed.) Peter Collier and Helga Geyer-Ryan (London: Polity Press, 1990), p.204.
21. Ibid, p.205.
22. Ibid, pp.206-7
23. Bettle London, *The Appropriated Voice: Narrative Authority in Conrad, Forster, and Wolff* (Ann Arbor: The University of Michigan Press, 1990), p.86.
24. Ibid, p.21.
25. Robert Scholes, 'Language, Narrative, and Anti-narrative,' in *On Narrative* ed. W.J.T. Mitchell (Chicago: Harvester Press, 1981), p.205.
26. See Abdul R. Jan Mohammed, 'The Economy of Manichean Allegory: The Function of Racial Difference in Colonialist Literature,' *Critical Inquiry* 12 (Autumn 1985). In a footnote Mohamed voices his central concern: 'I do not mean to imply that any writer who criticises Third World Cultures must be automatically condemned as a colonialist. For instance, Achebe's depiction of corruption in Nigeria in his novel *No Longer at Ease* (New York, 1961), is as complete and penetrating as any of Naipaul's characterizations. The crucial difference, however, is that while Achebe's representation is sympathetic and, therefore,

informative, Naipaul's reeks of contempt and reveals only the operation of colonialist mentality.', p.87.

27. Ibid, p.74.
28. Ibid.
29. Ibid, pp.75-77.
30. See Benita Parry, 'The Politics of Representation in A Passage to India' in *A Passage to India: Essays in Interpretation*, ed. John Beer (London: Macmillan, 1985), p.32.
31. Ibid, p.32.
32. My two principle sources for tracing the history of such debates in England are: P. Gardiner ed. *Theories of History* (New York: Pantheon, 1959), esp. pp.79-88, and Christopher Parker, English Historians and the Opposition to Positivism' in *History and Theory*, Vol.XII, No.2 (1983), pp.120-141. For the ideological effects of such debates within English society and its shaping influence on social values see, Catherine Gallagher, *The Industrial Reformation of English Fiction* (1932-1867) (Chicago and London: The University of Chicago Press, 1985) pp.187-218. Also for a 'neat' account of how the Determinism versus Free-will Controversy which rocked the English intellectual World for a great number of years in late 19th century and found its way into the Indian intellectual milieu, particularly in Bengal, see Sabyasachi Bhattacharya, 'Positivism in 19th Century Bengal: diffusion of European Intellectual Influence in India, in *Indian Society: Historical Probings in Memory of D.D. Kosambi*, ed. R.S. Sharma (New Delhi: ICHR, 1977), pp.337-356.
33. Kenneth Graham *Indirections of the Novel: James, Conrad, and Forster* (Cambridge: C.U.P., 1988) p.9. For a complex, and ambivalent use of language with subtle tonal and syntactic variations also see, Judith Herz 'Listening to Language' *A Passage to India: Essays in Interpretation* ed. John Beer (London: Macmillan, 1985), pp.59-71; Gillian Beer, 'Negation in *A Passage to India*:, pp.44-59; and Molly Tinsely, 'Muddle etcetera: Syntax in A Passage to India:, pp.71-81.
34. Important to mention here is Raymond Williams who thought the 'symbolic' excesses of the novel as an infirmity, which relegated it to the domain of 'a personal novel.' See Raymond

Williams, *The Long Revolution* (Harmondsworth: Penguin Books, 1965), p.308. In a similar vein, S.V. Pradhan argues that though Passage evinces the patterns of realism, it is not realist enough, as its symbolism is a quality characteristic of the decline of realism, and this is 'demonstrably true' of the novel. See 'A Passage to India: Realism Versus Symbolism, A Marxist Analysis' *Dalhousie Review* Vol.60, No.2, pp.301-17.

35. G.K. Das gives an account of how Forster's second visit to India in 1921-22 coincided with the momentous period of the Indian non-cooperation movement against British rule. He describes at length how Forster's reaction to the situation surrounding the Amritsar Massacre of the nationalist demonstrators in 1919 was 'reflected in the dramatization of the actual events in *A Passage to India*. He [Forster]' uses these events to portray an important historical truth about the decline of British India'... See G.K. Das, '*A Passage to India: A Socio-historical Study*' in John Beer, pp.2-15.

36. For this line of argument an authoritative text is Edward Said's *Orientalism*. See esp. pp.14-16.

37. See Frank Keromode's discussion of the effect of 'except for' and 'extraordinary' in this passage in 'The One Orderly Product' in *A Passage to India* (Casebook Series) ed. Malcolm Bradbury (London: Macmillan, 1970), pp.216-24 All references to the text are from the penguin edition, and given in parenthesis, unless otherwise indicated. Please see E.M. Forster, *A Passage to India* First published in 1924. (London: Penguin, 1936).

38. Many influential interpretations of the novel concentrate on this relationship between the cosmic and the mundane, particularly with reference to the opening chapter and its 'theme'. See, for instance, Barbara Rosencrane, 'A Passage to India: the Dominant Voice' in Hertz and Martin (ed.), *E.M. Forster: Century Revaluations* (London: Macmillan, 1982), pp.242-43.

39. Edward Said has an extended discussion of colonized 'space' in 'Representing the Colonised: Anthropology's Interlocutors' *Critical Inquiry* 15 (Winter 1989), pp.205-225. Modernism categorised as a purely 'literary' phenomenon continues to be discussed as a new achievement in expanding our consciousness of 'being' even when it was based on a direct colonial experience. The work of Albert Camus is praised for its definition and

intensification of 'the human condition' while the locale of this experience, colonised Algeria, is completely ignored. See Said's 'Narrative and Geography' *New Left Review*, 180 for an analysis of the crucial traffic between modernism and imperialist narratives.

40. E.M. Forster, 'The Mosque' *Abinger Harvest* (Harmondsworth: Penguin, 1936), rpt. 1976, p.45.
41. Ibid.
42. For details of the architectural aspects of the mosque, and its heterogeneous social meanings as they have changed historically, an excellent source is Hayat Salam-Liebich, *The Encyclopedia of Religion* (New York: Macmillan, 1987), pp.792-3.
43. This is shown by Oleg Grabar, *The Formation of Islamic Art* (New Haven: Harvester Press, 1973). Garbar's book is an analytic history of mosque architecture that also explores, quite interestingly, how Islamic form both employed and superseded the non-Islamic traditions under its influence. See esp. pp.74-81.
44. Ibid., p.79.
45. Ibid., p.81.
46. Quoted in Mahood, *The Colonial Encounter* (London: Rex Collins, 1977), p.77.
47. The 'Grand Narrative' of Imperialism has chided Indian Islam, particularly of the recent pre-British period, for its 'decadence', 'self-pity' 'pathos' and even 'fear psoychosis' emanating out of racial impurity and sheer lethargy. See M. Elphinstone, *The History of India: The Hindu and the Mohemmadan Period*, (London: John Murray, 1948): James Mill, *History of British India* (London: Stephenson and Spence, 1958) and John Dowson and H.M. Elliot, *The History of India as Told by its Own Historians*, 8Vols. 1867-77 Reprint. (Allahabad: Kitab Mahal, 1964).
48. See Gyan Pandey, *The Construction of Communalism in Colonial North India* (Delhi: OUP, 1990), pp.4-12.
49. P.N., Furbank, *E.M. Forster: A Life*, 2 Vols. (London: Harmondsworth, 1978), p.71.
50. See Moin Shakir, *Khilafat to Partition* (New Delhi: Kamalakar Publication, 1970), pp.13-16.

51. Ibid., p.13.
52. Ibid.
53. Quoted in Shakir, p.148.
54. Moin Shakir, 'Remembering Hasrat Mohani', *Mainstream* Annual Number, 1981.
55. Rafiuddin Ahmed. *The Bengal Muslims: 1971-106, A Quest for Identity* (Delhi: OUP, 1981), p.7.
56. For detailed information of these sources see Robin Lewis, *E.M. Forster's Passages to India* (New York: Columbia University Press, 1979), esp. chapter I and II.
57. Istiaq Ahmad, 'Consistency and Ambiguity in South Asian Islam' *Economic and Political Weekly*, August 12, 1989, pp.1829-30.
58. Gyan Pandey, (Op.cit), p.24.
59. I deal at length with the politics of 'secularism' in my discussion of Nehru in the next chapter. Tom Nairn raises this issue in a different context rather dramatically:
    The new middle class intelligentsia of nationalism had to invite the masses into history; and the invitation card had to be written in a secular language they understood.
    See Tom Nairn, *The Break-Up of Britain* (London: Version, 1977), p.77.
60. Eric Stokes, *The Political Ideas of British Imperialism* (London: OUP, 1976), p.28.
61. This line of thinking about the splitting of the enunciatory discourse of Imperialism is advanced by Homi Bhabha, 'Articulating the Archaic: Notes on Colonial Nonsense' in Peter Collier and Helga Geyer-Ryan (ed.)., *Literary Theory Today* (London: Polity Press, 1990), p.204.
62. Alain Robbe-Grillet, *Snapshots Towards a New Novel*. Trans. B.Wright (London: Edward Arnold, 1965), p.56.
63. Gillian Beer, 'Negation in A Passage to India' in John Beer (ed.) *A Passage to India: Essays in Interpretation* (London: Macmillan, 1985), pp.46-58.
64. Ibid, p.50.
65. Ibid.

66. Michael Orange comments on these words of Godbole: 'a noticeable feature of Godbole's explanation is Forster's satirical framing of it by Fielding's impatience, tiredness, and boredom, and to be anachronistic...'. The result is not, of course, to deprecate the Hindu's faith, but the process of explanation itself. See Michael Orange, 'Language and Silence in *A Passage to India*' in Das and Beer (ed.) *E.M. Forster: A Human Exploration* (Cambridge: CUP, 1979), p.158.
67. A post-modernist aesthetic, which takes the issues of ellipsis and discontinuity to its limits, would interrogate Forster's foregrounding of these textual mechanisms as being symptomatic of 'the fringes of human consciousness' or a marked 'absence' of it. Far from being a 'concept', or a 'theory', discontinuity has acquired a different analytic valence in post-modernist aesthetic. The notion of discontinuity, or 'rupture' in a more recent vocabulary, is a paradoxical one: because, as Foucault describes it in *The Archaeology of Knowledge*, trans. A.M. Sheridan Smith (London: Tavistock, 1972), p.9, it 'divides up the field of which it is the effect', it enables the historian-critic to individualise/identify different domains, but 'can be established only by comparing these domains' (p.9). And again, it is a 'displacement' in language which is always already present:

    One of the most essential features of the new history is probably this displacement of the discontinuous: its transference from the obstacle to the work itself; its integration into the discourse of the historian, where it no longer plays the role of an external condition that must be reduced, but that of a working notion; and therefore the inversion of signs by which it is no longer the negative of the historical reading (its underside, its failure, the limit of its power), but the positive element that determines its object and validates its analysis. (p.9)

68. I have discussed the bourgeois mode of liberalism in the previous chapter in its overtly imperialist, political and economic sense. For the Orientalist mode, which would engulf within its draconian hold more recent writers such as Rabindranath Tagore, Aurobindo Ghosh and Anand Coomarswamy, 'the other' was not merely a passive spectator, or an inert object waiting to be absorbed within the Orientalist epistemology. This

is, unfortunately, the impression Edward Said leaves us with in parts of his *Orientalism*. 'The other', on the contrary, seems to acquire an active, 'autonomous' role in the sense that once having inherited the larger structures of a transcendental guarantee that it must provide to the European 'self', it had the power to politicise these structures and inflect them for its own purposes. This particular inflection can be seen in the Gandhian intervention, not in its moral sense which has all along been emphasised, but in its reshaping the demands of the Orientalist mode.

69. Homi Bhabha, 'Articulating the Archaic: Notes on Colonial Nonsense', pp.204-6.
70. Jacques Derrida, *Of Grammatology*, trans. Gayatri Chakravorty Spivak (Baltimore and London: The John Hopkins University Press, 1974). See esp. Derrida's discussion on Rosseau and Levi-Strauss.
71. Gayatri Chakravorty Spivak, 'Translator's Preface', Of Grammatology, p.xvi.
72. Ibid.
73. Ibid.
74. E.M. Forster, *The Manuscripts of A Passage to India*, ed. Oliver Stallybrass (London: Edward Arnold, 1978), pp.242-3.
75. The reading of Adela's experience in terms of repression, sexual hysteria, frigidity, or fear of the body is, in fact, widespread. See Ronnie Frankstein, *Forster's Women: Eternal Differences* (New York: Columbia Univ. Press, 1975), pp.128-34, G.S. Amur, 'Hellenic Heroines and Sexless Angels: Images of women in Forster's novels' in V.S. Shahaney ed., *Approaches to E.M. Forster: A Centenary Volume* (Atlantic Highlands; NJ Humanities Press, 1981), pp.25-34, and Barbara Rosencrane, *Forster's Narrative Vision* (Ithaca: Cornell Univ. Press, 1982), p.207. In addition many critics associate Adela's experience with the condition of modern rationalism and the failure to recognise the importance of the heart, passions, and instincts. A different perspective on Adela's perception of the Experience as a rape associates it with the loveless or forced union symbolised by her engagement to Ronny. This line of thinking is advanced by Elaine Showalter, 'A

Passage to India as 'Marriage Fiction': Forster's Sexual Politics', *Women and Literature* Vol.5, No.2 (1977), p.3-16.

76. Michel Foucault, *The History of Sexuality*, Vol.I, trans. Robert Hurley (1978, New York; Vintage, 1980), pp.44-47, 104-51.
77. Patricia Joplin, 'The voice of the Shuttle is Ours' *Stanford Literary Review*, Vol.I, No.1 (1984), pp.25-53.
78. Catharine A. Mackinnon, 'Feminism, Marxism, Method, and the State: An Agenda for Theory' *Signs*, No.7 (1982), p.516. Also for a comprehensive understanding of how 'rape' enters as a 'trope' in the discussions under the rubric of critical legal feminism, see Hilaire Barnett, *Introduction to Feminist Jurisprudence* (London: Cavendish Publishing Ltd., 1998), pp. 167-202; and Jo Bridgeman and Susan Mills, *Feminist Perspectives on Law*: (Law's engagement with the female body) (London: Sweet & Maxwell, 1998), pp.391-442.
79. See Teresa de Lauretis' discussion of Foucault's failure to factor gender into his analysis in *Alice Doesn't: Feminism, Semiotics, Cinema* (Bloomington: India Univ. Press, 1984). Pp.92-94.
80. Catherine Mackinnon, *Signs*, p.516.
81. See John Berger, *Ways of Seeing* (London: BBC and Penguin, 1972), pp.46-47.
82. Mackinnon, 'Feminism, Theory, Marxism and the State: Toward Feminist Jurisprudence' *Signs*, No.8 (1983), p.654.
83. Ibid.
84. Ibid.
85. M. Foucault, *The History of Sexuality*, p.95. See also De Lauretis' exploration of Foucault's formulation in her discussion of male power and male resistance as playing by the same rules in *Alice Doesn't*, pp.91-92.
86. The *Punkhawalla*, within the space provided to him in the novel., cannot be understood to belong in the category of the '*subaltern*', since we do not get a single clue as to his thought or action. He is shown as a hermetically fixed object of our gaze, given over to the reader's vision, as plants in a botanical garden, or animals in a zoo are produced in select, manageable parts. Thus if we adhere to the collective's use of the term '*subaltern*', and its more general

emphasis of restoring his/her consciousness to history, we shall be disappointed by *Punkhawalla*.

87. The emergent class relations under British colonialism did not destroy the Hindu caste hierarchy, but rather, they were articulated with the older form of occupational status in what might be characterized as class-caste relations. Yet Christian missionaries, who were the first to admit untouchables to their schools during the latter half of the 19th century, sparked off what remains an issue of contestation: the access of untouchables to education. The issue of caste thus came under greater public scrutiny during Gandhi's efforts to end untouchability and bring the 'harijans' or the 'children of God' (which was his name for the untouchables) under the umbrella of Indian nationalism. However, as is well-known, Gandhi did not oppose untouchability as a fixed occupational status, which was in keeping with his ideas on moral duty. The caste system is very much in place today as the recent killings of the scheduled castes, particularly in Bihar, Madhya Pradesh, and Andhra Pradesh, apart from multiple ways of their subordination all over India, would suggest. However, the untouchables have rejected '*harijan*' as a name ascribed to them by Gandhi and out of upper-caste obligations. Instead, they call themselves '*dalits*' or 'the oppressed'. Forster's description of the Punkhawalla as a divine being thus carries resonance of the Gandhian appellation, '*harijan*'. Gandhi's re-naming of the untouchables, on the other hand, could be interpreted as a hegemonic nationalist strategy amounting to little more than an appropriation of '*harijan*' for the making of modern Indian nation-state.

88. See Reuben Brower's particular use of the concept 'iconic' in relation to the novel. He writes: 'It would be harder to find purer examples of symbolic expressions than ['mosque', 'Caves' and 'Temple']. They are obviously 'iconic'. For details, see Brower, 'The Twilight of the Double Vision: Symbol and Irony in *A passage to India* in Malcolm Bradbury ed. Casebook series (London: Edward Arnold, 1970), p.114. This ideology of the iconic, that is, of the reproducibility of the original, life-like image, picture of portrait is laid bare in many critical accounts. See Walter Benjamin's seminal essay on the irreproducibility of the original in a different context. W. Benjamin, 'The Work of

Art in the Age of Mechanical Reproduction' in *Illuminations* (1968), trans. Harry John (London: Fontana, 1973), pp.219-253.

89. See—Kumkum Sangari, 'Mirabai and the Spiritual Economy of Bhakti' in *Economic and Political Weekly* July 14, 1989, pp.1552.
90. Talal Asad, 'The Concept of Cultural Translation in British Social Anthropology' in James Clifford and George E. Marcus ed., *Writing Culture: The Poetics of Ethnography* (Berkeley: Univ. of California Press, 1986), p.4.

3

The Ghost in the Machine: Reflections on the Questions of Agency and Narrative Formation in *The Discovery of India*

I
The Status of the Text

Horace Walpole, in one of his famous lectures, said: 'It is not life that matters, but the courage you bring to it.' For Walpole the quality of life was to be measured by the degree of one's mental poise and determination. Many admirers, even critics of Nehru, I believe, have acknowledged his sense of poise and determination, his qualities of heart and head. Indeed very often, it is precisely these qualities of his personality, which have influenced their judgment of his work. Even serious studies on Nehru which have come up in the recent past have focused attention on his 'intention' and 'achievement'; whether, for instance, he compromised with capitalist bourgeois forces in planning for national development or whether his analysis of the Indian social and cultural formation was conditioned by an inexorable adherence to the progressive promise of science or scientific vision. However, qualities of head and heart, *and a person's achievements and intentions are not always the best resources to analyse and determine the effect of his work. The work, or text, which is a product of language, escapes life.* Edward Said in *Beginnings* puts it succinctly: 'With every advancing moment of the career the life seems impoverished as the text gains in reality on the basis of what Wilde called her own lines'[1]

It is *to the text*, rather than *to the man*, that we must turn, in order to understand and unravel the complexities and effects of Nehru's pronouncement. As we open *The Discovery of India*, we are greeted with this hiatus, the gap between a man's life and his work, in the preface. But ironically it is this very gap and the contradiction between the intention and range of possible meanings which the text attempts to repress. The preface has it:

> ... I recognise it [the book] of course, but not wholly: it seems almost that *I was* reading some familiar piece written by another, who was near to me and yet who was different. Perhaps that is the measure of change that has taken place in me. So I have felt about this book also. It is mine and not wholly mine as I am constituted today: it *represents* rather some *past self of mine* which has already joined that long succession of *other selves* that existed for a while and faded away, leaving only a memory behind.[2]
>
> (emphasis added)

In the above lines, written as they were about fifty eight years ago, we might sense a pre-figuration of what contemporary literary theory has described as the changing subject and the ever changing text. What kind of text is it ? Is it a history of India, as it is often made out to be ? No historian, not even an unorthodox or post-modernist historian can consider a text 'historical' which is such an assemblage of pell-mell events; here a detached, almost invisible writer seeking to analyse the course of events, there one who openly admits the personal longing of the author, meditating upon the India of his dream. A long critical commentary on industrialization and the planning commission is juxtaposed with a brooding over 'Life's philosophy,' 'Problems of human relationship' and 'Kamala, my wife.' The India of this text is therefore not merely an object of description or analysis: it even turns into a woman—a woman who finds comparison with the author's wife, Kamla:

> My past life unrolled itself before me and there was always Kamala standing by. She became a symbol of Indian women, or of woman herself. Sometimes she grew curiously mixed up with my idea of India, that land of ours so dear to us, with all, her faults and weaknesses, so elusive and full of mystery... Did I know her? [p.44]

Often the speaking subject or the narrator 'I' is distanced from the character 'I' who is an actor, or an active participant in the story of India. This is in keeping with the requirements of the plot of a 'historical' text which aims at an objective, retrospective narration. But often, as has happened in the above passage, *the distinction between the speaking subject and the acting subject is dissolved completely*. This double role of the speaking subject can be likened to a 'disseminatory act' of social narrative which Lyotard defines as the privileged role of the narrated, 'where the one doing the speaking speaks from the place of the referent. As narrator she [he] is narrated as well. And in a way she is already told, and what she herself is telling will not undo that somewhere else she is told.'[3] This narrative inversion makes untenable any supremacist or absolute nationalist claims to cultural mastery, for the position of control is neither monocular nor monologic. The signification of this narrative doubling of the subject of identification is borne out in Levi Strauss' description of the ethnographic act.[4] The ethnographic act demands that the observer 'himself' is a part of his observation and this requires that the field of knowledge—the totality of social fact—must be appropriated from the 'outside' like a 'thing', but a thing which comprises within itself the subjective understanding of the indigenous. *The subject has to split itself into object and subject in the process of identifying its field of knowledge* and the object is constituted, as Bhabha writes, 'by dint of the subject's capacity for indefinite self-objectification (without ever quite abolishing itself as subject) for projecting outside itself ever-diminishing fragments of itself.'[5]

In modern autobiography, the speaking subject is commonly conflated with the acting subject and the narration is kept in the first person. But autobiography as a genre is itself highly problematic. The form attempted by autobiography tries relentlessly to approximate that of a realist novel, inspite of the first person narration. The story to be told from the 'depths of one's heart' is *already inscribed in a language and in socio-cultural codes which the author reassembles in the form of his or her text*. The difficulty of keeping close to the form of a realist, proper, history is realised by the author of *The Discovery of India* himself—and in this regard, the book resembles those post-modernist texts where the element of irony or self-dramatisation and a playfulness that leads to subversion of one's own narration becomes significant. For example, we notice in the middle of the book a sudden retreat to a place where the text had begun—Ahmadnagar Fort. The switch in the temporal sequencing is definite, even strident, and authorial intervention, like the chorus in the Greek theatre, assumes the role of critical commentary on the course of events as well as on the state of narration itself:

> So during the past four months, in the course of this writing, I have occupied my mind with India's past records and experiences and out of multitude of ideas that came to me, I have selected some and made a book out of them. Looking back at what I have written, it seems inadequate, disjointed and lacking in unity, a mixture of many things, with the personal element dominant, and giving its colour *even to what was intended to be an objective record and analysis. That personal element has pushed itself forward*

> *almost against my will*; often I checked it and held it back, but sometimes I loosened the reins and allowed it to flow out of my pen... [p.509].
>
> (emphasis added)

By now, it should be clear that *The Discovery of India* cannot be treated merely as a historical text, though it does contain a large share of history. Neither is it fiction. Fiction in the conventional sense deals with invented characters that may heighten a sense of the real, but are in themselves not a part of the actual world. Nehru's difficulty in classifying the text in the conventional sense, once again anticipates contemporary literary theory which questions the distinction commonly made between historical, literary and autobiographical. What normally distinguishes historical and fictional narratives is their *content rather than their form*. The content of historical narratives is events that really happened and not imaginary events invented by the narrator. This implies that the form in which 'historical' events present themselves to a prospective narrator is supposed to be found rather than constructed. The form of the discourse, in conventional historiography, is taken as adding nothing to the actual events. It is considered to be a simulacrum of the structure and process of real events.

However, a careful analysis of the *form* of the historical and fictional narratives as has been made by contemporary theories of historiography and literary criticism, would show that *this division is brought into play by eliding the various functions of narrative which are implicit in all human discourse.*[6] Logical connections, chronologies, temporal sequences and factual description are as much constructed and enabled by the narrative, as are the rhetorical or poetic elements in a work of fiction. Hayden White, a contemporary theorist of historiography writes, for instance: 'narrative becomes a problem only when we wish to give the real events the form of a story. It is because real events do not offer themselves as stories that their narrativisation is so difficult.'[7] The logic of a historical narrative, its meaning or value, whatever it be, is derived from its manner of telling, its 'form' and the 'plot'. This redeems in good measure the anxieties and apprehensions of the author of *The Discovery of India.* What was an embarrassment to an author who regarded himself as having written a book that was not 'realist' enough, where the personal and the poetic elements tended to dominate the general run of description, can be turned into a reader's advantage.

The reader has now to analyse a text which has complex styles of narration embedded in it. This text has the merit of often running against the grain of its own logic and manner of telling. It is this particular paradox at the heart of the composition of the text which becomes decisive and curiously the book remains neither history, nor fiction nor autobiography and *finds itself a place among those dubiously privileged artifacts of pure writing or textuality which work to undermine the very distinction between history and fiction.*[8] In other words, *The Discovery of India* is a text which cannot sustain throughout the burden of a seamless, realist narrative and often explodes in heteronomous directions. This explosion serves to reveal those figurative mechanisms and narrative functions at work which finally produce or 'invent' the effect of coherence in the story. Read in this light, *The Discovery of India* can be discussed as one of those rare texts in which the contradictions between the garb of modernity and a timeless continuity; a utopian international order and a rigid nationalism; a socialist state economy and a monopoly capitalism; collective, shared memories of a traditional life as against bourgeois liberal individualism; and finally the objective scientific method of inquiry into history and the ineluctability of the subjective, are dramatically 'resolved'. *These resolutions are achieved through the narrative and in fact they become the very substance that is produced by the narrative.* It is important at this point to assert that the literary and rhetorical devices which enter into narrative production do not simply function in the dimension of the aesthetic nor are they entirely governed by the will of the author. In fact the schemes of narrative production, as I will try to show in the next sections, are *inextricably woven into those of ideological production.*

It is impossible today to conceive of narrative without relating it to the larger conception of ideology. The relationship between the two is reciprocal. For example the emergence of fiction of classic realism, still the dominant popular mode in literature, film and television, coincides with the rise of industrial capitalism in Europe. Capitalism needs subject who work by themselves, who freely exchange their labour power for wages. It is in the epoch of capitalism that ideology emphasises the value of individual freedom, freedom of conscience and, of course, consumer choice in all the multiplicity of its forms. Classic realism, as a literary form, performs the work of ideology *not only in its representation of the world as a coherent and total reality, but also in shaping the consciousness of individuals who are regarded as the source of meaning, knowledge and action.* By suppressing the relationship between language and subjectivity, classic realism tends to offer as the obvious basis of its intelligibility the assumption that a character, unified and uncontradictory, is the source of his or her action. Subjectivity is thus a major—perhaps the major—'theme' of classic realism.[9]

Connate with classic realism and the emergence of the autonomous individual is the emergence of the autobiographical mode of narration. *Here the sense of a direct, unmediated access to reality is accentuated by the aura of the living voice.* The illusion of transparency of the narrative voice, however, is not restricted to autobiography alone, though it may appear at its worst in it, and is common to all narrative forms complicitous with the ideological system in which they are produced. Roland Barthes in his analysis of narrative forms points this out:

> Our society takes the greatest pains to conjure away the coding of the narrative situation: there is no counting of the number of narrational devices which seek to naturalise the subsequent narrative by feigning to make it the outcome of some natural circumstances and thus, as it were 'disinaugurating' it... *the reluctance to declare its codes characterises bourgeois society* and the mass culture issuing from it: both demand signs which do not look like signs.[10]

The emotional devices, the tone, and the psychic structures that are called into play by an autobiography remain largely unanalysed and are taken to be natural and integral to a person's life, even in those critical studies which may have otherwise paid meticulous attention to the details of economic and social production of individuality. Jerry White's complaint about the invisibility of capitalism in people's autobiography runs somewhat along this line:

> At its worst autobiography can reinforce capitalist values so that the whole tone is politically bland and negative and unprovocative. They give us moving insights which enrich the brotherhood of man and boost the self confidence of working people but it all seems to take place in a social vacuum.[11]

What White and Barthes put under scrutiny is human experience which they seem to imply precedes narrative. Moreover, they emphasise how capitalism works upon a notion of experience that continues to be preserved in an individual's memory even when an ideologically determined public discourse devalued or absorbed it. There are, of course, literary critics who would go to the extent of arguing that *narrative must claim the focus of attention for waging an ideological and class-struggle, that it must become the site of cultural intervention today for understanding relations of power.* While such a position of a cultural critic might appear to be dubious to a sociologist, or hard-boiled Marxist, it cannot be overemphasised that as we shift our attention from the world to the text, the field (of enquiry) is suddenly shot through with a new provocative light.[12]

The above consideration of the close nexus between narrative and ideology would lead one to examine the specific kind of narrative formation in *The Discovery of India.* In India, as against in Europe, classic realism could not come to its own, despite several attempts to indigenise it from the second decade of this century onwards. A stultified form of capitalism under the impact of colonial economy proved to be inadequate to generate a genuine middle-class reading public. The almost total absence of Industrial capitalism on European lines in the late nineteenth and early twentieth century India did not demand the narrative production of a new, autonomous self. Although colonial English education did create a few isolated cultural pockets modeled on the English liberal values and English literary and aesthetic taste, they remained a microscopic minority when set against the popular traditions and cultural variety of the entire Indian sub-continent. The contemporary popular modes in literature were dominated by story telling: epics, parables, myths, devotional and lyric poetry and pastoral romance constituted the core of literature. Even in Premchand and Sharatchandra—the pioneers of 'novel of purpose' who introduced the novel form in India along the English lines to attack the 'decaying walls of orthodoxy' and 'religious and sentimental dogma'—we easily discern the elements of story telling, fables and myth, which ran counter to the overt purpose of depicting the events in themselves.[13] Very often the authorial voice intervened in such novels either to preach a moral at the 'end' or to draw a parallel from some well-known religious epic, or *puranic* story to corroborate the 'realism' of the story. Consequently, *realism as a literary form, and a bourgeois private readership as its corollary, remained relatively unknown in India well upto the 1930s.*

However, by the time *The Discovery of India* came to be written, an intellectual climate for realism was beginning to set in. Spurred by full-blown nationalist ideals of democracy and freedom, it was part of a writer's responsibility to prepare a truly patriotic, conscientious, free individual citizen, who would understand the import of belonging to his or her nation. Of course, such nationalist consciousness was not altogether free from its internal contradictions. It is visible in Premchand's mature novels where the narrative resolution sometimes leaves a reader baffled; as ambiguities and doubts about the course of events preclude a neat 'solution', or 'moral', of the story.[14] But even as contradictions of cultural nationalism, in form as well as in content, came to a sharp focus and demanded attention, the form of literary realism, and a certain kind of naive historicism—to accumulate facts, and to allow them to speak for themselves—had gained acceptance and power within the academy.[15] An educated reader in India was expected to have developed a taste for expressive realism, after having purged the dross of sentiment, horror, fables and myths that constituted literature of the early period. Nationalism indeed required of its citizens that they cultivate specific habits of thinking and living so that they could naturally and freely accept their role for national development. And, *this could be achieved only by a 'realistic' or 'objective' and 'scientific' assessment of the nation's cultural resources, its history, tradition and heritage.*

This was, then, the setting for the writing of *The Discovery of India*. However, as I have tried to argue earlier, if a seamless, realist narrative was not possible, and as it eventually teemed into a curiously heterogeneous and ambivalent combination of rhetorical, poetic and realist styles of story telling, the demand for such narrative as well as its effects upon the reader should be carefully considered. The *role of such hybrid narration in shaping the new politico-cultural space of the nation is absolutely crucial,* even if we do not dismiss out of hand the attempt made by various other nationalist discourses to produce the 'idea' of the nation as a unified, continuous and homogeneous narrative of a particular race, linguistic group, ethnic community, or all of these put together.[16] The attempt to 'find' a coherent and systematic discourse of the national obscures from our vision, if anything, the liminality and ambivalence that 'haunts the idea of the nation, the language of those who write of it and the lives of those who live it'.[17] It is hybridity and, one might add, liminality and ambivalence of the nation which emerge from a growing awareness that (in spite of the indubitability of the attempts of the historians to trace the origins of the nation as a sign of its insertion into modernity) the time-frame of a nation involves a much more heterogeneous and transitional socio-cultural, reality. Benedict Anderson in his *Imagined Communities* express this idea as the nation's 'coming into being.'

> If nation-states are widely considered to be 'new' and 'historical', the nation-states to which they give political expression always loom out of an immemorial past and... glide into a limitless future. What I am proposing is that nationalism has to be understood, by aligning it not with self-consciously held political ideologies, but with *large cultural systems that preceded it, out of which—as well as against which—it came into being.*[18]
>
> (emphasis added)

It is my purpose to explore the hybridity of *narrative* itself in the construction of the discourse of the nation in *The Discovery of India.* To analyse such a formation means, however, not merely to consider the figure of the nation in its transitional history, or in its conceptual indeterminacy. Equally important are the *effects* of such narration on the ideological and political control, on class alliances, social order, the comfort of belonging to a caste, race, community or religion: on the vicarious pleasures of consumerist invention of tradition and the hidden injuries of legal democracy, and economic progress. *Thus, to encounter the nation as it is written stages a plentitude of cultural and social consciousness along different temporalities*, more in tune with the partial, over-determined process by which textual meaning is produced through the articulation of hybridity in narrative. This approach to the coming into being of the nation interrogates the traditional power of those magic words/concepts long associated with the objects of knowledge in the national history—people, culture, democracy, secular, communal, tradition, unity, diversity, heritage, to name only a few—whose enunciative values often rely on their representation as holistic concepts located within an evolutionary narrative of historical continuity. To take the nation at its own word through its narrative address implies, on the other hand, attention to its language and rhetoric which can change the field of meanings and symbols associated with national life, turning the 'Janus-faced' nation into a figure of prodigious narrative hybridity in the process of the articulation of its constitutive elements. Here meanings may often be partial and history may be only beginning, or half-made, and the cultural authority might be much more diffuse and uncertain than what we may have suspected. With such an understanding of the performativity of the narrative hybridity and ambivalence of the nation, one might apply 'analytic pluralism as the form of critical attention appropriate to the cultural effects of the nation.'[19] The analytic of the nation takes on here a form of cultural elaboration in its most productive sense; it becomes a force for the enactment, guidance, exclusion and subordinations, as well as the diffusion, ambivalence, displacement, and condensation of discourses. Such productive form of elaboration alone can give us a rich sense of the nation as one of the major structures of ideological representation *within a larger global production of the discourse of modernity.* The cultural boundaries as they can be seen to be delimiting the space of the nation in *The Discovery of India* can thus be acknowledged *as containing thresholds of meaning that must be contested, crossed, erased, interrogated and translated in the ongoing process of cultural production*. The task of the critic then is not merely to acknowledge such contested grounds of meaning and narration in the text, and to demonstrate them in their fullness, but also to comment on the stakes beneath such formations of cultural politics.

II

The Discovery of National Time

William Hazlitt, while writing about the English nation, made a case for the rational necessity of patriotism. The feeling of patriotism, he argued, must transcend the narrow political interests of particular communities and locales, in order to realise the lofty ideals of universal justice and harmony. To Hazlitt:

> Patriotism, in modern times, and in great states, is and must be the creature of reason and reflection, rather than the offspring of physical or local attachment. It was once said by an acute observer, and eloquent writer (Rousseau), that the love of mankind was nothing but the love of justice; the same might be said, with considerable truth, of the love of our country. It is little more than another name for the love of liberty, of independence, of peace, of social happiness.[20]

Nehru's 'love of our country', (like Hazlitt's twin principles of reason and reflection) is a concept that must demonstrate a legitimate place and time for his country's 'natural' inhabitants: *the people of India*. The colligatory principles of his narration must therefore bring into play a battery of representational devices which define and create a new space for the nation. Here is *Nehru asking his countrymen to 'recognise' that new space:*

> Sometimes as I reached a gathering, a great roar of welcome would greet me: *Bharat Mata Ki Jai*-Victory of Mother India! I would ask them unexpectedly what they meant by that cry, who

> was this Bharat Mata, Mother India, whose victory they wanted? My question would amuse them and surprise them, and then, not knowing exactly what to answer, they would look at each other and at me. I persisted in my questioning. At last a vigorous *Jat*, wedded to the soil from immemorial generations, would say that it was the *dharti*, the good earth of India, that they meant. What earth? Their particular village patch, or all the patches in the district or province, or in the whole of India? And so question and answer went on, till they would ask me impatiently to tell them all about it. I would endeavour to do so and explain that India was all this that they had thought, but it was so much more, the mountains and the rivers of India, and the forests and broad fields, which gave us food, were all dear to us, but what counted ultimately were *the people of India, people like them and me* who were spread out all over this vast land... and as this idea slowly soaked into their brains, their eyes would light up as if they had made a great discovery' [p.48].
>
> (emphasis added)

This is quite a remarkable passage in the mode in which it imagines India in that it ostensibly creates a 'place' for its silent interlocutors. *Bharat Mata*, Mother India, was not a nation-state for the great cultural reformers of the nineteenth century India such as Rammohan Roy, Bankimchandra Chatterjee and Vivekananda.[21] The problematic of their cultural discourse lay elsewhere. Their effort was primarily to demonstrate how the traditional elements of culture in India had the strength not only to match the scientific criterion set up by the west to qualify as a civilised society, but also to circumvent the structural limitations of western culture itself. The implied audiences/readers of such discourses were invited to verify for themselves the validity claims made by these speakers/writers. *The specificity of Nehruvian discourse lies in the extension of the above problematic.* It effects a semantic shift in the domain of meanings customarily associated with expressions such as *people and Bharat Mata* and *resituates them narratively within the framework of the modern nation-state.* A Bankimchandra, or a

Vivekananda intent on proving the cultural superiority of India to the west is replaced by a modern state builder. The nation as mother comes to him as part of a political language which was exploited variously by the Indian National Congress. *Such language does not figure in his own scientific paradigm of economistic rationalism but, and this is very significant, such language is assumed to be one with what the masses,* 'the people of India' *speak.* Hence, the victory of the nation meant the victory of the whole people, 'people like them and me'. The reader is not told why s/he should not accept the version given by the *Jat* who associated India with the earth. By an unstated narrative gerrymandering modernity replaces the country as modernity is reproduced within the new politico-cultural space created for *Bharat Mata.*

The imaginative geography of the nation as a collective whole draws upon the religious symbolism of the earlier period whenever necessary, as we witness in the deployment of the image '*Bharat Mata*'. The religious semiotic of 'Hindu revivalism' in nineteenth century India which carried utopian representation of India *is replaced by a secular modernity which subordinates customary social and cultural habits to the demands of a new, hierarchical civil society.* It is also possible to see this as a progressive bourgeosification of the older, idealistic humanism. It might as well be seen as a part of 'a process of feminisation of society which replaces the law of the father (the older types of patriarchies cognate with the absolutist order) by autonomous subjects regulated by internalised representations'.[22] In addition to all of these, however, this is made possible by a fundamental transformation in the narrative and/or form of representation. The birth of the nation is characterised by, as evident from *The Discovery of India,* an inherently heteronomous discourse which reveals, on closer examination, more about the secrets of its own figurative mechanisms, rather than a coherent message about the intended object of its description. Hedged rather than interrogated by the variability of its discourse, the narrative of the nation lives on even as it responds to extreme socio-political and cultural pressures on it. For it works within a society as part of the effort to know (and thus, in part, and at several removes, to control) a particular social field. Being embedded within a society, it assumes and works on a set of disparate social connections mediated by the promotion of an overarching national type, or a national character. With these observations we have arrived at the precise moment of the enunciation of *The Discovery of India* and the power of its narrative manoeuverability. To illustrate:

> What is this India, apart from her physical and geographical aspects? What did she represent in the past? What gave strength to her then? How did she lose that old strength? And has she lost it completely? Does she represent anything vital now, apart from being the home of a vast number of human beings? How does she fit into the modern world?
>
> ...Before the future came there was the present, and behind the present lay the long and tangled past, out of which the present had grown. So to the past I looked for understanding.
>
> India was in my blood and there was much in her that instinctively thrilled me. And yet *I approached her almost as an alien critic,* full of dislike for the present as well as for many of the relics of the past that I saw. To some extent I came to her through the West, and looked at her as a friendly Westerner might have done. *I was eager and anxious to change her outlook and appearance and give her the garb of modernity.* And yet doubt arose within me. Did I know India?—I who presumed to scrap much of her past heritage? There was a great deal that has to be scrapped, that must be scrapped; but surely India could not have been what she undoubtedly was and could not have *continued a cultural existence for thousands of years,* if she had not possessed something very vital and enduring, something that was worthwhile. What was this something [pp.50-53]?
>
> (emphasis added)

At the centre of the discovery lies an unfathomable and ineffable 'secret', yet the narrative contingencies have to turn this mystique into an object of proper description—an object with a past, present and future. It is the need to understand her in the context of the 'modern world' ('How does she fit into the modern world?') which becomes the central motif for laying out a narrative scheme for the story of India. The narrative logic does not base itself on verisimilitude. It does not claim truth value for what it is going to discover. At the outset, the plot makes it amply clear that it is not the truth, but the need to integrate 'her' to the modern world that will occupy the focus of narrative control. The use of the first person pronoun 'I' vivifies the personal stake and commitment just as it dissolves any claim to an 'objective' or 'universal' understanding. However, the 'I', the narrator, is accorded the axis of timelessness from where he can see the past unfolding into the present, and the present laying down the foundation for the future. An erratic shift and reversal in the tense of description from 'was' to 'is' or 'did' to 'does' is a pointer towards the creation of a new sense of time by the plot, or by the narrative scheme.

To understand this compression of 'time' by the plot in fiction, we need to consider briefly Paul Ricoeur's treatment of *narrative time.* For Ricoeur, every narrative combines two dimensions in varying proportions: the chronological and the non-chronological. The first may be called the episodic dimension which characterises the story as made out of events, whereas the second would be the configurational dimension in which 'the plot construes significant wholes out of scattered events'[23] The configurational dimension would ensure that 'to tell and to follow a story is already to reflect upon events in order to encompass them in successive wholes.'[24] *It is the subtle combination of these two modes of representation, the episodic and the configurational, which creates a sense of time, and imparts a form of structure to the story.* Ricoeur's charge against recent theory of history and literary criticism, is that it has not taken cognizance of the configurational dimension of narrative as it 'takes it for granted that the surface grammar of what [they] call the 'plane of manifestation' is merely episodic and therefore purely chronological'[25]. This omission tends to deprive narrative activity of its inbuilt complexity, or its two fold characteristics of confronting and combining the sequence and pattern in various ways. `Narrative historians and structuralists, since they overlook the configurational dimension, come to the conclusion that 'the principle of order has been found at the higher level of a-chronological models of codes'[26] thus sharing a common prejudice in not seeing that 'the humblest narrative is always more than a chronological series of events and that in turn the configurational dimension cannot overcome the episodic dimension without suppressing the narrative structure itself'.[27]

The temporal implications of this two-fold structure of the plot are striking as the narrative function brings us back from a mere 'reckoning with time' to 'recollecting' it, or 'historicity'. By virtue of the episodic, narrative time tends towards linear representation in several ways: first, the 'now' and 'then' structure, that provides an answer to: 'what next?' suggests a relationship of exteriority between different phases of action. Secondly, episodes constitute an open-ended series of events that allow the reader to add to the 'now', 'then' and 'so on' of the narrative structure, and thus these episodes appear to follow one another, in accordance with an irreversible order of time, common to all human perception. In other words, this structure creates the effect of an irreversible order of time.

The configurational dimension, however, displays certain effects with respect to time which might be opposed to the episodic. Its arrangement turns the succession of events into significant wholes which are the correlative of the act of grouping together. These significant wholes may be 'translated into one thought'[28] Thought, according to Ricoeur, will imply a wide range of meaning depending upon the context of the narrative. It might characterise, for instance as in Aristotle's Poetics the 'Theme' (dianosia) that accompanies the fable or plot (mythos) of a tragedy. It could also designate the 'point' of the biblical parable since parable allows us to translate it into a proverb, or an aphorism. The term 'thought' might apply as well to the colligatory terms used in history writing such as 'the Industrial Revolution' or 'the Renaissance', which enables us to perceive a set of historical situations or events under a common denominator. The correlation between 'plot' and 'thought' thus supercedes the 'now' and 'then' and 'so on' structure of mere succession. However it would be a 'mistake' 'to consider 'thought' as a-chronological.'[29] The time of fables and parable is more deeply temporal than the time of episodic narrative. The configurational dimension also superimposes on the narrative, what Kermode's celebrated phrase 'sense of an ending' implies. As soon as a story is well-known, whether it is a popular narrative, traditional fable, or even the national chronicles of the founding events of the given community, retelling/recounting replace a mere telling. In such cases to follow a story is less important than to apprehend the well-known 'end' as implied in 'beginning' and the well-known episodes as leading to 'this end'. Here time is not apprehended by the teleological structure of the judgment which pulls together the events under the heading of 'the end'. This is, on the other hand, a strategy of judgment by which time experience is brought back from ordinary time, or 'within timeless', to 'repetition'. 'It is as though recollection converted the so-called natural order of time'.[30]

By reading the end in the beginning and the beginning in the end, once can learn to recapitulate the initial conditions of a course of action in its terminal consequences, thus the significance of the plot in narrative, with which we began our consideration of time, lies not merely in establishing human action, or course of events 'within time', but also 'within memory.' Memory repeats the course of events according to an order which become the counterpart of linear time between a beginning and an end.

This function of memory, that is, repetitiveness, applies to the sense of 'future' as created by narrative time. In a detailed discussion of Heidegger's concept of historicity and time,[31] Ricoeur argues that the finite aspect of time as 'stretching along' or as 'extended' between birth and death comes from the radical structure of temporality as governed by the structure of 'being towards death'. The impulse towards the future is, at the deep level of temporality, a finite movement to the extent that 'all genuine expectations (are) limited from within by being-towards death'.[32] Thus, through repetition (memory) the character of time as stretching-along is rooted in the unity of time as future, as the backward move towards the past is retrieved in the projection of a future and the endlessness of historical time is grafted on the finite structure of being-towards-death.[33]

In the passage quoted above from *The Discovery of India*, we discern two levels at which the story of India is put into a temporal structure. At the episodic level, the text creates a realm of events which pass each other in a succession to give the impression of 'the continuity of a cultured existence for thousands of years'. Moreover, it is this particular 'tradition', of a 'continued cultured existence of thousands of years' which has to overcome the temporary obstacle put forth by the present, an unhappy interlude in her long history (colonial rule), only to rejuvenate itself in future, when 'she would find herself again' and 'the world also will survive the horror of today and build itself a new on fresh foundations.' In Nehru's recounting of this long succession of events—beginning from the Indus Valley Civilization, moving forward to the period of great epics, the *Mahabharata* and *Ramayana*, through the great classical period of the Guptas and Mauryas, and the 'dark age' of the medieval Mughals, down to the modern period of

Tagore, Vivekananda and Gandhi—*historical time itself becomes episodic.* Every civilization, the argument runs, has its periods of growth and decay. After a long period of magnificent growth, the old springs of vitality and innovation of the Indian civilization gradually dried up and it was at this particular historical conjecture that the clash occurred between the West and East, resulting in the domination of the West over the East. Thus here *the sense of time is created by the periodicity of historical events, which reflect a corresponding stage of vitality, growth, decay or rejuvenation of civilization.*

The configurational dimension of this narrative, however, is more subtly worked into the fabric of the story. It deploys a battery of 'thoughts,' and 'themes' which are made to stand automatically for time, either in anticipation, that is, in the *utopian mode,* or in loss and recovery as in the *nostalgic mode.* Both these modes of narration are imparted a naturalness, an organic quality which seems to elude the fabric of the narrative. So we are told that the inner strength, vitality and synthesis of varied cultures represented the 'unity in diversity' of Indian civilization. The 'garb of modernity,' the 'unhappy interlude,' the 'decaying walls of tradition' and the 'scientific temper' are those 'events' of the plot which effect a repetition, as they lead to a visualisation of wholeness at the 'end' of the story.

We discern, as these 'events' are grouped together, either in contrast or continuous, a sense of wholeness, a sense of order and completion *whose logic precedes narration.* This being so, the story can be repeated endlessly, irrespective of the specificity of 'events' or 'contexts'. The temporal structure which groups these events together and the form of the narrative that accompanies it is supposed to be found naturally; it is *immanent* in the very nature of things. This particular 'order' of form, however, sets at rest, anxieties thrown up by the narrator in the passage such as: 'India was in my blood... and yet I approached her almost as an alien critic... I was eager and anxious to change her outlook and appearance and give her the garb of modernity, and yet doubt arose within me. Did I know India?' The sense of irony built here into the narrative which creates, a rupture, between the subject and object of description is subtly reworked into its form, imparting a sense of continuity and order which renders the specificity of an event, or the narrator's location in time and space, irrelevant to the over all scheme of the narrative.

The Discovery of India can thus be discussed as a construction of the 'present' which creates a *double axis of temporality* to establish an explicit link between the reader's and the writer's present and a common historical past. The sense of time which is forged by the narrative is further accentuated by Nehru's exposition of the common tradition of India. We therefore, turn our attention in the next section to a discussion of the cultural heritage or common Indian tradition.

III
Tradition

To understand tradition as it is explicated, forged, discovered by a text—each in various combination can be displayed by a text—is to pay close attention not merely to the recuperating as an ideological process, but also to the structuring of historicity, and its multiple forms of reflexivity as they are embedded in a text. Tradition is often represented by narratives as analogous to, indeed interchangeable with, repetitive human action whose forms can be congealed into myth. Even while we try to understand how the synchronic structure of a myth may be opened up and its symbolism set out or enacted as a series of motivated signs within the dimension of contemporary history, or genealogy, we must at the same time, be able to observe the application of genres, the inflection of motifs or symbology, and their formal composition. We can thus recognise the narrative strategy whereby an inherited 'historical' action or event is transfigured and inscribed in an ideology. As Marx wrote of this epiphanous meditation: 'When men produce their existence in the form of praxis they represent it to themselves in terms of fiction...[34]

The referent of narration or representation, namely human action, is never raw or immediate reality but an action which has been symbolised over and over again, with the ongoing material and cultural urgencies of each period. With the rising tide of nationalism in India, which coincided with the writing of *The Discovery of India* there was, as there still continues to be, a tendency to bring myths and legends, structures of feeling embodied in symbols, and other revelatory icons to the surface as part of the *Indian tradition.* Tradition thus shows itself as living tradition... It shows itself seeking beholders, native and foreign. The nationalist's deployment of meaning of symbology can thus be interpreted *as a case of infusing life into a frozen mass of cultural and social practices so that they gain contemporaneity and an urgency that allows them to be deployed for the historical task of nation-building.* Nehru performs this task by locating and interpreting tradition.

Writing about the two great epics of ancient India, namely, *Ramayana* and *Mahabharata* for example, he cuts them loose from their changing historical and interpretive contexts, and infuses them with a symbology of mystical continuity, capable of holding the diversity of Indian imagination together. The result is often a covert transformation and co-option of the 'masses' to a *Brahmanic*, nationalist purpose. To illustrate:

> I do not know of any books anywhere which have exercised such a continuous and pervasive influence on the mass mind as these two dated back to a living force in the life of the Indian people. Not in the original Sanskrit, except for a few intellectuals, but in translations and adaptations, and in those innumerable ways in which tradition and legend spread and became a part of the texture of a people's life. They represent the typical Indian method of creating all together for various degrees of cultural

> development, from the highest intellectual to the simple unread and untaught villager. They make us understand somewhat *the secret of the old Indians in holding together* a variegated society divided up in many ways... [pp.102-3].
>
> (emphasis added)

How did these epics promote unity and 'cultural development', one might ask? Inscribed in the logic of cultural unity and development is the bold, now oft-repeated argument of our contemporary cultural milieu that tradition symbolised by ancient myths and epics is the *natural cultural ground* of a nation, that it enkindles the awakening of a people to their national self-consciousness which has always existed at a *deep psychological level.* But on closer analysis of these processes of naturalization we may discover that the sheer act of handing down a tradition, whatever be its mythic dimensions and functional scope, introduces change: 'Traditions which we today believe have long pedigrees may on an historical analysis be found to be an invention of yesterday.[35] Like the discourse of nationalism and its several cultural languages, tradition turns out to be a contemporary politico-cultural, and *imaginative artifact that sutures over gaps and creates what might be called a social imaginary.*[36] It draws on the past, and indeed might use very ancient and very 'ethnic' or 'indigenous' materials, but the structures and the politics it draws upon, are laid out today. The psychological timelessness of the epics, and their uncanny hold on the so-called people's imagination in Nehruvian discourse, can be shown as constantly recreated: contested, fractured, elaborated, re-distributed, re-enacted, as new resolutions in regard to the politics of the traditional are negotiated or effected.[37] In fine, tradition is always in process, its imaginative geography always dislocated, and its affective space forever in danger of violation by other 'alien' spaces. Its closure, therefore, is never complete, never total.

In Nehru's handling of tradition we find enacted, a series of discourses which might potentially cancel each other; they are, on the other hand, held together by imaginative power, by the force of the magic idea of synthesis and by India's 'tryst with destiny' as it were. He writes, for instance:

> The discovery of India is tremendous; it is obvious; it lies on the surface and anybody can see it. It concerns itself with physical appearance as well as with certain mental habits and traits. There is little in common between the *Pathan* of the north-west and the Tamil in the far south. Their racial states are not the same, though there may be common strands running through them; they differ in face and figure, food and clothing and of course language... The *Pathan* and the Tamil are the two extreme examples, the others lie somewhere in between. *All of them have their distinctive features, all of them have still more the distinguishing mark of India* [p.470]
>
> (emphasis added)

The reason for identifying a common 'distinguishing mark of India' was that the 'people' of India were the exclusive legates of a national heritage which lay in a cultural tradition almost five thousand years old. The essence of this tradition consisted in a dynamics which acknowledged the contradiction in the specific situation, not by destroying the individual components but by modifying and reconciling them. This 'impulse' not only pervaded the interpersonal interactions of men and their attitude to the world but was also congealed in the divergent patterns of social, economic, and political life, and in their maintenance. As Nehru puts it:

> Some kind of a *dream of unity* has occupied the mind of India since the dawn of civilisation, that unity was not conceived as something imposed from outside, a standardisation of beliefs. It was something deeper. The widest tolerance of belief and custom was practised and every variety acknowledged and encouraged. During the 5,000 years there were invasions and upheavals but

the basic thrust towards unity and harmony was maintained [p.472].

The above logic of a single tradition of unity, however, must accommodate both contradiction and silences which arise from different geographical, religious, linguistic and cultural domains. Such processes of accommodation are sometimes marked by a switch of the genre. We move to a consideration of grand narrative of Democratic Secularism in India to understand these processes.

IV
Gandhi and the Discursive Regime of 'Mass Politics'

Nehru's analysis of Gandhi is one of the most important features of his discovery of India. He presents Gandhi as the singular force who transformed the nature of the Indian national movement. Nehru portrays the Indian scene *before* the 'arrival' of Gandhi as the one of horror, misery and total hopelessness, where the people had lost their bearings: 'We seemed to be helpless in the grip of some all powerful monster; our limbs were paralysed, our minds deadened' [p.378]. The peasantry was no better. The middle classes, the intelligentsia, 'who might have been beacon lights in the enveloping darkness, were themselves submerged in this all-pervading gloom' [p.378]. While the peasants starved, yet centuries of an unequal struggle against their environment had taught them 'to endure' and even in poverty and starvation the peasant had 'a certain calm dignity, a feeling of submission to an all-powerful fate.' But the case of the middle classes was different. 'Incompletely developed and frustrated, they did not know where to look, for neither the old, nor the new offered them any hope..... Like derelicts, frantically seeking some foothold of security for body and mind and finding none, they floated aimlessly in the murky waters of Indian life' [p.379].

Against this background of degradation and gloom, no one seemed to have a clue to the right path of action. 'What could we do?' asks Nehru! There seemed to be no way to pull India out of the 'quagmire of poverty and defeatism which sucked her in.' For long generations, he laments, the Indians had offered their 'blood and toil, tears and sweat,' and this process had eaten its way deep into the body and soul of India, poisoning every aspect of our life, like the 'fell disease which consumes the tissues of the lungs and kills slowly but inevitably' [p.379].

The narrative strategy in such description is to evoke a mood of loss, a total absence of thinking and action in India, which is portrayed in the metaphors of disease and paralysis. The metaphorical is conflated with life itself, as human condition, inborn, endemic. Nowhere in such portrayal, in spite of the much appreciated sense of history in Nehru, do we get a sense of the counter-currents, of resistances and oppositions to the dominating socio-cultural and political frameworks. Several peasant movements against local landlords as well as the British which came up with a rare organisational ability and skill, are treated by Nehru with astonishing silence.[38] Indeed in his narrative focus on Gandhi as the undisputed leader of the 'masses', we discover a conflation of the Indian National Congress with all that was 'radical' and 'subversive' in the contemporary Indian scene. So he writes:

> The Congress led by Gandhi represented not only the nationalist urge of India, which had grown with the growth of the new bourgeoisie, but also to a large extent proletarian urges for social changes... Within the Congress, Socialists and Communists found a place and could influence Congress Policy... [pp. 417-18].

Nehru's flirtation with Marxist vocabulary makes it clear in no uncertain terms that a single national party, that is the Congress, alone has the power to represent the 'urges for social change.' And this power is derived from the 'scientific' understanding of the Indian socio-cultural ethos. Other representations of the Indian nation, which were emerging around the same period, and had emphasised different elements of culture and ideology in their analysis of the Indian history are rendered invisible. So, for instance, B.R. Ambedkar[39], Jayaprakash Narayan,[40] Ram Manohar Lohiya[41] or M.N. Roy[42]—leaders of considerable strength who had widely different positions on the Indian past and present and for whom the 'people' were not a homogeneous mass of undifferentiated quality but, as they showed in their work, were placed in a hierarchical relation of power along the caste, class, regional and linguistic axis—are met with total silence. Such occlusions are not fortuitous. They are an elaboration of the point made earlier that the terrain of a nation is always in a process of distribution and re-distribution; its time always subject to manipulation; its mode of address, and its narrative form forever in need of adaptation as new cultural and ideological equations are forged. It is in the light of such 'evidence' that we should study Nehru's representation of Gandhi—the charismatic leader—'who changed dramatically the destiny of India and her people'.

To clear the ground for Gandhi's arrival, like a heavenly voice foreboding the end of all misery and torture, the narrative must weave the contemporary events in bold metaphors of binary oppositions: of light and darkness, pain and relief, knowledge and ignorance, health and disease and life and death, which conceals beneath its rhetorical surface the rather ordinary run of disjointedness, fractures, resistances, shifting manoeuvres and alliances with the British power in India. *The ideological is thus inscribed in the narrative form, as a generic displacement from autobiography to lyrical story effects the production of the 'real' Gandhi. Gandhi's magic descent is set against the foregoing pall of gloom:*

> And then Gandhi came, he was like a current of fresh air that made us stretch ourselves and take deep breaths; like a beam of light that pierced in darkness and removed the scales from our eyes; like a whirlwind that upset many things, but most of all the *working of people's minds*... the essence of his teaching was fearlessness and truth, and action allied to these, always keeping the welfare of the masses in view.... So *suddenly*, as it were, that black pall of fear was lifted from the people's shoulders, not wholly of course, but to an amazing degree. As fear is close companion to falsehood, so truth follows fearlessness... It was a *psychological change*, almost as if *some expert in psycho-analytical methods had probed deep into the patient's past*, found out the origins of his complexes, exposed them to his views, and then rid him of that burden... Gandhi influenced millions of people in India in varying degrees; some changed the whole texture of their lives, others were only partly affected, or the effect wore off; and yet not quite, for some part of it could not be wholly shaken off [p.380].
>
> (emphasis added)

This particular, and selective representation of Gandhi needs to be attended to, since it would appear that most contemporary analysis of Gandhi from various critical positions are also caught in it, one way or another.

Ashis Nandy has discussed Gandhi, for instance, as the initiator of a new style of cultural politics, which he chooses to designate as 'critical traditionalism.' Gandhi presents a *true alternative* to colonialism by refusing to accept the cognitive categories of modernity and progress released by the colonialist 'world-view':

> [Gandhi] rejected history and affirmed the primacy of myths over historical chronicles. He thereby circumvented the linear pathway from primitivism to modernity, and from political immaturity to political adulthood. This was his way of grappling with colonial racism...[43]

The problem with such a formulation is not that it is 'ahistorical', for history cannot be accepted as a transcendent meta-category of all knowledge; but that, it takes the Gandhian statement at its face value. Such rhetorical evaluation fails to account for the various ways in which 'an alternative Gandhian politics' emerged on the Indian national scene. Neither does such a position show in its analysis how the Gandhian dissolution of the current western epistemology was 'accepted', or even understood, by the 'innocent victims' of colonialism. Short of making these connections, Nandy's rhetoric of equating Gandhi with the folksy, non-modern, childlike, or androgynous elements of 'Indian culture' replicates Nehru's strategy seen earlier. It can lapse into an uncritical glorification of Gandhi the man, without paying attention to the richness, and often contradictory receptions of the Gandhian theory. The psychological, or agentive then completely obscures the contextual or discursive production of Gandhi. To illustrate again:

> Not only did every Westerner and Westernized Indian who came in touch with Gandhi refer at least once to his child's smile, his admirers and detractors dutifully found him childlike and childish respectively. His 'immature' attacks on the modern world and its props, his 'juvenile' food fads and symbols like the spinning wheel—all were viewed as planks of a political platform which defied conventional ideas of adulthood.[44]

Marxist analysis of Gandhi, however, erred on the other side. They too, like Nehru and other Congressmen, first of all, accepted the 'mass-appeal' of Gandhi and his ability to launch a mass-movement at will, and stop it arbitrarily. They saw in Gandhi their 'greatest historical enemy', as the one who had mobilised vast masses of working class and peasantry to fight a battle on behalf of the nationalist bourgeois. Contemporary Indian communists, in order to expand their political base, tried to work out 'strategies' for reducing Gandhian appeal.

This is borne out by Dange's study of Gandhi in *Gandhi vs. Lenin* and Santi Devi's articles in the journal of Comintern, *Imprector.* While intending an analysis of Gandhi, these studies often confused the consequences of Gandhian politics with the understanding of the historical reasons of his success. M.N. Roy, one of the first Indian Marxists to produce a competent materialist analysis of Indian society of the colonial period, could not escape this trend either, though his assessment of Gandhi shows an internal contradiction. In one of his early articles in *Imprector* he appreciated several features of Gandhian method. Through the non-cooperation movement, 'the agrarian movement, the proletarian movement and the nationalist movement are moving concertedly towards one object, that is, national independence.' Congress was then perceived by him as 'the acknowledged head' of the nationalist movement. Gandhi had tried 'to break the class insularity of (the Congress) and to make it truly representative of the national aspirations of all classes of Indians.' Roy even thought Gandhian Satyagraha to be '*much more dangerous than an armed uprising* which can always be met face to face and put down'.[45]

After the Ahmedabad session of the Congress, Roy's assessment of both Congress and Gandhi began to change. Congress had, according to him, graduated in political consciousness; it had ceased to be a 'debating society' for lawyers but it should not convert itself into an organ of merchants and manufacturers. If it did and became the political apparatus of the propertied class, 'it must forfeit the title to the leadership of the nation'.[46] Non-cooperation had already failed; the *charkha* 'has been relegated to its well-deserved place in the museum.. the spirit of the people can not be raised by such impotent tactics, nor is the government terrorised'.[47]

It is not easy to appreciate how from 'the only method of struggle', and one 'superior to even armed struggle' Gandhian ideology and practice degenerated into 'an impotent tactic.'

Roy's line hardened further in his book *India in Transition.* He wrote: 'Gandhism is the acutest and most desperate manifestation of the forces of reaction trying to hold their own against the objectively revolutionary tendencies contained in the liberal bourgeois nationalism.'

Eventually, in Roy's assessment of Gandhi, we find a mechanical application of classical Marxism to Indian history, which perceives Gandhi as an 'agent' of the propertied bourgeois, or sometimes, even if diametrically opposed to the former, as a force of reaction. It was not possible for the Marxists, and that includes later writers like Rajni Palme Dutt and E.M.S. Namboodripad, to ask questions regarding the validity and success of Gandhi outside the given classical Marxist categories of interpretation.[48] In such scheme of things, Gandhi became for them either an irritating enigma or too simplistically a mere agent of some classes who used his power of communication uniquely to mobilise the Indian peasantry. From the foregoing, it is clear that these writers retain the Nehruvian conceptualisation of Gandhi even though the effects of Gandhian intervention in regard to the historical progress might be perceived differently by different groups.

A departure from the above conceptualisation of Gandhi came with the 'neo-Marxists' such as Partha Chatterjee and Sudipta Kaviraj in the 1980s. Chatterjee's reading of Gandhi transforms him into a 'figure' who launched for the first time in the history of Indian nationalist thought, a total critique of the very foundations of civil society, 'one which arises from an epistemic standpoint situated outside the thematic of post-Enlightenment thought'.[49] It was a critique, in fact, of the 'entire edifice of the bourgeois society'.[50] Its continually expanding and prosperous economic life, based on individual property, the social division of labour and the impersonal laws of the market; its political institutions based on a dual notion of sovereignty in which the people in theory rule themselves, but are only allowed to do so through the medium of their representatives; its spirit of innovation, adventure and scientific progress, its rationalisation of philosophy and ethics and secularisation of art and education—all of these were put under the sword. As early as in *Hind Swaraj*, claims Chatterjee, 'Gandhi launches a thoroughgoing critique against each of these constitutive features of civil society'.[51]

Gandhi's criticism in *Hind Swaraj* is pitched at a level far beyond the constitutional, social or political. He does not accept the argument that effective combinations are formed among individuals and groups sharing self-interests, and that institutions of representative democracy will ensure that the government will act in ways, which are, on the whole, in the common interest of the entire collectivity. Besides, for Gandhi, *the legal fiction of equality before the law and the supposed neutrality of state institutions only have the effect of perpetuating the inequalities and divisions which already exist in society.* Politics has no role in removing those inequalities or cementing the divisions. In fact, this very process of law and politics creates a 'vested interest' among politicians, state officials, and 'legal practitioners' to perpetuate social divisions, and indeed to create new ones.[52]

By contrast, *it is only when politics is directly subordinated to a communal morality that the minority of exploiters in society can be isolated by the people and inequalities and divisions removed.* As a political leader, therefore, 'Gandhi counterposes against the system of representative government an undivided concept of popular sovereignty, where the community is self-regulating and political power is dissolved into the collective moral will'[53]. Chatterjee cites Gandhi to reiterate this point as a part of Gandhian political theory.

> The power to control national life through national representatives is called political power. *Representatives will become unnecessary if the national life becomes so perfect as to be self-controlled.* It will then be a state of *enlightened anarchy* in

> which each person will become his own ruler. He will conduct himself in such a way that his behaviour will not hamper the well being of his neighbours. In an ideal state there will be no political institution and therefore no political power.[54]

What appears to be initially a critique of western civilization, turns out to be later on, a total moral critique of the fundamental aspects of civil society. The critique is not that of Western culture or religion; nor is it an attempt to establish the superior spiritual claims of Hindu religion. In fact, to quote Chatterjee:

> The moral charge against the West is not that its religion is inferior, but that by whole-heartedly embracing the dubious virtues of modern civilization, *it has forgotten the true teachings of the Christian faith.* At this level of thought, therefore, Gandhi is not operating at all with the problematic of nationalism. His solution too is meant to be universal, applicable as much to the countries of the West as to nations such as India... Not only that, what is even more striking, but equally clear, is *that Gandhi does not even think within the thematic of nationalism.* He seldom writes or speaks in terms of the conceptual frameworks or the modes of reasoning and inference adopted by the nationalists of his day, and quite emphatically, rejects their rationalism, scientism and historicism.[55]

The critique of civil society, moreover, does not emerge out of a consideration of the historical contradiction of civil society as perceived from within it. Quite unlike any of the European romantics, Gandhi is not torn between the conflicting demands of Reason and Morality, Progress and Happiness, Historical Necessity and Human Will. This idealisation of a peaceful, non-competitive, just and happy Indian society of the past, according to Chatterjee, 'could not have been a romantic longing for the lost harmony of the archaic world,'[56] because, unlike romanticism, Gandhi's problem is not conceived at all within the thematic bounds of post-Enlightenment thought. He was not troubled by the problems of reconciling individuality with universalism. Gandhi shared neither the spiritual anguish, nor indeed the aestheticism of literary romantics of his time. Instead, his moral beliefs never seemed to lose that almost obdurate certitude which men like Tagore, or Jawaharlal Nehru, found so exasperating.

However, if Gandhian response to civil society, modernity and consequent colonial institutions were to be seen as of a piece with the 'traditional intellectuals,' sharing pre-capitalist categories of thought, one could hardly explain the 'tremendous power' Gandhi exercised on our national imagination. It would be grossly erroneous to regard Gandhi as merely another peasant intellectual. To understand Gandhi, Chatterjee contends, one must analyse his theory and practice in relation to the development of Indian bourgeois nationalist thought. Gandhism was

> an ideology conceived as an intervention in the elite-nationalist discourse of the time and was formed and shaped by the experience of a specifically national movement. It is only by looking at it in that historical context that it becomes possible to understand the *unique achievement* of Gandhism: its ability to open up the possibility for achieving perhaps the most important task for a successful national revolution in a country like India, viz. *the political appropriation of the subaltern classes by a bourgeois aspiring for hegemony* in the new nation-state. In the Indian case, the largest popular element of the nation was peasantry. And it was the Gandhian ideology which opened up the historical possibility for its appropriation into the evolving political structures of the Indian state.[57]
>
> (emphasis added)

In Chatterjee's statement of Gandhi we find a certain shift in the mode of analysis. Far from seeing Gandhi as an enigma, a force of reaction, or an agent of the propertied classes, he regards him as a figure capable of critiquing the entire edifice of the bourgeois civil society. It was here that he 'appealed to the masses', but also, and it is crucial, in this task he seemed to be ironically siding the bourgeoisie themselves. Gandhi is seen as 'appropriating the subaltern classes' in the development of a national revolution—a battle fought not for them, but on behalf of them.

We do not still get a sense of how it was possible, or could have been achieved. From Chatterjee's analysis, while we learn in detail about the Gandhian epistemological critique of the civil society and its attendant institutions, yet *it is not clear how and why the phenomenon of 'mass politics' or the subordination of the subaltern classes to a bourgeois nationalist purpose through Gandhi, resulting in a so-called 'passive revolution', became successful.* For lack of such explanation we must regard Gandhi either as an outstanding cultural and political force *per se,* or attribute a conspiratorial logic to him by which he somehow succeeded in aligning the masses for a 'passive revolution'. In fact, Congress leaders themselves, and that certainly includes Jawaharlal Nehru, were intensely aware of the ideological and class implication of such a national-struggle. Much before the appearance of *The Discovery of India* Nehru had written in 'Whither India':

> Again, whose freedom are we particularly striving for, for nationalism covers many sins and includes many a conflicting element? There is the feudal India of the princes, the India of the big *Zamindars*, of the professional classes, of the agriculturists, of the industrialists, of the bankers, of the lower middle class, of the workers. There are interests of foreign capital and those of home capital, of foreign services and home services. *The nationalist answer is to prefer home interest to foreign interests but beyond that it does not go.* It tries to avoid disturbing the divisions or the social status-quo. *It imagines that the various interests will somehow be accommodated when the country is free.* Being essentially a middle-class movement, nationalism works chiefly in the interest of that class. It is obvious that there are serious conflicts between

various interests in a country, and every law, every policy which is good for one interest may be harmful for another.[58]

(emphasis added)

It is hard to imagine that Gandhi was unaware of the above argument as put forward by Nehru. Yet, if he still chose to persist with the Congress-led national movement, was it simply because he considered it a 'practical necessity' in the face of Imperialism or was it perhaps because he had the tremendous support of the masses, cutting across class and caste-barriers, who after independence, would have helped him to resolve the internal crisis? Put either way, we are still with the familiar psycho-empirical categories of understanding the Gandhian phenomenon. *A larger conception of ideology,* one that goes beyond treating it as motivated by certain individuals, false consciousness, or so-called objective interests of certain classes might help us deflect the form of these questions and look for responses to the 'Gandhian nexus with the masses' in a different light.

Sudipta Kaviraj apparently finds one way out of this impasse by wresting Gandhi from the realm of interests and ideologies, and assigning him a new value in the field of culture. Culture, of course, is also one way of understanding the politics but is not entirely reducible to it. It is the uniquely symbolic style of Gandhian 'cultural power' he argues, which must be opened up and analysed before we can come up with critical responses to the success of Gandhian politics.[59]

A stubbornly 'rational inquiry' alone cannot make us understand the cultural power of Gandhism and 'its ability to fashion weapons of political struggle out of unorthodox material... Gandhi's politics were formed out of an irreducible combination of cultural and political strategies in which what you do and the way you do it are inextricably mixed... Resolved into its parts, it appeared laughable and simplistic; as a totality, it was after all, *the only strategy that worked against British imperialism...*[60]

Kaviraj finds the source of such a political strategy in the 'subtlety of Indian culture'[61] which, according to him, is a culture of great inflections containing 'an enormous repertoire of gestures symbolising action, from insults to defiance, gesture of great subtlety and inflection'[62]. Subtlety of a culture, however, is not a matter of literacy alone. Gandhi's political style, therefore, 'consciously tried to gather up elements' from the rich repertoire of Indian culture and from 'other aspects of Indian life in which effectiveness had been tried for centuries, and applied them to the untried field of politics.'[63]

Seen in these terms Gandhian politics was neither obscurantist, nor impotent. *Rather it was a subtly indigenous and cultural style, which does not justify itself in terms of the other but effects a breaking down* of the barrier between the political interlocutor and his audience. The result of all this was that, to quote Kaviraj:

> He [Gandhi] created a political culture which relied heavily on what can be called the *pre-discursive*, a play on symbols and meanings which already said a great deal to an audience before the actual speaking began... The elaborate theatre of simplicity was not a matter of personal idiosyncrasy, they constituted small but wholly credible everyday gestures of belonging, which formed in their totality a deeply political act. *It did through a personal symbolic style what a purely rationalist discourse could have imperfectly accomplished*...It use was double-edged as it put not only the British on the wrong foot but also his [Gandhi's] Indian political adversaries.[64]
>
> (emphasis added)

At the first sight Kaviraj's resounding conclusion—'it did through a personal symbolic style what a purely rational discourse could have imperfectly accomplished'—appears to strike the same note as Nehru's virtuoso performance when Nehru thought that the reason of Gandhi's success lay in his 'magical power' and 'tremendous inner reserves.' But a more critical probing will dispel the ostensible similarity of their positions. Kaviraj's position on the other hand may appear, after Fredric Jameson, to represent Gandhian intervention as an historically unique phenomenon in that it tried to bring to the surface those elements of Indian culture which had not yet been captured by the realm of the symbolic. The power of the symbolic lies, according to Jameson, in historicising narratives of the unconscious which are repressed by the reifying practice of ideology.[65] In the Gandhian case, the specific use of the Indian cultural material, taken from outside the dominant historic-cultural narratives, caused a crucial perceptual shift to allow the identification of the 'utopian impulse' of 'people' with their collective objective conditions in history. Kaviraj's explanation of the Gandhian success story certainty adds a new dimension to the existing interpretive strategies. He draws our attention to the cultural forces operating independently of a reductive economic, conspiratorial forces or merely class-based logic. The repertoire of a culture-system often consists of vastly undifferentiated and unconscious elements, which wait for a conscious historical ordering and explanation, and may be worked to ambivalent, divergent ends. *The Gandhian intervention lay in opening a new dimension of the cultural unconscious* and in linking it with the mobilisation of the vast number of people across various types and classes for the national struggle, or even in the interests of 'indigenous identity formation' against imperialism.

However, to extend such interpretation—even as generous as this one—to Gandhi and his 'nexus with mass politics,' does not seem to take us very far. For, there is no empirical evidence to suggest that Gandhi, or Gandhian practice, was a unitary phenomenon in the popular imagination of his times. Neither can such a practice, within itself, be seen as uniform, and unmediated, appearing to the deeper recesses of the 'minds' of people by a unique interplay of indigenous symbols and meanings.

On the other hand, one might, equally forcefully, argue that the 'force' of Gandhian practice was an ideological manoeuvre created for the containment of variously conflicting interests, to precipitate a new cultural space of the 'people' who would belong to an Indian nation, yet to be born. To say this does not mean automatic acceptance of a Gandhian cultural hegemony, or a national milieu, where the 'people' participated willingly, with their own consent, in the Gandhian style of cultural politics. As Shahid Amin has shown in his excellent study of Gandhi, the peasants did not always understand Gandhian practice in his non-violent terms.[66] Nor did the figure of 'Mahatma' become a legend suddenly, without a direct support of the Congress nationalist press often hand in glove with the local politicians landlords and the money-lenders.[67] Seen in these terms, one can surely make a viable case for the making of Gandhian practice as an historical and cultural phenomenon at cross-purposes. While, on the one hand, it seemed to challenge and interrogate the colonial mythologies of civil society, its institutions and civic practices, as well as the foundation of colonial epistemology, it also on the other hand helped create forces of domination which cancelled the raising of other pertinent questions in regard to the role of 'moral' solutions and the 'people' to whom they were addressed.

In Nehru's treatment of Gandhi it is this particular dilemma, which is sought to be glossed over, by accepting him as an over-arching figure with mysterious force, but at the same time, neglecting to court his critique of the civil society. The civil society, as it had emerged in the pre-independence India in the later half of the nineteenth century, was coeval with modern bourgeois forces and while it challenged the authority and rule of British Imperialism, *it borrowed from them the cognitive and cultural structure of domination and adapted these structures sufficiently* to suit a national-struggle for independence. *The Discovery of India* can be therefore *read metonymically* as creating a discourse for the consolidation of the civil society in its *strategic displacement* and ultimate elision of the Gandhian critique of the civil society. While it accepts, and even glorifies, Gandhi the man as a *national hero,* it undercuts the foundation of the Gandhian critique of the emerging national culture. We move on to the next section to consider certain aspects of the civil society, which appear in the text as integral features of a modern nation.

V
Secular Democracy, Legality and the Politics of Communalism

In the preceding pages we considered how the rhetorical devices of narrative in *The Discovery of India* forged a link between the various forms of early anti-colonial struggles (often expressed in the uprisings of the local populace against the landlords, or the religious movements against an exploitative colonial system) with a modern national, and Indian consciousness. Such ideological engineering aimed at *creating a narrative form* which shows a natural, transparent connection between time and language. But the road to temporal and linguistic unification was not a smooth one in this text. It followed a tortuous route, bifurcating along the way several times, and tapering off sometimes without further links. One such major link of the text, or a *cohesive cultural code, is secularism.*

In 'Secularism' Nehru discovered that magic which promised to cure all the ailments of a beleaguered Indian traditional society. 'Splintered' into various ethnic, linguistic, religious and cultural types, the contemporary Indian ethos had to be transformed internally to match the true scientific temper and the democratic spirit of a modern nation. For Nehru *secularising India was in essence, a task equivalent to civilizing it*, thus conferring upon it the respectable status of Modernity and

Reason which were the twin fundamental conditions of an incipient national democracy. At the same time, however, he was only too well aware of the role of traditional loyalties and religion in the domain of politics. The result was the invention of a new idiom, a new linguistic and cultural expression, which would tap the ontological force of traditional religion without its various esoteric and extraneous trappings. He quotes Romain Rolland very approvingly to fashion his own understanding of religion:

> [There are] many souls who are or who believe they are free from all religious beliefs, but who in reality live immersed in a state of super-rational consciousness, which they term socialism, communism, humanitarianism, nationalism and even rationalism. *It is the quality of thought and not its object* which determines its source and allows us to decide whether or not it emanates from religion. If it turns fearlessly towards the search for truth at all costs with single-minded sincerity, prepared for any sacrifice, I should call it religious...[68]

Nehru adds:

> I cannot presume to fulfill the conditions laid down by Romain Rolland, but on these terms I am prepared to be a humble camp follower of the Grand Army.[69]

The 'quality of thought' in search of Truth is supplemented surreptitiously by the doctrine of secularism which is seen as more 'advanced' and 'democratic' than the traditional societies based on religious values. Nehru observes:

> Our constitution lays down that we are a secular state, but it must be admitted that *this is not wholly reflected in our mass living and thinking*. In a country like England, the State is, under the constitution, allied to one particular religion, the Church of England, which is a sect of Christianity. Nevertheless; the state and people there largely function in a secular way. Society, therefore, in England is more advanced in this respect than in

India even though our constitution may be, in this matter, more advanced.[70]

Secularism in India emerged in the gap between loyalties to traditional religious communities, and the requirements of building a modern nation state. As is well-known, colonial India saw the persistence of many pre-capitalist economic forms and attendant social diversities. It contained a vast range of regional conditions, cultures and interests. But in the post-colonial phase the Indian people experienced a combination of modern and, in many ways the continuation of colonial, as well as pre-colonial modes of domination. Thus a new cohesion developed around existing foci of loyalty such as caste, language and religious community, even as a new modern national consciousness was not fully developed. *At this interface of the traditional and modern* the concept of secularism, or the Indian version of a western form of secularism, comes into play.[71]

What such a concept tends to do, particularly when it is allied to 'modernity' and 'scientific temper' (both Nehru's terms) is to reduce different socio-cultural customs, religious practices, and experiences of various communities *to the play of a predetermined nationalism and communalism in the larger narrative of Indian history.* It chooses to *delegitimise* or *thwart* the diverse religious ethos of the Indian people by designating them as 'communal.' Communalism appears in contemporary political discourse, and particularly in *The Discovery of India* as one of the main 'problems' to be wiped out, to overcome, in the development of a self-governing, national and democratic polity. Nehru tried to identify the 'causes' of the 'communal behaviour,' especially among the Muslims in India and his analysis is remarkably similar to that of the colonial machinery which first employed the term 'communal' to designate a religious type in India. *The Discovery of India* illustrates how the 'communal' question is inextricably linked to the techniques and discourses of modernisation and of an incipient secular nation-state which borrows its understanding of polity from the dominating frameworks of knowledge produced by the colonial experience:

> The Mughal rulers were strong *as long as they put themselves in line with the genius of the nation* and tried to work for a common nationality and a synthesis of the various elements in the country... The Muslims who came to India from outside brought no new technique or political and economic structure. In spite of a religious belief in the brotherhood of Islam, *they were class bound and feudal in outlook.* In technique and in the methods of production and industrial organisation they were *inferior to what prevailed in India.* Thus their influence on the economic life of India and the social structure was very little... Since British rule came to India, Moslems have produced few outstanding figures of the *modern type.* They have produced some remarkable men but, as a rule *these represented the continuation of the old culture and tradition and did not easily fit in with modern development.* This incapacity to march with the changing times and adapt themselves culturally and otherwise to a new environment was *not of course due to any innate feeling.* It derived from certain historical causes from *the delay in the development of a new industrial middle class, and the excessively feudal background of the Muslims* which blocked up avenues of development and prevented the release of talent... [pp.277-83; p.413].
>
> (emphasis added)

At bottom Nehru's argument is three-fold: first, Mughal rule degenerated only when it tried to neglect the national mainstream of India. The Indian tradition, or 'national genius' in Nehru's phrasing, lay in a unique, almost mystical, continuity which always assimilated the diverse, disparate, even contradictory socio-political and religious forces into a single wholeness of Indian culture. The euphemistic phrase 'Unity in Diversity' is extrapolated from the parlance of standard, Brahmanic Hinduism, and redisposed, secualarised into the continuity of the great Indian tradition which was supposed to evince equal respect to all religious sects and belief-systems. Second, the condition of Muslims in the colonial period is perceived as one of *backwardness,* though this is not due to an 'innate feeling'; it is not endemic, or inborn. The 'backwardness' can be attributed to the lack of development of modern culture, and the refusal of the Muslims to part with their traditional, feudal ways of life. The 'feudal' background, Nehru argues later in the book, leads to several problems, the most dangerous of all being a 'fear psychosis' or 'minority consciousness' among the Muslims of India. *This fear, or lack of security, lack of development, and the inability to foster a scientific temper, is the main 'cause' of the communal behaviour or communalism-*

Third, Nehru applies the existing framework of Marxism to an understanding of religion, particularly Islam. This led him to believe that *an industrial middle-class is the sine qua non for the onward march of history.* In this scheme of things Muslims fell behind in the race for progress since they, unlike most Hindus, did not learn from the English system of education, and other Western institutions of self-development. Communality among Muslims, arose as a result of this lag between the 'requirements of changing time' and a stubbornness to yield to the Age of Reason which was also, according to Nehru, a true index of the universal spirit. Nehru's *specific contribution* thus lies in introducing the element of universal rationality in the contemporary discourse on 'communalism' or religious types in India.

Several critiques of the phenomenon of secularism or the process of secularization of Indian society since Nehru have been put forward. It is not possible here to go into a detailed enumeration of all of them. Instead, one can analyse the phenomenon reflecting at the same time on various critical positions which seem significant. According to Ashis Nandy, the modern state 'always prefers to deal with religious ideologies rather than faiths'[72]. By 'ideologies' he means religion as a sub-national, national or cross-national identifier of populations contesting for or protecting non-religious, usually political or socio-economic, interests. Such religions as ideologies get identified with *one or more texts* which, 'rather than the way of life of the believers, then become the final identifiers of the pure form of religion.' The texts help anchor the ideologies in something seemingly concrete and delimited, and in effect provide a set of manageable operational definitions.

Secondly, because such process of secularisation of society is seen to be coeval with a simultaneous process of colonisation in India, there has grown a tendency to view the older faiths of Asia through the eyes of evangelical Anglican Christianity and its various offshoots, or its mirror image in the orthodox modernism propagated by Fredric Engels and Thomas Huxley. *Because this particular euro-centric way of looking at faiths gradually came to be associated with the dominant culture of the colonial states,* it subsumes under it a set of clear polarities: centre versus periphery, true religion vs. its distortions, civil vs. primordial, and great traditions vs. local cultures. Because of its singularly modernising and civilising impulse secularism obfuscates the growth of varied cultures. In fact it has little to say about cultures. It is definitionally ethnophobic and frequently ethnocidal, unless of course cultures, and those living by cultures are willing to show total subservience to the modern nation state and become ornaments or adjuncts to modern living.'[73] The 'orthodox secularists' such as Jawaharlal Nehru 'have no clue to the way a religion can link up different faiths or ways of life according to its '*own configurative principles.*'[74] Implicit in their definitions of secularism, however honestly held (as might be the case with Nehru), is the belief that *managing* the public sphere is a science which is essentially *areligious* and that religion, to the extent that it is opposed to the *Baconian* world-image of science, is an open or potential *threat to any modern polity.*

Thirdly, the concept of secularism is responsible for producing definition of a modern 'self' which is incompatible with fluid, and multiple ways of *realising the self* in the traditional Indian cultures. Such a self, which can be conceptually viewed as a configuration of selves, invokes and reflects 'the configurative principle of religion-as-faith.'[75] *It is a negation of the modern concept of selfhood acquired partly from the Enlightenment rationality, and partly from a rediscovery of previously recessive elements in the Indian traditions.* Religion-as-ideology which is a by-product of secularisation, on the other hand, works with the concept of well-bounded, mutually exclusive religious identities, and is compatible with a clearly individualised self, separable from the 'non-self' of religion-as-faith. One can, for instance, decontaminate Hinduism of its folk elements, turn it into a classical *vedantic* faith, and then give it additional teeth with the help of Western technology and secular state craft. Thus it is hoped that the Hindus can take on and ultimately defeat all their external and internal enemies, if necessary by liquidating all forms of ethnic plurality and religious 'non-selves', first within Hinduism and then within India, to equal western *Man* as a new universal type. *The new nation-state, in the secularist scheme, begins to perceive traditional faith and its attendant non-selves as a danger to the technology of statecraft and political and social management of the society. The new nation-state thus performs the same function as the colonial cultural and political machinery once did to the 'distant cultures' which came under their domination.* It accepts them at best as 'things' or 'objects' to be studied 'engineered', ghettoed, museumised or preserved. This *secular state of mind,* in sum, is the basic format of the *internal colonialism, which* is at work today. Nandy's antidote to the ideology of secularism is religious faith, or an active celebration of 'non-self' as argued earlier. It is from non-modern India:

> from the traditions and principles of religious tolerance encoded in the everyday life associated with the different faiths of India, that *one will have to seek clues to the renewal of Indian political*

> *culture...* It not only means tolerance of religion but also a tolerance that is religious. It therefore squarely locates itself in traditions, outside the ideological grid of modernity.'[76]

Nandy's position is powerful enough to show the crucial nexus between the emerging modern nation-state, its democratic legal set up, its technocratic management of social and cultural space of peoples, and the process of secularisation, which creates modern selfhood. However, *it is his 'solution' to the problem, that is, an uncritical invocation of 'religion-as-faith' or 'traditions of tolerance', which needs to be put under a careful scrutiny.* We will return to these issues once we have examined a few other contemporary positions on 'secularism', particularly from the left. Writing in 1966, E.M.S. Namboodiripad offered a coldly practical interpretation of ruling class, secular nationalism:

> The dominant ruling group at the centre tried to establish a fake 'unity of the Nation' by denying the right of every nationality and social group to have equality of opportunity and status in a democratic set up... The so-called 'struggle between nationalism and the fissiparous forces'—the struggle in the name of which the leaders of the ruling party are trying to beat the opposition forces into submission—is a *fake* 'struggle'. It is the means through which the dominant section of the bourgeoisie is trying to maintain its domination not only over the working people but even section of their own class. The slogan of 'communal harmony' and 'national unity' is the weapon with which the dominant monopoly group tried to bring their competitors into submission.[77]

Namboodiripad's is one of the earliest Marxist interpretation of Indian secularism and it leaned heavily on the economic forces, as the key factor in the determination of a 'fake' cultural phenomenon. Secularism of the ruling elite, in this scheme of things, is mere hypocrisy, a mystification intended mainly for *international consumption.* This position is important for its unequivocal emphasis on the direct involvement of the state and its cultural machinery in the production of the official discourse of secular-nationalism—which is an attempt to dictate the terms of the debate between warring cultural and socio-economic groups.

Such interpretations tend to elide completely the subterranean, below-the-official, or semi-official, transactions of secularism. In a similar view Miller points out in his 'Six Theses':

> The state, whatever its intentions and desires, is indubitably a political machine. It creates divisions, conflicts, interests, alliances, expectations, frustrations, and heightened consciousness just as much as society does. No legislation, or lack thereof, can constitute nationality, uniformity, even-handedness...[78]

Thus, the state, which claims to love all and hate none, is at best 'hypocritical'. It enables the ruling elites to entertain the fantasy of power without responsibility for the exercise of power:

> The secular state mystique ultimately lets the state off the hook, as it encourages it to blame the (unfortunate) affairs of things entirely on society and not to take responsibility for its own deeds and non-deeds.[79]

One way out of this Mechiavellian role of the state is to ask the state machinery *itself* to use its power with discretion and appropriateness. There can be no such thing as equal respect for the content of all religions. 'In truth', as Anil Nauriya points out, 'there can be equal respect only for the universal or humanist element in each religion and that too only to the extent to which we can discover it'.[80] Beyond that one can have equal respect for all religions, or *being untrue to other values,* say humanism.

According to this style of criticism, a state reflecting a true understanding of 'humanism' or 'universal rationality' is not neutral or indifferent to religion and does not treat all religions with respect. It confines the respect to certain underlying elements of religion. This inevitably means that the state 'must differentiate one religious impulse from another even within an individual religion.'[81] Further, such a state is neither religious, nor against religion. It provides instead an active critique of religion. A 'clue' to the understanding of this conception of the relationship between state and religion is to be found in a comment made by Marx on the democratic state in his article on the Jewish question. According to Marx:

> The democratic state, the true state, does not need religion for its political completion. On the contrary, it can discard religion, because in it the *human foundation of religion* is realized in a secular way.[82]

For those Marxists in India who saw the liberal strains of Nehru's secularism overriding his commitment to a socialist transformation, here lies '*the dialectical relationship between state and religion.*'[83] There is no escape from making differentiations *within* different and diverse religious stimuli. The 'humanistic' is to be separated from the 'non-humanistic', and this requires *judgement on the part of the state.* Such a state, involving as it does, a more activist or interventionist view of secularism, could be expected to utilize the human foundation to confront the non-humanistic practices associated with religion, at least so far as these impinge upon social life as a means of social control. The role of the state is not to promote or oppose any religion but to grow out of it for the goals, which are truly human.

For an historical understanding of secularism, one may recognise the 'necessity' of this phenomenon for the elite who aspired to speak for the Indian nation to the colonial masters. The British, as Nehru painstakingly emphasised time and again in his writings, refused to recognise any 'national' entity in India, but insisted on dissolving it into a myriad particularities of caste, tribe, region and religion. On the rebound from this particular British stubbornness, elite secularism, according to Ravinder Kumar, who specifies three major stands in it, 'was a necessary ideological strategy'.[84] However, as Nehru realised promptly, it was equally necessary to mobilise the support of traditional groups along the caste, regional, linguistic and religious lines—the traditional loyalties as they are euphemistically called—for a nationalist struggle. Indeed such popular mobilisation of the peasantry, working classes, and the low-castes was sought. But the creation, consolidation, recognition and affirmation of diverse communities did not necessarily lead to a critical or 'autonomous' consciousness. It worked on the other hand, as Sumit Sarkar has argued in detail, to install a way-station on the royal road to the ultimate nationalist consciousness.[85] The phenomenon of wooing the 'traditional loyalties' is dramatically put by Nairn:

> The new middle class intelligentsia of nationalism had to invite the masses into history; and the invitation had to be written in a language they understood.[86]

Nehru's language, on the contrary, is not the one which would *invite* masses to 'understand' the implications of his goal. His effort is directed to find a *resonance,* a reciprocating chord of identity from each group. So he writes:

> The diversity of India is tremendous: it is obvious; it lies on the surface and anybody can see it. It concerns itself with physical appearances as well as with certain mental habits and traits. There is little in common between the *Pathan* of the North-West and the *Tamil* in the far South. Their racial stocks are not the same, though there may be common stands running through them; they differ in face and figure, food and clothing, and, of course, language... The *Pathans* and the *Tamil* are two extreme examples; the others lie somewhere in between... It is fascinating to find how the *Bengalis*, the *Marathas*, the *Gujratis*, the *Tamils*, the *Andhras*, the *Oriyas*, the Assamese, the *Canarese*, the *Malayalis*,

> the *Sindhis*, the *Punjabis*, the *Pathans*, the *Kashmirs*, the *Rajputs*, and the great central block comprising the Hindustani speaking people, have *retained their peculiar characteristics for hundreds of years,* have still more or less the same virtues and failings of which old tradition or record tells us, and yet have been throughout these ages *distinctively Indian,* with the same *national heritage* and the same set of *moral and mental qualities...* [pp.63-64].
>
> (emphasis added)

This emphasis on unity, the distinctive Indianness, inspite of tremendous differences across cultures, economic, social and religious differences, is the *leit motif* of Nehru's official version of secularism. And this is held in constant tension with his own, 'personal' understanding of religion which moves away from an acknowledgement of the religious impulse in public, as we saw earlier. This duality, and ambivalence characteristic of the Nehruvian text enables one to realise that a belief in secularism—of whichever type—for its own sake, was not the *only* or *unique resource of the legitimation of political power.* This discourse appeals to a wide variety of motivations and beliefs systems. He found it desirable to invoke elements of history, tradition, caste, charisma, legality and religion equally, to sustain a secular and national unity. These heterogeneous narratives on secularisation can be seen to be working alongside the other, equally significant, strands: they together constitute the appeal of his 'voice', even as they refuse to cohere into a logical, or consistent pattern of arguments. Belief in *constitutional democracy* and/or *legality,* derived consciously from the British parliamentary system provides an example parallel to the phenomenon of secularism. For an understanding of this phenomenon we should place it in the historical context of the political economy which sustained the flowering of a bourgeois form of constitutional democracy, and more particularly, a Nehruvian interpretation of its legal and political machinery.

Long-term structural compulsions on Indian politics since the arrival of colonial economy, and the choices of both the ruling block of propertied classes and the unorchestrated 'subaltern' classes, arise in several well-known ways: first, the inclusion of Indian economy in the capitalist international market and its division of labour; secondly, the received structure of colonial economic retardation and socio-political formations; and thirdly, the fundamental choice exercised by the leadership of the new Indian state in favour of a capitalist strategy of economic growth through a set of basic legal and constitutional reforms. These structural compulsions often led to the characterisation of India as a 'late' or 'backward', post-colonial capitalism which functionally uses various enclaves of pre-capitalist productive forms.[87] It is in this context that we have recognised Indian state as a 'bourgeois state'. It may be further qualified by three, mutually supportive, senses: first, when we say that a nation-state is 'bourgeois state', this refers in some way (though this particular way can be very different in various historically concrete cases) to a state of dominance enjoyed by the capitalist class, *or a coalition of classes dominated by the bourgeoisie.*[88] Secondly, the *state form* is bourgeois, that is, the sense in which we speak of the parliamentary democratic form as being historically a bourgeois form of government. This is not just a matter of registering that such forms historically arose during the period of rising capitalism in Europe (or what is more loosely called these days the period of Enlightenment in Europe) and spread out through a process of 'cultural diffusion'. Rather one would have to look very carefully, for 'a stronger, structural connection between bourgeois hegemony and this form of the (democratic) state.[89] It arranges a disbursing of advantages in a particular way, and the democratic mechanism works as a usefully sensitive political index as to when the distribution of disadvantages, which is bound to happen and intensify in a capitalist economy, is becoming politically insupportable. *This is an example of Marx's hypothesis that democracy was the most appropriate, indeed a tailor-made form, for capitalism.* Besides, this also lays down norms of management of the conflict of various interests in a way that even though political grievances accumulate, their *political articulation* does not assume a pitch and form which makes the minimal stability required for capitalist production unobtainable.

In the third, and much more solid form, the Indian state is bourgeois in that it expresses and ensures the domination of the ruling coalition bloc and helps in capitalist reproduction, and a subordinate reproduction of other types of economic relations by imposing on the economy a deliberate order of capitalist planning. *Those directive functions that capital cannot perform through the market* (either because the market is not very powerful in its network, or because such tasks cannot be performed directly by market pressures alone) *the bourgeois state performs through the legitimised directive mechanisms of the state.*

India has then a bourgeois state in three different senses and a bourgeois format of the state, or the bourgeois character of its legal system, property structure and institutions of governance, are clearly evident.[90] These are revealed in the framing of the Indian constitution *which lays down that patterns of laws can direct social relations rather than reflect them.* It can be said that the Indian capitalist class exercises its control over society neither through a purely moral/cultural hegemony of the *Gramscian* type, nor a simple coercive strategy on the lines of satellite states of the third world. It does so by a coalitional strategy carried out partly through the state directed process of economic growth, partly through the allocational necessities indicated by bourgeois democratic political system. It follows that in the realm of politics too, as in the field of economic relations, the Indian bourgeois could not be accorded an absolute supremacy, because of the undeniable prevalence of pre-capitalist political forms in our governance, particularly in the political life of a vast majority of rural India.

The above observation nullifies the view that the state of India, which was about to be set up after the crumbling of the British Empire, has been merely an *expression* of class relations, rather than a *terrain* of accommodative interests and ideologies. This helps us to understand better that capital alone, apart from the bureaucratic-managerial-intellectual elite and the rural magnates operating largely through the pre-capitalist forms, has not been *independently* dominant in Indian state. It is, on the other hand, a long term political coalition which ensures a joint group domination. Such a coalition, it can be argued, is not *an effect*, or an *accidental* attribute of a dominance, it is its *condition.*[91]

Such a minimum 'political economy' argument is necessary for an understanding of the ambivalence apparent in Nehru's discourse which appealed to a wide variety of resources to seek legitimacy. It helps us understand why Nehru could never pitch his argument in a single direction, and confront directly the weight of forces acting upon the incipient Indian nation state. *The equivocal fluidity of his rhetoric* very often shrouds the shifting nature of alliances that constitute the nature of relation between the public and private, legal and cultural domains.

Today, with the departure of the British, and the establishment of the institution of formal democracy, the modes in which legitimacy may be sought have been somewhat changed—but the *implicit contradiction* between communities *which have to be simultaneously affirmed and transcended has, if anything, deepened*[92]. And it is ironic indeed that it should be the institutions of democracy which drive the ruling coalition blocks with their commitments to secularism to periodic compromises, in village and *taluka*, north and south, with various and variably noxious kinds of 'non-secular' mobilisation.[93] It has been suggested that electoral imperatives of institutional democracy themselves might be contributing significantly to the process of social fracturing by reinforcing the inherited patterns of 'vertical mobilisation.'[94]

Apart from these specifically political compulsions, one should be able to *examine the historical linkage of official secular doctrine with the process of capitalist transformation in India.* Secularism in this context becomes 'the cutting edge of the ideological drive to clear the public space of hindrances to the unfettered pursuit of profit, an attempt to clear the field of traditional loyalties that have, under the new dispensation, become suddenly dysfunctional'[95]. At the same time, however, the nexus between capitalism and the process of democratic secularisation of society is an uneasy one because the promise it held out to humanity—'a confident this-worldliness' in Nehru's phraseology—has contradictions inherent in it. The compulsion of electoral politics and the crucial role of 'traditional loyalties' of various ethnic and religious communities severely constrain capitalist ambitions. Secularisation thus begins by offering religion a 'bargain' of privatisation—the relegation of religion to an exclusively personal domain—but a bad bargain in that the offer cannot be accepted the whole hog. The cherished space of modernity and capitalist order is, so often, invaded by the outcast religious types, even as these religious communities serve as axes of manipulation and control of the communal politics for the ruling group. Even as we recognise the intrinsic functionality of the traditional bonds of religion, caste and community—those same traditional groups and collectivities which appear from one location, 'communal' but which might as well be modes of resistance to the heartless violence of capitalist secularism, there is no pristine innocence of pure faith, or religion-as-faith in Ashis Nandy's formulation, to pull us out of the politics of secularism. It is curious that Nandy's solution to the vacuous, official secularism and the entire urban-industrial vision of life that it brings along with it, is confected out of the same essentialised religion that went into the making of the toxin in the first place. What is needed here is not an uncritical invocation of the pre-modern or non-modern traditional societies or syncretist faith, even if they seem not to have completely lost their function in the context of contemporary political calculation, but a reaffirmation of the *sustaining role of 'public space' in a manner which does not allow the commodification of religion in the capitalist market.* The community of shared experiences of a world that manifests itself more often in ambivalences and lack, rather than fulfilment and accord, must continue to project its competing and mutually antagonistic interests in the face of 'secular' and 'national' unity.

Secularism takes a complex turn when its discourse combines very effectively, the so-called 'private' domain of religion with the 'public' sphere comprising law, or more precisely, the rule of law. Such a discourse has both an individualising and a totalising form of power *simultaneously*[96]. The technique of individualisation lies in creating a new form of subjectivity whose force is derived from self-recognition. Similar to the technique which originated in Christian institutions, *secularism addresses the individual as a unique, coherent whole, whose salvation in the world of every day reality was based on acting with the consent of his or her conscience.* The recognition of conscience must be consistent with the law of truth which is *internal* to each individual. This form of power thus cannot be exercised without knowing the inside of people's minds, without exploring their souls, and without making them reveal their 'innermost' secrets. It implies a *knowledge* of the conscience and the ability to direct it. It is coextensive and continuous with life; it is linked with a production of truth—the truth of the individual himself. However, and this is significant, the discourse of secularism does not lead an individual to his or her salvation in the next world. Unlike the pastoral power of the Christian missionaries, secularism, when allied to the modern nation-state, plays upon different meanings of the word salvation. Salvation is replaced by welfare or well-being, that is, sufficient wealth, standard of living, security, protection against accidents. Consequently, a series of 'worldly' aims take the place of the religious aims of the traditional pastorate. It is this 'ecclesiastical' function of secularism—function extending far beyond the confines of traditional organisational religion—which is deployed by the modern state.

As Michel Foucault noted in one of his last interviews, the modern state should not be considered.

> as an entity which was developed above individuals, ignoring what they are and even their very existence, but, on the contrary, as a very sophisticated structure, in which individuals can be integrated under one condition: that this individuality would be shaped in a new form and submitted to a set of very specific patterns.[97]

The individualising power of secularism is combined with totalising procedures, as for example, law. The secular law addresses a variety of people as a bundle, or homogeneous mass thereby enabling a smooth management of collective life. In Nehru's recounting of the story of India we find a sudden switch from the construction of private, conscientious Indian citizen to the 'unconstitutional' procedures adopted by the British, who 'distorted' law in order to blunt the actualisation of such a citizen. In refuting the allegation that the Congress agitational methods were 'unconstitutional' Nehru celebrated the wide significance of the word 'constitutional' in countries with democratic constitutions. The notion of constitution, or legality, he wrote,

> controls the making of laws...protects liberties... checks the executive.... Provides democratic methods of bringing about changes in the political and economic structure.[98]

Legality or constitutionalism thus performs four critical functions. First, it provides a framework of powers and limitations for the exercise of legislative competence. It thus provides a grammar, for the law-making political activity. Second, legality ordains the protection of liberties of citizens always threatened by the dominating power of the few. It is a prime function of constitutional legality to define the nature and scope of these freedoms and the ways in which these may be enjoyed without hindrance and also to define ways in which, collectively, the pursuit or exercise of freedom enrich rather than impoverish, sub serve rather than subvert, the overall scheme or structure of *distribution of freedom.* Third, constitutions provide for orderly changes in political structure not just through the guarantee right of adult suffrage but through the politics of accountability embedded in the freedom of speech and press and of association. Fourth, constitutions provide frameworks for development and endow governing groups with capabilities to alter the framework.

None of these requirements of legality, claims Nehru, 'was fulfilled by the colonial government'. *Colonial law was only an adjunct to the repressive and arbitrary powers of the executive.* Nehru's critique of British law appears in the following passage:

> When these (British) laws can be promulgated by an irresponsible executive at the shortest notice, the word 'legal' simply means the will of that executive and nothing more. Ordinarily that will be obeyed, willingly or sullenly, because the consequences of disobedience are unpleasant. But for any one to say that he will always obey it means abject submission to a dictatorship or irresponsible authority, the surrender of his conscience, and the impossibility of ever gaining freedom, so far as his activities are concerned.[99]

This critique throws up three additional features of 'legality'. First, the law is more than 'the will of the executive' in a *truly democratic society.* Since the executive power is created by the constitution, it can only be exercised *for constitutional* and *no other* ends.

Second, the law's time is *political,* hegemonic time. Laws ought not to be brought into being 'at the shortest notice'. Law's time instead is a time which creates space for consultations: calls for revisions in original legislative proposals, and for *democratic* deliberation.

Third, the title that law carried to legitimacy and obedience is structured by norms of legality. Willing obedience is, indeed, 'sullen', not conscientious, when animated by the desire to avoid unpleasant consequences. Implicitly, Nehru is pointing to belief in *legality for its own sake*—an internationalisation of the authority of the laws as a motive for compliance. To articulate it differently, it is an effort towards hegemony rather than sheer dominance by force, which according to Nehru, characterises the colonial state.

Nehru's critique of the Indian liberals was that they worked within the legal-administrative framework laid out by the British, and were unable to stretch the *conditions* which shaped the contours of legality. The 'mentality' reflected that of a 'good country house servant' who does not contest the legitimacy of the British treating 'India as a kind of enormous country house... that they owned'[100] The liberals thought of changing *merely* the mode of administration whereas what was needed as a *new state* which would *transform the condition of legality,* and would break through its colonial frameworks. A new Indian state won by *Swaraj* did not mean that 'everything continues as before, only with a darker shade.'[101] The author of the *Discovery of India* is only too well aware that full-fledged notions of legality emanate from the conditions of the colonising western nations. He acknowledges that:

> Our challenges to the British version of legality, history, economics and administration in India grew, and yet we continued to function within the orbit of their ideology...[102]

It was this awareness which enabled Nehru, as Upendra Baxi puts it, 'to variously operationalise the eight attributes of legality in the formulation of the Indian constitution. In many respects, he (Nehru) moved India, through this effort, outside the orbit of... English Ideology...'[103] But the inflection of English law also meant *to transgress legal discourse altogether and take refuge* in the parlance of 'history', 'tradition', 'heritage' or mere convention to make the case for a strong nation. As Baxi has argued, the deviance from the merely 'legal' or 'constitutional' becomes all the more frequent in the post-colonial phase, to seek legitimacy from 'the competing notions of traditions and charisma'[104] outside the frontiers of institutions he himself had helped in building in an earlier period. For Baxi it is frustrating became the overall legacy that Nehru bestowed us was one in which a *modernised state armed with modern science was considered critical for Indian development*, but modern law was often considered an obstacle to such development. The constraints which Nehru perceived in pursuing the path of legality as an end in itself and the justification he offered paved the way for a legal and constitutional culture which, more or less *forfeited the role of the law or belief in legality* as the mosaic of motivations sustaining political authority.[105]

(emphasis added)

The 'forfeiture' of legality is yet another powerful instance of the fractional discourse of modernity—discourse which Nehru has to simultaneously affirm and reject. As analysed in the earlier sections, Nehru's predicament, determined largely by the existing coalitional political economy, is that of a free prisoner—a contradiction in terms. He inherits the paradigm of an economist-scientific rationalism only to inflect it further by an invocation of 'feudal' categories of tradition and cultural heritage. The burden of his modern India imparts a colourful variety to his narrative, but a variety which is engulfed by the draconian tripartite of class, nation and community. Nehru's famous notes on 'The Basic Approach—which grew out of a keen awareness of 'real' dangers facing India: we have too many fissiparous tendencies for us to take risks'—founded upon the process of democratic secularisation which, as we have seen, inevitably involves fission, and along with it *the creation of majorities, the isolation of minorities, in an economy of representation of the nation which is best suited to the coalitional form of Indian politics.*

In sum, the narrative of *The Discovery of India* presents a dramatic split between what its author-narrator sets out to do: to recount the story of India which is optimistic, tragic, exultant, and ironic at the same time—and what gets done through the recourse to an analysis of the multi layered and diverse texture of the story. History, as we saw in our analysis earlier, becomes an infinite expanse of events waiting for potential nomination into significance. To grasp it, one must give it the order of a narrative. Every history, in that sense, is a construction, one out of many possible meaningful, intelligible, but *non-equivalent ways of giving it an order of unity and difference of events.* The remarkable thing about Nehru's narrative, however, is that while it effects significant displacements in the framework of modernist thinking imbibed from a liberal, economist paradigm, *it remains heavily dominated by the very structure of power it sought to repudiate.* In addition the multiplicity of his narrative which is characterised by the hybridity of genres, serves ultimately to consolidate the appropriation of many competing and unfinished stories of the Indian people into the life of a single nation marching forward to a universal, secular humanism. And all this was achieved, in the name of Reason and Progress.

In the overall analysis one discovers how each constitutive element of the text contributes to its design or structure. The inherently heteronomous mode of narration as discussed in the first section brings into play an array of key concept-metaphors which first appear to be autonomous but on a close analysis, fall into a pattern of the grand narrative of the making-of-a nation, that is, India. The creation of a national time and national past by narrative device merges imperceptibly into India's cultural heritage or tradition. Similarly the figuration of Gandhi-the-man (which marks a departure from the inherited colonial domination and initiates a new politics of the national) emerges within a careful narrative framing as one who does not stand opposed to the modern civil and scientific basis of re-writing India's story. He is in fact shown as the complementary 'other' of the truly rational and modern, thus contributing to a predetermined telos of synthesis of the ancient and modern, spiritual and scientific, all combining into the great mission of India. Thus considered we finally arrive at the most crucial and intrinsically ambivalent concept-metaphor, namely, secular democracy which incorporates both the 'modern' Indian citizen-subject and the collective 'traditional' identity of India by appealing simultaneously to a wide range of ethical, social, cultural and religious types cutting across classes and various political contradictions, assimilating them into a single vast and unified nation as whole.

If one were to look for possible 'flaws', 'omissions', 'constraints', or 'motives' in Nehru's narrative—(though it is not a very desirable task to perform: what is available to us today by way of critique was not available in Nehru's time)—it can be stated in his defense *that nationalist thought has never emerged as the antagonist of universal Reason in the arena of world history*. To attain this position, it will need to supercede itself. For ever since the Age of Enlightenment, 'Reason in its universalising mission has been parasitic upon a much less lofty, much more mundane, palpably material and singularly insidious force, namely the universalist urge of capital.'[106] To the extent that Nehru's nationalist narrative opposed colonial rule, it administered a check on a specific political form of metropolitan capitalist dominance. The nationalist ideology does not possess the apparatus of knowledge to challenge the legitimacy of the marriage between Reason and Capital. Nationalist ideology on the other hand, tends to 'resolve' the conflict between the metropolitan capital and the 'people' by absorbing the political life of various communities and nationalities, into the body of a single, homogeneous nation-state. Protected by the cultural-ideological sway of the identity between the nation and the state capital continues its 'passive revolution' by assiduously exploring the possibilities of marginal development, using the state as the principal mobiliser, planner, guarantor and legitimator of productive investment.[107]

The Discovery of India, in the ultimate analysis, proves to be a fascinating and powerful narrative of the making of a nation. Fascinating, because of its remarkable and charming construction. Nehru is indeed an incomparable storyteller, attracted by history's great spectacles as well as its silent, invisible transformation of the conditions of life. He is an observer of immense sensitivity with a fine sense of drama. Rarely does he lose his soft personal voice, or let his reader forget that it is an individual's way of making sense of history. At the same time, his narrative is immensely powerful in its subtle and dexterous employment of the 'cunning of reason'. It conceals beneath its surface as much as it reveals about its own mode of construction. And that indeed is a great source of its appeal.

Notes

1. Edward Said, *Beginnings: Intention and Method*. (New York: Basic Books, 1985), p.253.

2. Jawaharlal Nehru, *The Discovery of India* (Delhi: Asia Publishing, 1945; first edition). All subsequent reference to the text are from this edition unless otherwise indicated.
3. J.F. Lyotard and J,L. Theband, *Just Gaming*, trans. Wlad Godzich (Manchester: Manchester University Press, 1985), p.41.
4. C. Levi-Strauss, *Introduction to the Work of Marcel Mauss*, trans. F. Baker (London: Routledge, 1987).
5. Homi K. Bhabha. 'Dissemination: time, narrative, and the margins of the modern nation: in Homi K. Bhabha (ed), *Nation and Narration* (London and New York: Routledge, 1990), p.301.
6. For an excellent review of this literature—the changing role of representation in historical analysis and its dialogue with literary theory—See Hans Keller, 'Narrativity in History: Post-Structuralism and Since' *History and Theory* (September 1987), pp.1-29. Also in the same issue of the journal see John Rusen, 'Historical Narration: Foundation, Types, Reason,' pp.87-97.
7. Hayden White, *Tropics of Discourse: Essays in Cultural Criticism* (Baltimore and London: The Johns Hopkins University press, 1978).
8. Jacques Derrida's work is of course the best known example of 'pure textuality'. Also, Paul de Man's highly ironic and playful style contributes to a 'permanent revolution' in generic classification. See, for instance, Jacques Derrida, *Disseminations* (Chicago: Chicago University Press, 1985), and Paul De Man, *Allegories of Reading; Figural Language in Rousseau, Nietzche, Rilke and Proust* (New Haven: Yale University Press 1979).
9. Georg Lukacs has the distinction of positing reader subjectivity as the high point of all realist literature. The great artists of realist narrative such as Scott, Balzac and Tolstoy, according to Lukacs, invariably recount incidents as they are experienced by the principal characters whose fates are historically significant. Events have subjective meanings, shared by the principal character and by the reader who identifies with him. See Georg Lukacs, *Writer and Critic* (London: NLB, 1970) especially pp.120-127.
10. Roland Barthes, 'Introduction to the Structural Analysis of Narratives' in *Language and Language Use* (London: Heinemann Educational Books, 1980), pp.244-249.

11. Jerry White, 'Beyond Autobiography' in Raphael Samuel (ed.), *People's History and Socialist Theory* (London: Routledge and Kegan Paul, 1981), p.36.
12. Susie Tharu, 'Oral History, Narrative Strategy, and the Figures of Autobiography' in Meenakshi Mukherjee and Sudhakar Marathe (eds), *Narrative Forms and Transformation* (Delhi: Chanakya, 1986). Drawing upon a close analysis of the narratives Tharu concluded:

    '...Women are oppressed not only economically and politically but in the very forms of reasoning, signifying and symbolic exchange of culture.... They are oppressed by the apparatus of narrative...' (p.195).

13. Meenakshi Mukherjee, *Realism and Reality: The Novel and Society in India* (New Delhi: OUP, 1985). Also see her discussion of Premchand's *Godan* in 'Narrative Discontinuities: The Paradox of Godan,' Marathe, Mukherjee (ed.). *Narrative Forms and Transformations* (New Delhi: Chanakya, 1986). Mukherjee shows how inspite of Premchand's overt intention to write a novel in the mode of realism, the discourse gives way to the traditional 'Indian' style of narration. Often the realist mode of narration breaks into parables, or authorial sermonising. Also a description of the city life in the mimetic mode, as differentiated from the description of village-life, appears to be superimposed on the 'plot' of the story.
14. For a detailed discussion of contradictory aspects of Indian nationalism as they appear in the mature novels of Premchand, see Sudhir Chandra, 'Premchand and Indian Nationalism' *Modern Asian Studies,* Vol.16, No.14 (1982): 601-21.
15. This is suggested by Ayappa Pannikar in his 'foreword' to *The Growth of the Novel in India,* ed. P.K. Rajan (Delhi: Abhinav, 1989), pp.v.xi.
16. In the face of Muslim self-assertion after the formation of the all India Muslim League, the goal of making India an exclusive nation of Hindus went far beyond the realm of 'practical' politics. A subtle modification was therefore introduced by Aurobindo. Reacting sharply to the emergence of the Hindu Mahasabha in Punjab, he wrote:

Under modern conditions India can exist only as a whole... what geographical base can a Hindu nationality possess? Our ideal is an Indian nationalism, largely Hindu in its spirit and traditions, because the Hindu made the land and the people and persists, by the greatness of his past, his civilization and his culture and his invincible virility, in holding it, but wide enough also to include the Moslem and his culture and traditions and absorb them into itself. Sri Aurobindo, *Collected Works*, vol.2 (Pondicherry, Aurobindo Ashram, 1972), p.62.

17. Homi K. Bhabha, 'Introduction: Narrating the Nation', *Nation and Narration* (London and New York: Routledge, 1990), p.1. Sudipta Kaviraj writes: 'There appears to exist a necessary inversion in *nationalist historical discourse*: ordinary popular consciousness regards this search for history as a search for the past narrative of a *community already constituted*... It is by telling these stories, by this construction of the past that this community, in exactly this shape and form, comes into existence. It is partly *this narrative consciousness that determines the being of a Nation*.' See S. Kaviraj, 'On the Structure of Nationalist Discourse' in *State and Nation in the Context of Social Change,* ed. By T.V. Sathyamurthy (Delhi: OUP, 1994), p.320 (emphasis added)
18. Benedict Anderson, *Imagined Communities* (London: Verso, Press, 1983), p.19.
19. Edward Said, *The World, the Text and the Critic* (Cambridge, Mass: Harvard University Press, 1983), p.171.
20. *The Complete Works of William Hazlitt*. Ed. P.P. Howe (London: Dent, 1930-4), Vol.4, pp.67-8.
21. Vivekananda, for instance, delivered the following speech to a group of young men and women in Madras after his historic success as a religious preacher and exponent of Hinduism in the West:

    Children of India, I am here to speak to you today about some practical things, and my object in reminding you about the glories of the past is simply this: Look back as far as you can, drink deep of the eternal fountains that are behind, and after that look forward, march forward, and make India brighter, greater, much higher than she ever was. Our ancestors were great. We must first recall that. We must learn the elements of our being, the blood that courses in our veins; we must have faith in that blood and consciousness of past greatness, we must build an India yet greater than what she has been...

The Complete Works of Swami Vivekananda, Vol.III (Calcutta: Advaita, 1960), pp.285-6.

22. Simon During 'Literature—Nationalism's Other? The Case for Revision' in Home Bhabha (ed.), *Nation and Narration*, p.143.
23. Paul Ricoeur, 'Narrative Time', *Critical Inquiry* (Autumn 1980), p.178.
24. Ibid.
25. Ibid.
26. Ibid.
27. Ibid.
28. Ibid, p.179.
29. Ibid.
30. Ibid.
31. Martin Heidegger, *Being and Time*, trans. John Macquarrie and Edward Robin (New York: 1962).
32. Ricoeur, p.182.
33. Ibid.
34. Quoted in F. Jameson, *Marxism and Form* (Princeton J.N., 1971), p.279.
35. Romila Thapar, *Cultural Transaction and Early India: Tradition and Patronage* (Delhi: Oxford University Press, 1987), Thapar writes:

I would like to look at those constituents of Hindu communal ideology which claim legitimacy from the past, namely that there has always been a well-defined and *historically evolved religion* which we now call Hinduism and an equally *clearly defined Hindu community*.... The modern description of Hinduism has been largely that of a brahmana dominated religion which *to gather itself in a somewhat paternalistic pattern a variety of sects* drawing a range of Buddhists, Jainas, Vaishnavas, Saivas and Saktas... the text and traditions were viewed as inspirational, initially orally preserved, with multiple manifestations of deities, priests but no church, a plurality of doctrines with a seeming absence of controversies and all this somehow integrated into a single religious fabric.

...Scholarship (has) *tended to ignore the significance of the popular manifestations of religion in contrast to the textual*...the two epics, the Mahabharata and Ramayana, frequently treated as primarily the religious literature of the vaishnavas, are originally epics, civilizational symbols. They were, at one level, carriers of ethical traditions and were used again by a variety of religious sects to propagate their own particular ethic, a situation which is evident from the diverse treatment of the theme of the Ramayana in Valmiki, in the Buddhist Vessantara and Vamacharyam of Vamalasuri. The epic versions were also used for purposes of political legitimation. The primarily vaishnava religious function of the epics develops gradually and comes to fruition in the second millennium A.D. with clearly defined sects worshipping Rama or Krishna coinciding with the development of what has been called the puranic religion. Subsequent to this were various tribal adaptations of the Ramayana and these were less concerned with the Vaishnava message and more with articulating their own social fears and aspirations.

Also see her, 'Imagined religious communities? Ancient History and the Modern Search for a Hindu Identity', *Modern Asian Studies,* Vol.23, No.2 (1989), pp.216-7 (emphasis added)

36. In Lacanian vocabulary, the Imaginary involves a misrecognition through which the individual identifies with his or her unified image in the mirror. When applied to the realm of social relations, the corresponding stage involves a deflection of the specular 'I' into a social 'I' as the ego replaces I as the 'subject' of the imaginary relation to the object.

    See Jacques Lacan, *Ecrits: A Selection* trans. Alan Sheridan (New York: Norton and Co., 1977), pp.1-7.

37. The building of a nation involves crating an 'affective' space. Tharu and Lalita in their study of the formation of gender

relations as they are mediated by the demands of a nation-in-making, say:

It is important, therefore, as we attempt to understand the representational practices of the nation and the politics of gender implicit in them, to plot out the terrain as one which is constantly being re-formed; equally important to conceive of as they are composed. In distinct contrast to other critical efforts to define an ancient and timeless 'Indian sensibility' or locate the 'authentic Indian' our attempt here is to plot the nation and nationality, not as an essence, but as a historically constituted terrain, changing and contestable, and its citizen-subjects as always 'in process'.

See 'Introduction', *Women Writing in India, 600 B.C. to the Present Vol.II. The Twentieth Century*, ed. Susie Tharu and K. Lalita (New York: The Feminist Press 1993), p.53.

38. Although *The Discovery of India* is silent on the peasant uprising, Nehru's position on it is not hard to discern. In his earlier book, *An Autobiography* (Reprinted Delhi: OUP, 1980) he writes that the peasants, left to their own devices, often rebelled. But these 'upheavals' were only 'symptoms of a deep-seated unrest' (p.63). Where they lasted, the countryside would be 'afire with enthusiasm' (9,51), and the peasants would seem 'to expect strange happenings which would, as if by a miracle, put an end to their long misery' (p.52), But the uprisings 'were always spontaneous and localised... The Indian *Kisans* have little staying power, little energy to resist for long' (p.62).
There is enough historical evidence by now to contradict the thesis that peasant insurrections were purely spontaneous and unpremeditated affairs. Indeed their initiatives went against the interest of the Indian National Congress, and its 'passive revolution:. For historical details see Gyan Pandey, 'Peasant Revolt and Indian Nationalism: the Peasant Movement in Awadh, 1911-1922' in Ranajit Guha ed., *Subaltern Studies*, vol. I (Delhi: OUP, 1982), pp.143-97: and Majid Hayaat Siddiqui, Agrarian Unrest in North India: *The United Provinces, 1918-22* (New Delhi: Vikas, 1978). Ranajit Guha in his much celebrated essay 'The prose of Counter-Insurgency' *Subaltern Studies*, Vol.II (1983), writes:

To rebel was indeed *to destroy many of those familiar* signs which the peasant had learned to read and manipulate in order to extract a meaning out of the harsh world around him and live with it. The risk in 'turning things upside down' under these conditions was indeed so great that he could hardly afford to engage in such a project in a state of absent-mindedness (pp.1-42).

39. Ambedkar's position on political rights for untouchables, articulated in testimony to the Simon Commission, urged joint electorates for both the Depressed Classes and the *Muslims* but with adult suffrage and reserved seats, as well as some special attention to the education and employment of the Depressed Classes in government positions. In the midst of the 'Clamour' in London in the 1932 Round Table Conference where every minority demands an election process in which they alone would elect their representatives, Ambedkar changed his position to one demanding separate electorate for Untouchables.

    Gandhi opposed Ambedkar in London, but his most effective opposition came later in 1932, after the Communal Award of the British government granted separate electorates. Gandhi began a fast unto death in the cell in the Yeravada Prison in Poona, with the insistence that the award engineered by the British to separate the 'Untouchables' from the Hindu society be withdrawn. An entire book on this episode by Pyarelal entitled *The Epic Fast* (Ahmedabad: Bhatt, 1932) which tells the story from the Gandhian point of view illustrates the dramatic impact of the Gandhi-Ambedkar clash. Ambedkar's side of the Poona fast and a general polemic against the Gandhian and Congress position was published later. See B.R. Ambedkar, *What Congress and Gandhi Have Done to the Untouchables* (Bombay: Thacker and Co., 1945). Ambedkar's full program is detailed in 'The Annihilation of Caste' First published in 1936 and reprinted in *Dr. Babasaheb Ambedkar: Writings and Speeches,* vol. I Bombay: Education Department, Government of Maharashtra, 1959). Also for an excellent exposition of Ambedkar's side vis-à-vis Jawaharlal Nehru and Gandhi, see Marc Galanter, *Competing Equalities: Law and Backward Classes in India* (Berkeley: University of California Press, 1984).

40. Jayaprakash Narayan, who founded the Congress Socialist Party in 1934 along with Acharya Narendra Dev and later broke away

from the Congress party on ideological issues, had his own theory of the nation and social change. See his *Nation Building in India* (Varanasi: Navchetana Prakashan, 1957), especially Chapter VI 'The Concept of Nationhood', pp.377-428.

41. Ram Manohar Lohia (1910-1967) also helped in the formation of congress socialist party and launched an English weekly *The Congress Socialist.* If 'Culture' and 'Caste' in the Indian Context can be said to be the 'unthought' of Indian Marxism, Lohia was one of the earliest to broach these issues. He denounced the policy of economistic determinism, and a bureaucratic rationality which sustained it. He was one of the staunchest and earliest critics of Nehru to emphasise that Nehru was unable to understand the close connection between advances in European technology and British imperialism in India. In his book, *Wheel of History* (Hyderabad: Samta Vidyalaya, 1955) Lohia writes:

The industrial revolution in Europe and what followed it belonged to a unique historical situation, incapable of repetition in Asia and Africa. Too little land and too many men and too few tools are mark of Asia, so that application of the technique of mass production is utterly impossible... political and economic ideologies must be related to concrete historical situation and no greater tragedy can occur than to think of capitalism or communism and even socialism unrelated to history and geography. Existing technology made possible by the imperialist control which European Civilization exercises over the rest of the world is no longer valid. The Bessmer process in Europe for instance, which was a basis for developing its industry fructified with the opening of the Suez Canal and proved prosperous when a sector of Indian agriculture was commercialised. This historical process proceeded in such fashion that every industrial and technical advance of Western Europe, which led to greater concentration of capital, was paired correspondingly by a dynamics of an empire-colony relationship. *The technology of modern Europe is an imperialist technology in origin and in current substance is incapable of reproduction all over the world* (P. 60). (emphasis added)

Elsewhere Lohia writes about the 'making of a different nation from that of the imagination of Mr. Nehru...' It is worth quoting him at some length:

A vested interest socialism (as advocated by Nehru) talks of political and economic revolution alone, meaning thereby the award of increased wages of bonus on the lowest level and the destruction of private property in factories and the like on the highest level. Even in Europe of changing classes, *such a 'revolution' would keep intact the distinction between manual workers and those with the brain.* In India of fixed castes, this distinction would spell ruin to the health of society. Workers with the brain are a fixed caste in Indian society; together with the solider caste, they are the high caste. Even after the completed economic and political revolution, they would continue to supply the managers of the State and of Industry... that is why the intelligentsia of India which is over-whelmingly high-caste, abhors all talks of a *mental and social revolution of a radical change in respect of language or caste or the base of thought.* Five thousand years have gone into the building of the undisputed 'merit' (of the upper caste). A true doctrine of equal opportunity would have to undo the work of five thousand years by giving *preferential treatment* to the lower castes. *India's political parties, Congress or Communist are, under Mr. Nehru's leadership, thoroughly hostile to the award of preferential treatment* on any large scale. They denounce it as a caste-motivated measure while they are themselves viciously caste-ridden, perhaps unknowingly... (emphasis added) Rammanohar Lohia, *The Caste System* (Hyderabad Samta Vidyalaya, 1964), p.97.

42. Manabendra Nath Roy (1887-1945) was a most 'remarkable failure' in the history of the Indian national movement. I discuss his position in some detail, particularly in relation to Gandhi, in the main body of this section.
43. Ashis Nandy, *The Intimate Enemy* (Delhi: OUP, 1983).
44. Ibid., p.55.
45. See M.N. Roy, 'An Indian Communist Manifesto' in G. Adhikari (ed.), *Document of the History of the Communist Party of India,* vol.II. (Delhi: People's Publishing House, 1971), p.346.
46. Ibid., p.349.
47. Ibid.
48. See Rajni Palme Dutt, *India Today* (Bombay: People's Publishing House, 1949).

49. Partha Chatterjee, *Nationalist Thought and the Colonial World: A Derivative Discourse?* (Delhi: OUP, 1986), p.100.
50. Ibid., p.90.
51. Ibid., p.91.
52. Ibid., p.92.
53. M.K. Gandhi, 'Enlightened Anarchy: A Political Ideal' *Collected Works of Mahatma Gandhi* (New Delhi, Publications Division, 1958), Vol.x., p.18 quoted in Chatterjee, p.93.
54. Partha Chatterjee, p.93.
55. Ibid., p.100.
56. Ibid.
57. Ibid, p.102.
58. *Selected Works of Jawaharlal Nehru*, 15 vols. (New Delhi: Orient Longman, 1972-82), vol.3,p.3.
59. Sudipta Kaviraj, 'The Heteronomous Radicalism of M.N. Roy' in *Political Thought in Modern India*, edited by Thomas Pantham and K.L. Deutsch (New Delhi: Sage, 1986), p.229.
60. Ibid.
61. Ibid.
62. Ibid.
63. Ibid.
64. Ibid., p.230.
65. Fredric Jameson, *The Political Unconscious* (London: Metheun, 1981). For Jameson, the recovery of the symbolic is coeval with the waking of the collective unconscious. See esp.pp.17-23.
66. Shahid Amin, 'Gandhi as Mahatma: Gorakhpur district, Eastern U.P., 1921-2' *Subaltern Studies*, Vol.III, pp.1-62.
67. Gyanendra Pandey has also argued that the myth of Mahatma was deliberately created by the congress leaders, including Jawaharlal Nehru. Taking the specific example of the peasants in the Awadh region in Uttar Pradesh, who had started a massive rebellion against the Zamindars in 1921, Pandey argues that the rebellion was sought to be suppressed at the behest of Jawaharlal Nehru who invoked the supremacy of the Gandhian non-violent methods. In Faizabad Division Nehru asked the peasants to 'give

up organising meetings...' and although the recent *Rent Act* had made their position worse, they should 'pay their rents and keep the welfare of the country in view... You should give up organising meetings as well as disturbances and *leave it to Gandhi to win Swaraj'* See Gyan Pandey, 'Peasant Revolt and Indian Nationalism', *Subaltern Studies,* Vol.I., pp.157-159.

Pandey also gives a fascinating British report on the rising figure of the Mahatma which is worth quoting in full:

The currency which Mr. Gandhi's name has acquired even in the remotest villages is astonishing. No one seems to know quite who or what he is, but it is an accepted fact that what he orders must be done. He is a *Mahatma*, or a *Sadhu*, a *Pandit*, a *Brahmin* who lives at Allahabad, even a *Deota.* One man said he was a merchant who sells cloth at three *annas* a yard... It is the curious instance of the power of a name. The curious thing is that as a general rule Gandhi is not thought of as antagonistic to the [British] government, but only to the Zamindars. The reformed councils are just a rise of the Zamindars. We are for Gandhiji and the Sarkar [They say]...

Generous remissions of land revenue would be the first requisite (to avert the Kisan Movement)... If the land tenure Act is tackled in a liberal manner as the first Business of the new council, Mr. Gandhi's name will probably fade from peoples memories as quickly as did that of the Germans after the first excitement at the outbreak of great war. (Government of India, Home Department, Political Branch Deposit, Feb.1921. Signed P.Biggane. Quoted in Pandey, p.159)

68. Extract from Nehru's Presidential Address to the Lucknow session of the Congress held in April 1936. Quoted in Asghar Ali Engineer, 'Secularism and Nation Building' *Jawaharlal Nehru Centenary Volume.* (Delhi: Oxford University Press, 1989), pp.212-22.

69. Ibid.

70. Quoted in S. Gopal (ed.), *Jawaharlal Nehru: An Anthology* (Delhi: OUP, 1980), p.330.

71. For an elaboration of this statement see Gyanendra Pandey, *The Construction of Communalism in Colonial North India* (Delhi: OUP,) 1990. See particularly pp.302.

72. Ashis Nandy, 'The Politics of Secularism and the Recovery of Religious Tolerance', *The Book Review*, vol. XIV, No.6, pp.233-9.
73. Ibid., p.23.
74. Ibid.
75. Ibid., p.24.
76. Ibid., p.29.
77. E.M.S. Namboodripad, 'The Programme Explained'(Calcutta: Dec.1966), quoted in F. Frankel, *India's Political Economy* (London: Polity Press, 1978), p.343.
78. Miller, 'Six Theses on the Question of Religion and Politics in India Today', *Economic and Political Weekly* (July 25), 1978, p.2172.
79. Ibid.
80. Anil Nauriya, 'Relationship between state and Religion: Antinomies of Passive Revolution: '*Economic and Political Weekly* (February 25), 1989, pp.405-6.
81. Ibid.
82. Quoted in Nauriya, pp.405-6.
83. Nauriya, p.406.
84. Ravinder Kumar, 'The Secular Culture of India' *Nehru Memorial Museum Library* (NMML), *Occasional paper*, No.18, p.21.
85. Sumit Sarkar, *Modern India 1985-1947* (Delhi: Macmillan, 1983), p.84.
86. Tom Nairn, *The Break-up of Britain* (London: Verso, 1978), p.340.
87. This is developed by Sudipta Kaviraj, 'A Critique of the Passive Revolution', *Economic and Political Weekly* (Nov.1988), pp.24-31.
88. Sudipta Kaviraj, p.2430 argues that the form of 'democracy' which arose historically in India after the colonial experience, is an instance of the thesis developed by Marx that it is the democratic form which suits the capitalist mode of production most properly.
89. A discussion on this is presented by Chhatrapati Singh, *Law between Anarchy and Utopia* (Delhi: OUP, 1985), esp. pp.72-110.

Also see Rajeev Dhavan and Thomas Paul (ed.) *Nehru and the Constitution* (The Indian Law Institute: Delhi, 1992).

90. Ibid.

91. Ibid.

92. An historical understanding of the coalition or alliances between various classes [which would roughly correspond to high caste as well] is crucial to the analysis of the development of national democracy in India. Traditional Marxist accounts of the ruling coalition suffered because they saw the bureaucratic elite as being too straightforwardly subordinate to the power of the bourgeoisie, and saw what was basically a coalitional and bargaining relation as a purely instrumental one... See Kaviraj, p.2439.

93. Alok Rai, 'Added Only in Parts: Strange Case of Indian Secularism', *Economic and Political Weekly* (December 16, 1989), pp.2771-73.

94. Ibid.

95. Alok Rai, p.2771.

96. Contemporary discussions of Human Rights, especially in the context of India, which otherwise show a great deal of complexity in the formulation and framing of the question of 'rights' vis-à-vis the State, do not seem to pay enough attention to this issue of subjectivity, or more precisely, the *techniques of the formation of subject employed by the State, where secularism is a key trope.* See, for instance, Upendra Baxi, *The Future of Human Rights* (Delhi: Oxford University Press, 2002); Charles Taylor 'Conditions of Unenforced consensus on Human Rights' *The East Asian Challenges for Human Rights* in J.R. Baner and Daniel Bell (eds.) (Cambridge: C.U.P., 1999) and R.M Unger, *What should Legal Analysis Become?* (London: Verso, 1996).

97. Michel Foucault, 'The Subject and Power', *Critical Inquiry* (Summer 1982), p.783.

98. *Jawaharlal Nehru: An Autobiography* (Reprinted, Delhi OUP, 1980), pp.422-3.

99. Ibid., p.432.

100. Ibid., p.417.

101. Ibid., p.419
102. Ibid., p.427
103. Upendra Baxi, 'The Recovery of Fire: Nehru and Legitimation of Power in India' *Economic and Political Weekly* (January 13, 1990), p.108.
104. Ibid., p.108.
105. Ibid.
106. Partha Chatterjee, *Nationalist Thought and the Colonial World.* p.168.
107. Ibid., pp.168-9.

4

Salman Rushdie and the Irreconcilable 'Longing for Form' in *Midnight's Children*

I
Preamble

Salman Rushdie's fiction compels our [the subject-position of a non-definitive, even if culturally subjugated reader] attention to the basic proposition that the problems of meaning, form and representation that beset the 'third world' are indeed very different from the slippage of meaning and of the 'real' which confront academic discourses arising from Europe and North America. Despite a call for the 'provincialisation of Europe' in certain quarters it can hardly be overemphasised that both meaning and the need to locate meaning are conjunctural; and hence, the so called universal problematic of hermeneutics can also be seen as a narrowly historical one. The post-modern cultural paraphernalia along with the valorization of the collage, and fragmented, quicksilver ways of seeing and knowing have become the 'frame' through which the historical and cultural products of the 'third world' are placed and assessed in the fast growing global markets. Rushdie's highly stylised narrative may well have become the prototype of a new genre: a metafiction of the 'third world' literature where mythic and historical, fabulous and rational, comic and ironic, jostle all too easily into a spectacular pastiche of non-mimetic forms.

II
Modernism and the Politics of Textuality

There are many strands interlocked in Rushdie's narrative style. It might, at first sight, appear to be a parody of the epic, the realist and the autobiographical modes that jostle too rapidly in traditional Indian folktales, and *puranic* modes of storytelling. In this medley of 'surprise' and 'innovation' there is a definitive sense in which Rushdie carries forward the modernist problematic of knowledge and representation. The fragmentation of the individual subject within the modernist project of 'alienation' is deftly transformed into a post-modernist aesthetic of dispersal of meaning. In Rushdie's text the organising role of individual perception, which had earlier legitimised perspective and the cohesive concept of 'art', has lost its ability to bind the fragment into a whole. Indeed both the idea of 'art' and 'perspective' are interrogated and unmade by Rushdie's post-modernism. All the same there are distinct ideological and historical continuities between a liberal-modernism and the polyphonus, 'carnivalesque' post-modernism of Rushdie. Let us pursue this parallel briefly.

Liberalism undertook a transformation of the internal epistemological crisis of the West and sought to project this crisis as the ontological essence of the East. In other words, the internal contradiction between classes at 'home' and between the metropolitan capital and the colony (which has assumed ideological form of debate between free-will and determinism, or between reason and the irrational) were resolved by a liberal-modernist ontology of the soul whose source was India, or more generally, the spirit of East. As Williams points out, modernism is 'governed by the unevenness...of a class-society, which along with its mobility and dislocation finds a house within the imperial metropolis leading to a characteristic experience of estrangement and exposure'.[1] Such an experience is then catapulted into an act of cultural self-definition made at a time when colonial territories are being reparceled and emergent nationalisms are beginning to present the early outlines of 'decolonisation'.[2] The easy, freewheeling absorption of modernism in the act of cultural definition coincided with, and indeed was dependent upon, a rigorous documentation, inventory, and reclassification of 'third world' cultural products by the museum, library and archive.[3] Thus considered, modernism as a literary and cultural phenomenon is unthinkable without the archive, for the archive is repository of the net results of the political and economic relations of colonialism.[4] The destabilising of the image effected by literary modernism is extended by post-modernism as it continues to invade the mysterious, inarticulate or simply-anti-mimetic forms of the 'third world'.

As the colonial project of Industrial Capitalism is replaced by the subtle network of multinational capital, the ideological form through which legitimacy may be sought change, and become more diffuse than ever before. Post-modernism emerges at this juncture which is characterised by a *rapid textualisation* of the geographically 'lost' terrains and its much valorised skepticism can be viewed as both symptom and critique of the contemporary socio-economic formation of the West. The writing that emerges from this position, however self-critical or ironic, has a tendency to universalise its own epistemological preoccupations with the absence of meaning, the impossibility of history, the fracture of subjectivity or, more generally, the lack of a centre, in the text. And it is precisely here that the greatest paradox of the so-called 'third world' novel can be seen. Given conditions of illiteracy, economic and social deprivation and lack of reading time, the

English novel has been an elitist and minority form in developing countries like India in comparison with poetry, song and films. Almost inevitable, it has been the form through which a thin, foreign-educated stratum (however sensitive or committed to domestic political interest) has communicated to a metropolitan reading public. Empire, it would appear, has allowed cosmopolitan form to play a national role, only in an international arena. In a metafictional extravaganza Rushdie treats the story of an entire region, slowly coming to think of itself as one, with deep comic sarcasm, because in his perception an emerging nationalist politics is confined to the 'demagogy of a caste of domestic sell-outs and power-brokers' only.[5]

In a somewhat similar vein Aijaz Ahmed laments over the aftermath of 'decolonisation' of India:

> What we witnessed was just the British policy of divide and rule, which surely was there, but our own willingness to break up our civilizational unity, to kill our neighbours ...the major-fictions of the 50s and 60s... came out of that refusal to forgive what we ourselves had done and were still doing in one way or another, to our own policy.[6]

Fredric Jameson, in his essay on the 'national allegory' argues that the third world novel is for most part socially unrealistic and that it is unable to offer the satisfaction of a *Proust or a Joyce* with their 'rhythm of modernist/ innovation'.[7] Jameson is unable to perceive the different kinds of innovation at work here which result from creating a new aesthetic of socio-political contradictions. Rather, he perceives 'third world' literature simply as an important artefact or record. In the process he obscures its abundance, diversity, and *irreconcilable* contradiction—factors which enable its production—by reducing complex fictions to totalities that might be 'mapped'. To suggest as Jameson does that the corpus of third world literature 'as a whole' is caught in a derivative aesthetics of European realism, is to give air to the suspicion that while it can be described it is not worth engaging with. With these assumptions, the metropolitan reader is only too delighted—and surprised—to find authors like Rushdie who treat their material with sophistication and who reinforce dominant tastes in a characteristically dual fashion—not in reluctant submission to values branded on to the skin of their cultures, but as participants in a new world literature, with apprentice like devotion to a mind-boggling array of literary precursors across regions, traditions and styles, from Jonathan Swift, Milan Kundera, Gunter Grass to Garcia Marquez.

The problems of meaning, form and representation that beset the 'third world' are indeed very different from the slippage of meaning and of real which currently confront academic discourse of Europe and America. This, however, does not imply that one can find essential 'truth' of an indigenous variety by applying a more authentic method of inquiry, It is, on the other hand, to emphasise that both meaning and the need to locate meaning are *conjunctural;* and hence, the epistemological problem of the West is itself *a narrowly historical one.* As the world contracts into the western supermarket, an increasingly eurocentric perspective is brought to bear upon 'third world' cultural products. (This tendency has gained further poignancy after the Soviet collapse, and the anti-teleological, anti-master narrative dismay of Euro-American Marxism). The new post-modern cultural paraphernalia along with its quicksilver way of seeing and knowing, then, becomes the 'frame' through which the cultural products of the rest of the world are known placed and assessed in the global market.

There is however, a definitive sense in which the West expands, and its expansion is characterised by a marking out of 'economic zones' and a complex codification of cultural artefacts through which the peripheral third world cultures must respond to, and palpitate the centre. Centre-periphery perspectives such as Jameson's are in fact based on a homology between economic and cultural domination and relegate the 'third world' to an unenviable position of a permanent yet 'desired' challenge to the engulfing 'centre' of western sovereignty. And it must be emphasised that the literary form which takes birth at the site of such 'opposition' to the centre is a kind of parody, ironic laughter, pastiche, or other variations along the continuum of this genre.

Parody in the conventional sense has always had an ulterior motive. It is satiric mimicry of an act or discourse underwritten by 'reformist' impulse, or by the conviction that alongside the abnormal tongue one has momentarily borrowed, some healthy linguistic normality still exists. In the post-modernist application of this genre, however, any consciousness of foundational criterion, or norms of the non-deviant, or normal, or sane, is altogether absent. The genre is devoid of historical memory. For all these reasons, one might say that *pastiche, rather than parody*, is the appropriate form of post-modernist culture.[8] Pastiche is endless imitation bordering on speech in a deal language. To repeat a gesture thus drains it of its shock value and its ironic impulse, leaving nothing beyond brute fact. In replacing parody by pastiche late capitalism inverts its own logic and proclaims that if the artefact is a commodity, *the commodity can also be an artefact*.[9] Thus art models itself upon a commodity form which is 'already invested with aesthetic allure in a sealed circle.[10]

Reading *Midnight's Children* in the above context is a difficult task since this text responds to the post-modernist aesthetic in complex ways, pitching its textual politics often in no man's land between a parody and pastiche. To put it more positively while *Midnight's Children* attempts to parody the various forms of legitimisation of dominance embedded in the birth of a nation, that is India, its own style of representation resembles a sick joke at the expense of the subversive function of avant-garde art, whose major impulse was to dismantle the institutional autonomy of art and erase the frontiers between culture and political society, and return aesthetic production to its humble, unprivileged place within social practice as a whole[11].' For elaboration of this summary statement let us enter the labyrinthine textual universe of *Midnight's Children.*

III
Parody or Pastiche

Midnight's Children[12] has been widely acclaimed as a literary *tour de* force. It has won plaudits for its author, from critics throughout the Anglo-saxon world and has been awarded the prestigious Booker prize. Rushdie has been compared, at different times, to Gunter Grass and Gabriel Garcia Marquez whose influences, openly acknowledged, are evident in *Midnight's Children.* Saleem Sinai, the semi-autobiographical narrator and central figure in the book, has definite affinities with Oskar in *The Tin Drum* and perhaps it would not be difficult to find the Latin American equivalents of the sub-continent's generals in *Autumn of the Patriarch.*[13] Besides these surface analogies, some critics have also discovered Marquazian 'magic realism' in the novel. Foregrounding of style, syncopated dialogue, constant shifts of chronological sequence, a highly self-conscious and repetitive narrative mode and fusion of historical with fantastical—all point to a keen awareness of metafictional trends in fiction and a desire to break away from realism and from the assumptions governing the growth of the average Indo-Anglian novel. Rushdie's text exemplifies the oft-repeated principal that the reader half-creates the text she receives.

Art has already begun to mirror theory, and the implied contract between writer and reader is one whose small print the novelist is showing himself well able to interpret to his own advantage, and to turn into the defensive subject matter of his work. Thus the power-struggle is no longer between author, inner world, outer world and text. The reader has also entered the tussle and the novelist seem more than willing to 'share' in the reader's anxiety as well as assault on the intransigence of both art and life. It is difficult to avoid contemporary critical questions, most specifically, questions regarding 'reader-response' when approaching *Midnight's Children.* Rushdie carefully *builds them into* his narrative strategies. Theory about reading is forced to confront practice in writing if the text is to receive a serious discussion. The narrator Saleem Sinai points this out in an ironic sideways glance at the construction of his story:

> Reality can have metaphorical content. A thousand and one children were born: there were a thousand and one possibilities, which had been present in one place at one time before: and there were a thousand and one dead ends. *Midnight's Children* can be made to represent many things, according to your point of view: they can be seen as the last throw of everything antiquated and regressive in our myth ridden nation, whose defeat was entirely desirable in the context of a modernising twentieth-century economy: or as the hope of freedom, which is now forever extinguished ... [p.267].

The thousand and one midnight's children, born in the hour of Indian independence and possessed of various miraculous and magical talents, 'are both tellers and, like their Arabian analogues, tales.'[14] And this image of the writer as both master and victim of the so-called division between public and private spaces and materials, which has shaped his or her experience, and which the writer is in run attempting to shape, keenly informs the writing of the text. The reality of *public history, of private experience* is never reducible to the encompassing or absolutist forms that conventional writer may want to impose upon them. Therefore, Rushdie's protagonists, narrators and readers make 'imaginative' connections transmuting historical fiction into fact and vice versa, and when they gossip they are supposed to 'blend reality with imaginative truth, giving a *semantics*, a system of meaning *to the teeming events of history.*'[15] If the task of historical documentation is ponderously immense and dishonest, patterns of inner meaning can, according to the textual practice of Rushdie, only emerge from selective juxtapositions, partial viewing, re-creation, collage or, as Saleem Sinai puts it, by making 'pickles of history which possess the authentic taste of truth' [p.295].

The fragmentation of the narrative style permits to and fro temporal movement, and a capacious space to the chief narrator, Saleem. He is now with Tai, the boatman and his grandfather by the Dal lake in Kashmir, now with the language rioters in Bombay, now with the *Mukti Bahini* in Bangladesh, and now in Jallianwala Bagh witnessing the mass massacre by General Dyer's army, now back again with Padma, his chief interlocutor in a pickle factory, the site of writing for this novel. Such restlessness can only be accommodated by adopting a narrative style that permits fragmentation. The ideal mode of such discourse is '*Gossip*': an under-rated, conversational medium for private criticism gossip is used anew by Rushdie as a devastating literary weapon against the claims of historical truth and religious morality.[16] Within the linguistic space of the novel, Rushdie's native cassandras and '*Tiresiases*'[17] liberated by their fantastical powers to penetrate and dissolve several selves, to traverse time and space with ease, may 'home in unannounced on the most private of public moments'.[18] Multifarious births, copulations, tomfoolery, voyeurism, and regenerative deaths come within their purview. No wonder the act of narration itself seems to approximate to fine gossip. The narrator's own style can be likened to a character in the novel, named Durga, the washer woman, who stands as a metaphor for a rare gift of gossip:

> She was as full of gossip and tittle-tattle as she was of milk ...everyday a dozen new stories gushed from her lips. she was a monster who forgot each day the moment ended... Her name, even before I met her, had the smell of new things; she represented novelty, beginnings, the advent of new stories, events, and complexities [p.445].

Since gossip functions in Rushdie as exposé, common codes of verbal propriety are broken with impunity. Blasphemy, obscenity, and scatological detail can be justified for 'the inner story'. As it allows narration in scraps, shreds, fragments, one may take a short cut through to the delightful, scandalous or voyeuristic moments of a story, skipping the labourious tasks of making connection, and evading the dreaded term, causality. 'The one thing you learn as historian is just how fragmented and ambiguous and peculiar the historical record is,' remarks Rushdie in his Bandung file interview.[19] This is shown clearly in the novel by the metaphor of the *perforated sheet* through which Saleem's grandfather Aadam Aziz originally glimpses parts of a patient of his, who later becomes his wife. The point apparently being made is that the forever incomplete image of reality, of history, is apprehended only in bits, part by part, by reconstructing the missing links. As Saleem, the narrator puts it:

> So gradually Dr. Aziz came to have a picture of Naseem in his mind, a badly fitting collage of her severally inspected parts. Glued together by his imagination, she accompanied him on all his rounds, so that waking and sleeping he could feel in his finger-tips the softness of her ticklish skin or the perfect tiny wrists, or the beauty of the ankles... but she was headless because he had never seen her face [p.25].

The problematic relationship of the artist with the reality that one attempts to record is given fullest subsidiary embodiment in Saleem's uncle Hanif. He is film-director and script-writer obsessed with documentary realism in an industry whose Indian stock-in trade is illusion and fantasy, its products defined by Eastern Westerners enthusiastically patronised by Rashid, the rickshaw boy. Hanif's main ambition is to make a film about 'the ordinary life of a pickle factory' a task which presages the pickle factory, both literal and metaphorical, that Saleem eventually works up as representation of his successful compromise with art and life. Hanif's refusal to compromise his objective realist vision means that his script is never produced, and he is forced to work out the logic of his absolutist position in a secondary sphere of activity that is within his own keeping:

> My uncle Hanif played rummy dedicatedly; but he was in the thrall of a curious obsession—namely, that he was determined never to lay down a hand until he completed a thirteen-card sequence in hearts. Always hearts; all the hearts and nothing but the hearts would do. In his quest for this unattainable perfection my uncle would discard perfectly good threes-of-a-kind whole sequence of spades, clubs, diamonds [p.240].

For the artist who pursues comprehensiveness, pure sequence, and manipulative control, the cost is high and the eventual out come, even when it has the passing appearance of success, is failure. Thus Rushdie confronts directly the fallibility of the writer and the *partialness of vision.* Writing in the *London Review of Books,* Rushdie acknowledges that 'my India was just that ...a version and no more than one version of all the hundreds of millions of possible versions' and further reveals that 'this is why I made my narrator, Saleem, suspect in his narration: his mistakes are the mistakes of fallible memory compounded by quirks of characters and of circumstance, and his vision is fragmentary.'[20]

Narrative fallibility is thus qualified by the undeniable shape that Saleem's story, through a circuitous discourse of gossip, eventually assumes. This shape is supposed to be brought about by the engagement of narrator with listener,'[21] of Saleem with the surrogate reader Padma, within the novel. For if Saleem's uncertainties are a part of Rushdie's solution to the problem of authorial subjectivity and partialness, Padma to whom Saleem's story is substantially told and whose irascible presence fuels the momentum of his narrative, is another part of that 'solution'. The participatory but implicit contract that Rushdie has with his reader, a contract premised on the reader's knowledge of the conventions and deceptions of the narrative act, is ironically imaged in the relationship that Saleem has with Padma who has no time for the problem of the narration and wants straight, unburdened real stories in the here-and-now. Padma, named after the lotus Goddess, whose most common appellation amongst village-folk is 'the one who possesses dung' is model for the imperious reader. Constantly demanding completion of a story that has no end, narration becomes for her an irritatingly bewildering collection of circuitous leads:

> But here is Padma at my elbow, bullying my back into the world of linear narrative, the universe of what-happened-next... fighting down the proper pride of the successfull storyteller. I attempt to educate her. Things—even people—have a way of leaking into each other, I explain, like flavours when you cook... the past has dripped into me. Her shrug cuts me off.. [pp.38-39].

The need to effect a relationship between narrator and listener which will meet their conflicting priorities and inclusiveness is constantly deferred, even as it is openly acknowledged by Saleem. Deprived of a strong recipient for his kind of narrative, the narrator 'loses' meaning, the pursuit of which he has given at the novel's inception as his main impetus:

> How to dispense with Padma? How to give up her ignorance and superstition that necessarily counterweighs to my miracle laden omniscience? How to do without her paradoxical earthiness of spirit, which keeps—kept my feet on the ground? I have become,

it seem to me, the apex of an isosceles triangle, supported equally by twin deities, the wild God of memory and lotus Goddess of present [p.149].

Thus the reader/listener, deity of the narrator's present to whom he offers up the narrative, has equal status with memory. The 'eventual imminent marriage of Saleem with Padma, of impotent narrator with lustful reader,'[22] on which the novel ends, 'evokes in the unconsummated sexual terms that have defined throughout Saleem's dealings with Padma, the uneasy reconciliation of the often conflicting imperatives of author and reader.[23]

By dramatising the symbiotic relationship between narrator and audience, which grows out of that between a personal and public past on the one hand and a narrative present on the other, Rushdie asks for a *collaborative basis* for all literary activity. *Midnight's Children* then, is intended to be a novel concerned with the *imperfection of any narrative act*—a novel about the compromises which govern the relationship of writer with a reader who is supposedly hungry for 'linearity', and the impossibility of a 'reality', however much concerned with public history, that is not petrified into subjective form at the point at which a writer attempts to render it. In sum it is a novel whose *principal preoccupation* seems to be the *questioning of the credentials of the novelist* and of the illusory surface objectivity of the novel form. However, the issue is, who is it that insists on the *impossible demands* of reality, *or objective history*, or *wholeness*? On the other hand, by keeping the issue at the 'centre' of the novel, one might argue, Rushdie acquiesces to a world-view which underwrites the politics of the *proliferation of narrative desire to contradictory effects.* We will consider the implications of the politics of literary form at the end of this chapter after a brief discussion of other features of the technique explored by *Midnight's Children.*

Rushdie has a peculiar way of conflating history, memory and autobiography without of course interrogating in depth the critical assumption underlying each of these forms. The result is a fleeting *cinematographic montage* of several voices in amoeba like recurring fusion, forever contracting and expanding in concentric circles. This might leave a reader baffled, not of course for its lack of centre, or verisimilitude, but for its sheer grandiloquence. Tai, the storyteller, in the first section of the novel represents this majestic act as a fusion of the time-events and becomes the repository of 'racial memory':

> I have watched the mountains being born: I have seen emperors die... I saw that Isa, that Christ, when he came to Kashmir. Smile, smile, it is your history I am keeping in my head [p.16].

This marks the compressions of history in the figure of Saleem: 'I had been mysteriously handcuffed to history, my destinies indissolubly chained to those of my country'. Under alternating fission-fusion, his individual *identity* is by turn *fragmented* and enlarged by the interwined lives around him, engulfing the destiny of a whole nation. British images become Rushdie's obvious framework for linking 'autobiography' with India's recent history. Like Saleem, Shiva, his alter ego and rival, is born on the stroke of midnight. Saleem's mother started her labour pains exactly twenty-four hours earlier when Pakistan came into existence and Saleem's wife's son, by Shiva, is born at midnight of the day when Indira Gandhi clamped down Emergency Rule on India. Parvati's thirteen-day labour coincides with thirteen days of political tumult in India when Indira Gandhi, found guilty of malpractice during the election of 1971, refused to resign and later proclaimed an emergency. Parvati and Saleem, Indira and India—each undergoes a long-drawn travail. The parallel between Parvati (and Saleem's) travail and India's political tumult ends in a 'nightmare':

> Come on Parvati, push, push while Parvati pushed in the ghetto, J.P. Narayan and Morarji Desai... were forcing Mrs. Gandhi to push... the Prime Minister was giving birth to a child of her own... suspension of civil rights, and censorship of the press, and armoured-units-on special-alert, and arrest-of subversive-elements [p.419].

Births and prognostications, birth and symbols. Rushdie 'drives births home with a sledgehammer.[24] Saleem is the son of an Englishman and a Hindu street-singer's wife; he is brought up by a Kashmiri Muslim couple whose own child is given to the street-singer by Mary Pereira, a Goanese midwife who is influenced by her Marxist lover into contributing her mite towards the equalisation of classes; Mary Pereira, with her catholicism and paranoia, becomes Saleem's ayah. This obvious symbolism of *in between identities*, mixed ancestries and religious hybridity of India corroborates the narrator's earlier statement that events have always a tendency, like people, to leak into each other. And our willful effort to segment them into neat parts is an ideological process of *marking identities for political purpose.*

The treatment of time, however, poses a serious problem. At the surface, Rushdie evokes the 'mythic' dimension of time, which moves along repetitive circles symbolising frozen essences and nature. Such a view is vividly evoked in Saleem's description of Indian politicians, who in their desire for immortality, are 'clutching time in their mummified fingers and refusing to let it move'. Only when the British want to leave India does time move again—the sound of clocks ticking reverberates as Independence draws near. Saleem finds himself constantly resisting the urge to linearise, to narrativise in the historian's sense, at the same time as fervently *wishing to fulfill his and his nation's longing for form'* and to record for posterity, in writing the history of this 'nation of forgetters', which—because of its domination by others—is, as a nation, 'simply run (ning) out of steam'.

As Saleem writes, he rearranges events, misremembers dates, and creates causes and effects for 'real' events. For him, the truth of a story lies in its manner of narration and is a reflection of 'idiosyncratic process' of selecting events from memory:

> I say yet again 'memory's truth, because memory has its own special kind. It selects, it eliminates, alters, exaggerates, minimises, glorifies, and vilifies also; but in the end it creates its own reality, its heterogeneous but usually coherent version of events; and no sane human being ever trusts someone else's version more than his own.' Yes: I said 'sane' [p.211].

While memory is *privileged* over history, a sense of linear time, according to Saleem, is 'damaging'. He was 'the child of a father who was not his father; but also the child of time which damaged reality so badly that nobody ever managed to put it together again'. This leads him to follow the traditional 'Indian' urge to 'encapsulate the whole of reality'. This gradual change from history as an assemblage of fragments symbolised by 'the perforated sheet' of the first section, to the 'wholeness'/to the swallowing of lives, is signalled in the following passage:

> I am the sum total of everything that went before me, of all I have been seen done, of everything done to me. I am everyone everything whose being-in the world affected was affected by mine. I am anything that happens after I've gone which would not have happened [p.425].

This is part of Hindu transcendentalism *par excellence* which is supposed to be baffling to a 'western' mind for its *interpenetration* of the ordinary and extraordinary. These double strands also account for 'cyclic' and 'new' concepts of time in *Brahmanic* view of history, to be discovered in the *Vedas* and *Upanishads*. As Saleem remarks, 'no people whose word for 'yesterday' is the same as their word for 'tomorrow' can be said to have a firm grip on time'. One is tempted to argue here, as Kumkum Sangari does, that the synchronic time of the modern and the post-modern and its cognate vision of culture in the west takes shape through the conglomerative modality of collage as 'different times and different spaces are combined in a here and now that is everywhere at once.'[25] *Synchronicity*, which once negotiated and reparceled cultural colonialism, now enters the dominant discourses and institutions of the post-modern and becomes the joint apogee of a cultural post modernism and a consumer culture, 'the instant availability effect of the specialisation of the museum and of the push-button archive, as well as a matter of recurring renovation of style through new juxtapositions.'[26]

The second issue relates to *representation in history,* since questioning the basis of conventional history, and rational and familiar ties seem directly to lead to a disintegration of the individual, and eventually threaten the very existence of *subjectivity* in the novel. David Carroll, a theoretician of the post-modern moment in literary criticism, puts it succinctly:

> The uncertainty of the representation of the past when the origin and end of history are no longer assumed to be present, when the sense of direction of history is in question, cannot simply be dismissed as constituting a subjectivist view of collectivity (type) that depends on teleological views of history for its support. The derivation of the individual subject... the subject as unified presence... is problematical when history is not accepted in its 'domesticated', rational, metaphysical form as the optimistic resolution of contradictions.[27]

This received theoretical idea against representation seems to have two political consequences. On one hand, it seems to require us to discard the concerns and results of much post-modern inquiry if we are to pursue the play of representations in the world, where *the power of representation is something sought, indeed passionately struggled for, by groups* 'that consider themselves dominated by alien and alienating representation.'[28] An excellent example of this would be Edward Said's plea on behalf of the Palestinians who have been denied the *permission to narrate* their life-stories and the demands for a homeland.[29] On the other hand it encourages an 'ultra-leftist,' academic avant-gardism which assumes that any critic/writer working with 'representation' and its inevitably associated notions of narrative and history, must be repudiated and challenged unconditionally. Both of these positions deprive us of valuable critical resources and tend to paralyse our exercise of political and critical engagement into internecine warfare the further spinning of 'theory' without a sense of direction, and a context for change. Representation is after all a game where we are all willy-nilly caught and even the sharpest analytic work contains in it an element of representation, or simply narration.[30] The crucial issue which Rushdie's text evades, or fails to address properly, is: *representation by what means, to what purpose, with what effect*—pragmatic questions, not an essentialist dilemma about whether we have finally found something that will not prove, after all, to be representation just again.[31]

An equally significant issue, one which is cognate with representation, is the loss or disintegration of subjectivity. In *Midnight's Children* the 'theme' of fragmentation becomes predominant, as its narrator Saleem Sinai experiences, through an amoeba-like contraction and expansion of memory, the disintegration of self. His problems are restated, with an apocalyptic intensity heightened by the intervening four hundred page struggle with his own fragmentation, as seen in the novel's final paragraph:

> Yes, they will trample me underfoot, the numbers marching one two three, four hundred million five hundred six, reducing me to specks of voiceless, dust, just as, all in good time, they will trample my son who is not my son, and his son who will not be

> his, until the thousand and first generation, until the thousand and one midnights have bestowed their terrible gifts and a thousand and one children have died, because it is the privilege and the curse of mid-night's children to be both masters and victims of their times, to forsake privacy and be sucked into the annihilating whirlpool of the multitudes, and to be unable to live or die in peace [p.446].

This brings into a sharp focus the problem of the forms that time and temporality will assume in a post-modern culture, which is increasingly dominated by space and spatial logic. If indeed as Rushdie's last paragraph seems to suggest, the subject has lost its capacity actively to extend its pro-tensions and retentions across the temporal manifold, and to organise its past and future into coherent experience, it becomes difficult enough to see how 'the cultural productions of such a subject could result in anything but, as Jameson puts it, 'heaps of fragments'[32] and in 'a practice of the randomly heterogeneous and fragmentary and the aleatory.'[33] *This results in a kind of giggling euphoria* which determines the characteristic tone of the post-modernist farcical novel. Even as the bourgeois monad subject, formerly angst-ridden, nauseated by contingency, guilt, and fear gives way to a quasi-comic schizophrenic individual-effect, the politics of such a 'radical' shift in emphasis, from the *one subject-agent to that of subject-effect seems to be at best dubious.*

IV
'Magic Realism'

The third issue for consideration is a highly stylised deployment of the 'fabulous' or 'fantastic' in *Midnight's Children* as yet another important aspect of contemporary post-modernist metafiction.

The cultural heterogeneity of India is at once different from, and determined by, the linear history of the West. The simultaneity of the heterogeneous is an aspect of the age-old historical sedimentation that results from the co-existence over time of a large number of ethnic, religious, caste and social group, each laden with its respective cultural baggage of myth, oral narrative, magic, superstition, modernity, Cartesian education, folklore, and other specific institutional modes of production and reception of various knowledges. And this simultaneity, it must be said, is not merely a 'reality-effect' caused by the disjunction of native-histories and rationalism. It is rather an ongoing cultural and social practice born of a genealogy of miscegenation, assimilation, and syncretisation as well as of conflict, contradiction and displacement. Although a mixed formation often possesses an amazing degree of retentiveness and absorptive cultural capacity to resist radical subversion or change, it would be somewhat naive not to perceive in this hybridity the traces of difference and continuity. The piecemeal engagement with British colonial, and later American neo-colonial culture is difficult either to reject or to homogenise mainly because, first in a contradictory *way it is simultaneously owned and resisted;* and secondly, because of an uneven development set in motion by the various *Ideological State Apparatuses* coeveal with the rise of modern and national institutions land their penetration in the vast rural life of India, we have a complex and breathtaking collective *corpus of the pre-modern, modern and post-modern conjunctures in the present.* Coconuts crash on the nuclear reactors, bullock-carts jostling with mega-buses and computer controlled rockets, and of course, even as the traditional agriculture is invaded by the international export economics, elitist university academic groups routinely secrets Marxist, post modernist and feminist discourses. This is then, in short, the moment of a *hybrid simultaneity* of the 'post-colonial' India, a moment of living co-existence of variously empowering and signifying relation of meaning and practices.

Rushdie's literary intervention is marked precisely by this moment, and his invention of a new form, or to be more accurate, his particular style of 'magic-realism' must be viewed as both enabling and enabled by the 'context' described earlier. Our purpose, however, is not to quarrel over whether magic realism is progressive or reactionary, eastern or western, or direct consequence of post-modernist aesthetic, or a deviation from it. It would be, on the other hand, a much more interesting task to examine whether 'magic realism' as it appears in the text *reflects or engages with the moment* of a hybrid-simultaneity of India: if it does not, what are the politics of such omission? With these set of questions and propositions we can critically comment on the form invented by Rushdie—its digressions from realism, its inversion of linearity, and its proliferation of spatial images and differences invested heavily in the *invention of the fabulous, mythic and fantastic* modes of narration.

As for Gabriel Garcia Marquez, whose powerful narratives are often, if somewhat naively and uncritically, compared with Rushdie's, the real, historical and the fabulous are not antithetical terms. His fiction demonstrates how in a complex way Latin American history 'secretes the history of Europe and in turn renders it ironic.'[34] From Marquez's Noble Lecture (1982), it is obvious that real and marvelous are complementary terms, and he deliberately deploys the magical only where the so-called real is inadequate, oppressive, or redundant.[35]

Latin American history in his account is that which opposes a *simple and* direct reproduction of the past, but repeatedly raises the question of how it is to be known in order to recreate the present. In Foucauldian terms it is a *history of the present.* 'You can throw away the fig leaf of rationalism only if you don't descend into chaos and irrationality', writes Marquez.[36] The creation of arbitrariness, unfamiliar, distant, exotic and the peripheral in Marquez is the product of a genealogical relation and embodies a specific social situation. For example in *The Autumn of the Patriarch* we witness how different modes of production, social formations, and ways of seeing jostle in the large terrain of conflict, continuity, struggle and change, both indigenous and foreign. Big Mama emerges as an emblematic figure, and her power is described in 'Big Mama's funeral' as being at once, manorial, papal, electoral, and mercantile all at once, even as the pre-capitalist forms and practices initiated by Spanish Colonialism are shown to be redeployed by the emerging dominating frameworks of power. The cruelest killer in *The Autumn* of the *Patriarch* is Jose Ignacia Saenz de la Barra, the last scion of aristocracy and a sort of medieval prince of darkness'.[37]

Secondly, Marquez has an uncanny ability to ingest the potentially real, the desirable and the desired within the corpus of his *magic realism*, and that often brings the difficulty of distinguishing between fact and fiction. For example, do the incipient rebels in *The Autumn of the Partiarch* actually slice up and dine on the cooked corpse of their comrade? Similarly, are two thousand children really kidnapped and massacred because they have discovered how the General rigs the lottery so that he can win every time? These questions do not obviously have a direct yes/no answer; they rather inhabit a space of plausibility more real than the received 'real'.[38]

There is hence *nothing purely formal* in Marquez's choice of mode and narration. The enactment of the story in Marquez has a close parallel to the existing *modes of perception* as it leans heavily upon not the principle of surprise or innovation, or a rupture from the linear, but the continuing and shared structures of beliefs, ideas, songs, and narratives *within the lived reality of a community outside the text.* In doing this, even at its most exaggerated or fantastic inventions, the *shared social basis of the magical or fabulous is never lost sight of.* This renders it impossible to idealise or freeze a 'native' or 'folk' culture; because, after all, on close examination such inventions prove not only to be crafted from the contingent, but are unassimilably hybrid and open to manoeuvre. Stories exist inside a continuous social space within which they can be remodeled and recombined. In *One Hundred Years of Solitude,* for instance, the 'almost' two-hundred years old Francisco, sings the news in songs he has composed, accompanying himself with the same *archaic* accordian that Sir Walter Raleigh has given him in the Guianas. In these songs he 'told in great detail the things that had happened in the towns along his route ...so that if anyone had message to send or an event to make public, he would pay him two cents to include it in his repertoire.[39]

As a literary mode magic realism therefore is grounded in the real. Marquez's narrative figures a dynamic relation of past to future in which the present is perceived in terms of its transformative potential which embodies the variously visible and invisible possibilities of culture in the teeming capaciousness of the narrative itself. The narrative is 'open' only in the sense that it creates a space for transformative or *interrogative interventions* on behalf of those represented. It replicates the way in which various voices in their polyphonous interaction—marked by a shift between first, second, and third person, singular and plural speech—shape and are mutually shaped by their social relations. The stillness of repetition, or memory, whenever used as a figurative device is not merely a sign of horror or despair, but it also proves to be the active agent of historical sense and of political understanding of the present. In sum Marquez's magic realism is a mode *deeply anchored in the soil of Latin American history* and while it does often reject the rational encrustations brought into play by colonialist interventions in the writing of the past, it succeeds in digging beneath these encrustation to create new modes of narration *at once continuous with and removed from,* the pre-modern oral styles prevalent in Latin America.[40]

Returning to Rushdie's handling of 'magic realism' while it might be sensitive to some historic-political 'events' which acquire appropriately fantastic, or magical figuration in the text, it seems to lapse into a solipsistic, anti representational style, bereft of the multiple conjunctions of a usable past, indeed of historical agency both obvious and subcutaneous. Although Rushdie's narrative method attempts to combine the voluminous knowledge with a pre-authorised orality—Saleem reads out what is written to the non-literate Padma, just as he writes what he hears, and so tries to forge a new transaction between the oral and the written—the overall effect of such an effort, seeking to express transindividual, collective destiny of its people in a parody of both nationalist-real and the traditional-epic, seems to be a *new artifice:* a grafting of a (post) modernist aesthetic on Indian material.

And again, while Rushdie, like Marquez, sets upon a project that must exploit the received transformative capacity of pre-modern indigeneous narratives and readers, this project can hardly succeed in showing the social basis of the 'literary form' and in reworking reader-subjectivity. The totalising potential of his style does not seem to yield a desired axis to the contemporary hybrid writer and reader of the third world, who is open already too at two ambivalent world of bourgeois individual prespectivism and, to the collectivity of the folktale and epic forms of narration who is further *constructed within the traditional and international cultural systems.* To be hybrid and displaced is to be acutely aware of these questions, and to represent the weight of such genealogical sedimentation. The lived-in simultaneity of Indian social formations achieved through various kinds of *transformation*—by absorption, trickery, selective assimilation, osmosis and direct violence over a long period of history—is not merely a matter of facile heteroglossia, or a coexistence of different modes of perception. Though ostensibly forged within localised Indian social relation, Rushdie's grafting of the (post) modernist playfulness of genres, and interrogation of 'received knowledge' is amenable to use by the International system of cultural production with a keen roving eye upon the different, the novel, the surprising and the fantastic. By wearing its technique on its sleeve as it were—while displaying to the Indian middle class the doubleness of its parentage—the making of its urban and western habitat, its popular culture, and its existentialist despair, Rushdie's 'innovative' project threatens to undermine itself. Its cutting edges are blunted by its overwrought style; and its use of what Foucault called 'counter-memory' is drowned in the teeming interplay of voices. The fate of *Midnight's Children,* alas, in *many ways* is coterminous with the despairing fate of reading in our own times, though it is the last thing that Rushdie himself as author would have wanted.

To sum up, it becomes clear that a 'revival' of traditional modes of narration, and an experimentation with the new *per se* is not always effective, particularly when one is skeptical about the site of its reception. Traditional modes were themselves not an unequivocal guarantee of resistance to contemporary hegemonic structures of dominance and subjugation, and in fact could be interpreted variously as also a sign of consolidation of the repetitive feudal modes of cultural production in pre-colonial and colonial India. Added to this, finally, is the considerably embarrassing question of a writer's location and language. Writing from the western metropolis about India in English as 'a swallower of lives', to digest 'the whole of life', has a certain *inbuilt irony.* The fact that his sophisticated account cannot even be read by those whose narrative forms he seeks to display as subversive of dominating historical frames, is indeed ironic, and confirms the thesis that *immigrant hybridity* is a solidly class-based position. But that is also inevitably part of a metropolitan author's condition of writing. Unless one makes a conscious effort to bring about changes in these fundamental conditions of production of writing, authors such as Rushdie will continue to remain highly vulnerable to the cunning of reception and interpretation by the powerful communities abroad and at home.

Notes

1. Raymond Williams, *Writing in Society* (London: Verso, 1984) pp.221-3.
2. This is developed by James Clifford. For a critique and documentation of some aspects of this process, see his 'Histories of the Tribal and Modern Art in 'America,' Vol. 73 No.4 (April 1985), pp. 164-77. The so-called 'decolonisation' like its sister expression 'post-colonialist' may sound like a buzz-word coined by the academic-literary critics of contemporary 'first world' who often choose to ignore the International system of unequal cultural and literary production which runs parallel in many ways to the multinational commodity-production.
3. For a description of the post-modern cultural archive, see Hal Foster, Readings: Art, Spectacle, Cultural Politics (Post Townsend: Bay Press, 1985), pp.181-209.
4. Geoffrey Hartman describes the 'cultural supermarket' as 'a liberation not of men and women but of images (which) has created '*a theatrum mundi* in which the distance between Past and present, culture and modernity, truth and superstition is suspended by a quasi-divine synchronism.' See *The Fate of Reading* (Chicago: Chicago University Press, 1975), p.104
5. Timoth Brennam, *Salman Rushdie and the Third World* (London: Macmillan, 1989)p.27.
6. Aijaz Ahmed, 'Jameson's Rhetoric of Oerness and the National Allegory', *Social Text,* Vo1.17 (Fall 1987), p.22
7. Fredric Jameson, 'Third world Literature in the Era of Multinational Capital', *Social Text,* Vol. 15 (Fall 1986).
8. F. Jameson, 'Postmodernism, or the Cultural Logic of Late Capitalism' *New Left Review* (146), pp.52-111.
9. Terry Eagleton, 'Capitalism, Modernism and Postmodernism', *New Left Review* (149), pp. 60-73.
10. Ibid., p.62.
11. On the revolutionary function of avant-garde art, see Peter Burger, *Theory of Avant-Garde* (Minneapolis: University of Minnesota Press, 1984).

12. Salman Rushdie, *Midnight's Children* (London: Cape, 1981). All subsequent references belong to this edition of the text unless otherwise indicated.
13. For such comparisons see Patricia Merivale, 'Saleem fathered by Oskar: Intertextual Strategies in *'Midnight's Children'* and 'The Tin Drum' Ariel, Vol. 21, No.3 (July 1990), pp.5-21 and M. Keith Brooker, 'Beauty and the Beast: Dualism as Despotism in the Fiction of Salman Rushdie' ELH No. 57 (July 1990), pp.977-977. For a comparison with Rudyard Kipling and Rushdie see Richard Cronin 'The Indian English Novel: Kim and Midnight's Children in *Modern Fiction Studies* Vo1.33, No.2 (Summer 1987) pp.201-313.
14. Of these thousand and one tales of an Indian night, only five hundred and eighty-one survived to the age of ten, 'since 420... since time immemorial, the number associated with fraud, deception and trickery' (p.193) die at birth or in young childhood.
15. Rukmini Bhaya Nair, 'Text and Pre-Text: History as Gossip in Rushdie's Novels' *Economic and Political Weekly* (May 6, 1989), pp.994-1000.
16. Ibid., p.995.
17. Ibid.
18. Ibid.
19. Rushdie, 'The Bandung File Interview 'Channel 4 (Feb.1989) quoted in Nair, p.996.
20. Rushdie, 'Imaginary Homelands', *London Review of Books* (October 1982), p.18.
21. Keith Wilson, 'Imaginary Homelands' *London Review of Books* (October 1982), p.18.
22. Ibid., p.28.
23. Ibid., p.28.
24. Uma Parameswaram, 'Salman Rushdie's Art', *Ariel*, Vol. 14, No.4 (October 1983), pp.34-46.
25. This is Kumkum Sangari's critique of the notion of synchronicity, of 'spatial time' which is, according to her, privileged and depoliticised by literary postmodernism. See Kumkum

Sangari, 'The Politics of the Possible' *Cultural Critique* (Fall 1987), pp.157-186.

26. See Gayatri Spivak's reflections on the convergence of new economic order and principles of technological innovations that have fragmented the global village into so many unequal splinters. Economic citizenship based on the international finance markets, rather than in the individual nation states, has now become the site of authority and legitimacy for re-writing cultures. She writes: 'it is instructive that mining indigenous knowledges or the D.N.A. of the subaltern body, Transnational Organisations are aware that the real source is the smaller and remoter groups, historically distanced from the cultures of domination...' Gayatri Chakravorty Spivak, *A Critique of Post-Colonial Reason: Toward a History of the Vanishing Present.* (Calcutta: Seagull Books, 1997), p.403.
27. David Carroll, 'The Subject in Question:' *The Language of Theory and the Strategies of Fiction* (Chicago: University of Chicago Press, 1992), p.112.
28. The understanding of 'representation' in history is advanced by Jonathan Arac (ed.) *Postmodernism and Politics* (Manchester: Manchester University Press, 1986), p.xxi.
29. Edward Said and Jean Mohr, *After the Last Sky* (London: Faber, 1986).
30. See debates in History and Theory around the question of 'representation' and past in a special No. on 'Narrative and Representation in History' (September 1987) and Kumkum Sangari (ed.) 'Introduction: representations in History', *Journal of Arts and Ideas* (17-18 (1989),pp.3-9.
31. Dipesh Chakrabarty poses a similar problem of 'representation' in the writing of subaltern histories that do not lend themselves to an easy assimilation by the Marxist conceptual schema. However, for him this issue does not lapse into a mere celebration of 'difference' or a linguistic paly of 'binary oppositions' that seem to cancel each other. He writes: 'Subaltern histories will engage philosophically with questions of difference that are elided in the dominant traditions of Marxism. At the same time however, just as real labour can't be thought of *outside the global narrative of capital*—including the narrative of

transition to capitalism—though it is not grounded in the narrative...the outside I am thinking of is different from what is simply imagined as *'before or after capital' in historicist prose*. The outside is something that straddles a border zone of temporality, that conforms to the temporal code within which capital comes into being even as it violates that code, something we are able to see only because we can think/theorise capital, but that also always reminds us that *other temporalities, other forms of worlding, co-exist and are possible'*. See Dipesh Chakrabarty, *Provincialising Europe* (post Colonial thought and Historical Difference) (Princeton University press, 2000), p.95.

32. This is Jameson's phrase from 'The Cultural Logic of Late Capitalism' *NLR* 146, p.86.
33. Ibid: Also see an interesting position on this, albeit couhed in traditional Marxist critical idiom, as developed by Aijaz Ahmad. According to him the forms of narrativisation in Rushdie are diverse enough for critics to conjecture that they belong, in essence, to a generally non-western, specifically Indian forms of non-mimetic narration, so that they can be classified as 'third world' texts. However, as Ahmad puts it, 'the lines of descent from European modernism are too numerous. The necessary, though often unintended consequence of these approaches—the preoccupation with Rushdie's portrayal of the nation and the 'third world' on the one hand, with the digressive self reflexivity of his narrative technique on the other—has been the *obscuring of his ideological moorings* in the High culture of the modern metropolitan bourgeoisie as well as the suppression of a whole range of questions which have little to do with either 'the Nation' or 'the Third Word' but which remain central to the basic import of his narrative.' See Aijaz Ahmad, *In Theory: Classes, Nations, Literatures* (London: Verso, 1992).

    For an understanding of the invasion of the modern and the post-modern into the 'traditional', or better, the museumisation of tradition, Ahmad's remarks are pertinent to the mushrooming of '*culture study*' today. He goes on: 'What is new in the contemporary metropolitan philosophies and the literary ideologies which have arisen since the 1960s, in tandem with vastly novel restructurings of global capitalists investments, communication system and information network, is that the idea of belonging is itself being abandoned as antiquated false consciousness. The terrors of High modernism at the prospect of inner fragmentation and social disconnection have now been stripped, in Derridean strands of post-modernism, of their tragic edge, pushing that experience of loss, instead, in a celebratory direction: the idea of belonging itself is now seen as bad faith, a mere *'myth of origins'*, a truth effect produced by the Enlightenment's *'metaphysis of presence'* The Truth of Being, to the extent that truth is at all possible, resides now in occupying a *multiplicity of subject positions* and an excess of belonging' *In Theory*, pp.129-130 (emphasis added).

34. Lacan has declared, as we know, that when as children we learn language and are penetrated by the discourse of culture, a ghostly self takes shape around the alien words and names. But it is a self which has entered us, *not a self which we are.* This other non-linguistic self, inarticulate and sullen, lurks in the gaps between the words. This self is the old modernist, or even Romantic self, looking out through the bars of language, forever alienated, distanced and unhappy, *translating its deepest longing into the sleazy dis-course of its time.* See Jacques Lacan, *The Language of the Self*, trans, with notes and commentary by Anthony Wilden (Baltimore:The Johns Hopkins Press,1968). For Fredric Jameson, who borrows this notion of the self form Lacan to assimilate it within his Marxist scheme, even the glib, convivial, cultural, externally-constituted self is an object of ruthless inquiry in post-modernism. It is figuratively, if also clinically, *schizophrenic since it is constituted by the function of language; any breakdown in the signifying chain will breakdown the self as it breaks down meaning.* Personal identity then depends upon the interrelation of past and future with the present moment of consciousness. When the signifying chain snaps, everything then becomes for the schizophrenic an experience of pure material signifiers, a *series of pure and unrelated presents in* time. Jameson finds this Lacanian Schizophrenia adapted everywhere as a post-modern cultural style—in the language of poetry, music and architecture of our period.

35. See Kumkum Sangari, 'The politics of the possible, pp.157-186.

36. G.C. Marquez, 1982 Nobel, Lecture, 'Latin America's Solitude' in Julio Ortega (ed.) *Gabriel Garcia Marquez and the Powers of Fiction* (Austin: University of Texas Press, 1982), pp. 87-93.
37. Marquez, *The Fragrance of Guava*, trans, Ann Wright (London: Verso, 1982), p.31.
38. Sangari, p.160.
39. In an interview with Gena Bell-Villade, Marquez talks about the famous strike sequence in *One Hundred Years of Solitude* in these words:
    '—That sequence sticks closely to the facts of the United Front strike of 1928, which dates from my childhood—the only exaggeration is in the *number* of dead, though it does fit the proportion of the novel. So instead of hundred dead, I upped it to thousands... as my patriarch says: 'It doesn't matter if something isn't true, because eventually it will be' *South* (Jan.1983).
40. Marquez, *One Hundred Years of Solitude*, trans. Gregory Rabassa (Harmondsworth: Penguin, 1970), pp.52-53.

Epilogue

> Autumn Clouds, Vague and obscure;
> The evening, lonely and chill.
> I felt the dampness on my garments
> But saw no spot, and heard no sound of rain...

This book has ultimately found its place at the interface of literature and history. Most of the critics and writers whose voices have been heard in the course of this writing had something to say, implicitly or explicitly, about the relationship between literary texts and history, though their specific emphasis have varied a great deal and betrayed in turn their positions on the politics which a text is potentially charged with. The politics of a text implies here the understanding of a work from another time and place, and a sensitive listening to the set of questions it raises, and the 'answers' it provides for 'our' geographical and temporal location.

The three texts on India I undertook for interpretation revealed more about themselves: in the specific problematic they set up, the set of questions they raised, and the solutions provided in each case, than the world they sought to illumine. Although they could be read as 'autonomous' texts, with each setting up its own narrative scheme and range of devices of representation, I found them to be linked together in their journey on the grand road of liberal humanism, supported in each case by different cultural assumptions which represented a specific stage of the development of capital. Of course the links are not at all intrinsic to the textual design; they are forged by a critic's understanding of the political thrust which each text potentially represents, or actively brings into play.

Much has changed since the time of the writing of these texts, yet how alive the issues raised by them remain! Ironically they serve to corroborate the thesis that if you refuse to listen to the 'small' voice of history, you are condemned to repeat the worst of it. The specific forms which debates on caste, communal or gender questions in India today have taken, may be shown in their germinal stage in Forster's treatment of the figure of *Punkhawala* and the 'rape' sequence in *A Passage to India;* in Nehru's construction of secularism and the figure of Gandhi in *The Discovery of India;* and in Rushdie's strident dissolution of agency in all history, as evident from *Midnight's Children*. If these issues continue to echo in our minds, it is mainly because the dominant trends in historiography and literary criticism chose to engage only with the powerful and mainstream concepts of our times. The post-independence story of India, however, has confirmed the Freudian speculation that what we choose to repress out of 'fear' or 'historical necessity' beneath the pale of 'normal' and 'sane', comes back to us with a force several times that of the original moment. The much dreaded 'fissiparous tendencies' in Nehru's phraseology are nowhere more evident than in the continuously raging violence in Kashmir, the North-East and Gujarat; in the vociferous demand for reservation and right for representation by the so-called backward castes, and in the women's movement for equal 'rights' in all the spheres of human activity. The post-independence scenario in India has made it amply clear that crucial questions of cultural representation, caste, communal and gender discrimination, individual rights and citizenship cannot be adequately understood within the parameters of a hyper-critical negative hermeneutics of 'theory' which is after all an academic invention, however self-critical though it may be.

Ironically, thanks to the legacy of this 'theoretical' intervention since the 19th century, the intellectual material of the long history of several Indian Traditions, that should have been very familiar to us, have now been rendered opaque. This is of course the result, not entirely of 'Orientalist' transformations [and translations] of older life-worlds and its symbology, into the 'modern' and 'post-modern' concepts; or a result of mere 'application' of cognitive categories of social-science that have been nurtured in the cradle of the colonising mission of Europe. Rather, in addition to the second order Orientalism, and its attendant cognitive regime of the science of the social, it is also a certain desire to transform Indian nationalist project into a pedagogic 'reality'—to 'educate' people into a 'science' of management of their individual and collective lives according to principles of historicism and rationality—that has contributed to the opaqueness and distortions. For ultimately, one does not learn the 'truth' or 'reality' of a given situation by a mere straining of the mind or senses, by becoming an intellectual porcupine, as it were. On the other hand, the attitude of a healthy respect for 'the unknown', a certain quietness of mind in relation to the 'objective' world, and the willingness to go through completely the shock of the uncanny at the expense of the cold clarity of the surface—'virtues' associated with non-rational life worlds—that need to be stressed once again as vital elements of our present-day collective cultural repertoire.

As the great mathematician of all times A.N. Whitehead had put it:

> When you understand all about the sun and all about the atmosphere and all about the rotation of the earth, you may still miss the radiance of the sunset. There is no substitute for the direct perception....

Index